D1880911

Towards Understanding the Kashmir Crisis

Towards Understanding the Kashmir Crisis

Edited by

Shri Prakash
Ghulam Mohammad Shah

GYAN PUBLISHING HOUSE
New Delhi-110002

Towards Understanding the Kashmir Crisis
[*Anthology, Crimes, Politics*]

Rs. 690

ISBN: 81-212-0778-9

© Academy of Third World Studies, Jamia Millia Islamia, New Delhi

All rights reserved. No part of this book may be reproduced in any manner without written permission.

Published in 2002 in India by
Gyan Publishing House
5, Ansari Road
New Delhi 110 002
Phones: 3261060, 3282060, Fax: 3285914
e-mail: gyanbook@del2.vsnl.net.in
visit our website at: http://www.gyanbooks.com

Laser Typeset at Alphabet, Delhi
Printed at Chawla Offset Printers, Delhi 110 052

Contents

Foreword

It gives me great pleasure to introduce the first publication of the Academy of Third World Studies, JMI, in this millennium.

This volume is based on the papers presented at the three-day conference held at the Jamia Millia Islamia, New Delhi, in November 2000. It brings to light the complexity of the Kashmir issue, focuses on multiple themes, and reveals the several different perspectives on what constitutes the Kashmir imbroglio.

We are grateful to the Government of Jammu and Kashmir and the Indian Council of Social Science Research for providing financial assistance. We feel, moreover, beholden to Mr. Syed Shahid Mahdi, Vice-Chancellor, Jamia Millia Islamia, for his generous and fulsome support to our activities. The Academy has been on the move due to his patronage.

Mushirul Hasan, Director,
Academy of Third World Studies,
Jamia Millia Islamia,
New Delhi.

List of Contributors

1. **Majid Husain**
   Professor, Deptt. of Geography, Jamia Millia Islamia, New Delhi.

2. **Mohammad Ishaq Khan**
   Professor of History and Dean Academics, University of Kashmir, Srinagar.

3. **Noor Ahmad Baba**
   Professor and Head in the Department of Political Science, University of Kashmir, Srinagar.

4. **Nayana Bose**
   Currently working on Kashmir.

5. **Kamal Mitra Chenoy**
   Associate Professor, School of International Studies, Jawaharlal Nehru University, New Delhi.

6. **Shri Prakash**
   Academy of Third World Studies, Jamia Millia Islamia University, New Delhi.

7. **R.M. Pal**
   Visiting Professor, Academy of Third World Studies, Jamia Millia Islamia Univvversity, New Delhi.

8. **Balraj Puri**
   Director, Institute of Jammu and Kashmir Affairs, Jammu.

9. **G.M. Shah**
Lecturer, Academy of Third World Studies, Jamia Millia Islamia, New Delhi.

10. **Hari Om**
Professor of History, University of Jammu, Jammu.

11. **Dost Mohammad**
A.S. Bhat
Dost Mohammad is Professor, and A.S. Bhat is Reader in Department of Economics, University of Kashmir, Srinagar.

12. **M.S. Bhat**
Associate Professor, Department of Economics, Jamia Millia Islamia.

13. **Aijaz Ahmed**
Holds the Rajiv Gandhi Chair at the Jawaharlal Nehru University, New Delhi.

14. **Kshitij Prabha**
Associate Fellow, IDSA, New Delhi.

15. **Asghar Ali Engineer**
Chairman, Centre for Study of Society and Secularism, Mumbai.

16. **G.M. Wani**
Lecturer, Department of Political Science, University of Kashmir, Srinagar.

Introduction

Shri Prakash
Ghulam Mohammad Shah

It is no part of our brief to evaluate the book entrusted to our care. Our own views are expressed in our papers in this anthology. It would, however, be in place to mention the themes dealt with and summarize the conclusions reached by the contributors in the introduction. Kashmir is a much trodden subject, and, it is to the credit of the authors that they have still produced new insights on this theme. The title of the book does assume that there is a crisis in Kashmir but does not indicate its nature even broadly: whether it is political, economic, social or pertaining mainly to the sphere of law and order. An answer to this question is attempted in the various papers.

Majid Husain underlines the lack of adequate farming land reflected in the relatively high density of population in the Kashmir Valley proper — Srinagar 318, Pulwama 289, Budgam 268 as compared to the All India average of 216; the severity and length of the winter with its snow and below freezing temperatures limiting the farming to spring and summer months and increasing the demand for electricity for heating and lighting, all these are basic constraints which will exist under any political system or within any nation state. Similarly, the question of utilizing the waters of the rivers originating in Jammu and Kashmir and building of railways are issues affected by the geography or in aphoristic terms the lay of the land. In other words, the political dimensions of the Kashmir crisis, cannot override the specific nature of the developmental issues arising due to basic geographical factors.

Mohammad Ishaq Khan contends that Kashmiri nationalism had succeeded in uniting the mass of the Kashmiri Muslims and Pandits against the misgovernance of the Dogra elite. However, the tribal invasion and the inability of the Indian forces to liberate all of Kashmiri territory from Pakistan's control meant that 25 seats had to be left vacant for the representatives from Pakistan occupied Kashmir. This means that J and K's accession to India was ratified by a Constituent Assembly which was not fully representative of the whole of J and K. He is silent about the fact that even without these 25 representatives the two-thirds of those present and voting constituted an overall majority of the House and hence the decision of the J and K Constituent Assembly were taken on behalf of the overwhelming majority of the entire people of Jammu and Kashmir. Sheikh Abdullah recognized this fact, when in his agreement with the then Indian Prime Minister Indira Gandhi on November 13, 1974 he expressed in writing: "The State of Jammu and Kashmir which is a constituent unit of the Union of India shall in its relations with the Union, continue to be governed by Article 370 of the Constitution of India."[1] Still, Ishaq Khan's contentions are worth considering as a statement of an alternative point of view which continues to have currency.

Noor Ahmad Baba, a political scientist, traces the present phase of the crisis in his essay to the "impressive electoral performance" of Farooq Abdullah "in the valley in 1983" and his subsequent "unjustified dismissal in July 1984." According to him, it was during the President's Rule in 1986-87 that non-secular forces gained ground and later regrouped together under the name of the Muslim United Front (MUF). Such was the support enjoyed by the MUF that the very same Farooq Abdullah who had on his own won a landslide victory in 1983, now along with the Congress had in 1987 "to resort to large-scale rigging in order to secure a clear majority in the State Assembly." The sequel to the "rigging" was that groups of "young men who had actually worked during the 1987 elections on the side of the MUF" took to militancy and separatism and "provided a good opportunity to Pakistan to get involved in Kashmir as never before." A growing criminalization of

1. Justice J.S. Anand, *The Constitution of Jammu and Kashmir, Its Development and Comments*, Delhi, 1994, p. 112.

militants and repression by State agencies "further alienated the people from the existing political set up." Throughout Baba emphasizes the political nature of the crisis in Kashmir. It follows that the main elements of a possible solution too will be political — fair elections, resumption of normal political activities, and greater synchronization between local and All India politics.

Nayana Bose agrees that the crisis in Kashmir does not consist in unmitigated economic backwardness but differences between those who won and those who lost the elections to the National Parliament and the State Assembly as well as the subsequent intensity and focus of violence by the militants. She cites some data to show how "Kashmiris benefit from massive Central Government subsidies and are better off than their counterparts in the rest of the country; per capita household consumption is higher than the national average: Kashmir families buy mutton twice a week; the infant mortality rate is 70/1,000 as opposed to 90/1,000 in the Hindi heartland." Even as elections go the 1996 elections saw high voter turnouts often as much as 60 per cent. Then why the violence? Two reasons are suggested: (1) Pakistan's active involvement in attempting to bleed Indian resources. (2) The inevitably hard nature of counter insurgency operations. The cycle of terrorist violence and the state's anti-terrorist campaigns leading to several hundred soldiers and paramilitary forces deployed per militant or on the disputed borders is the result of the heavily armed Jehadis being smuggled across the Line of Control and the territorial annexations made by Pakistan and China.

Kamal Mitra Chenoy's Report on Human Rights violations in Jammu and Kashmir further analyzes the impact of violence in this unlucky region. He thinks that rigged elections have added to the numbers willing to act at the behest of Pakistani forces which have supported secessionism since 1948. According to estimates mentioned by him, almost 60,000 persons have died in militancy related violence and the counter operations "by the Army, para military forces, police and surrendered militants." However, as no period is mentioned during which these casualties occurred, one is left with the feeling that hard or accurate data is difficult to obtain in relation to human rights violations. Chenoy's assumption is that from all accounts in the media and by human rights investigators all official figures are gross underestimates of the actual incidence of human rights violations, and most of them are not investigated. He blames the powers granted to the Security Forces under the "Armed Forces (Special Powers) Act, 1958 [as amended in 1972]." Under Section 4(a) of the Act, even a non-commissioned officer can order his men to shoot-to-kill if he is of the opinion that it is necessary to do so for maintenance of public order. He wants this Act to be withdrawn, arguing that local laws are adequate to deal with Pakistan sponsored terrorism.

Shri Prakash's paper emphasizes how any effort at reopening the issue of Kashmir's accession to India will run up against the fact that not only did Jammu and Kashmir have a Constituent Assembly of its own, it was elected on the basis of adult suffarage and duly ratified the decision of Raja Hari Singh to acceed to the Indian Union, along with a Constitution which accepted the special autonomy granted under Article 370 of the Indian Federal Constitution.

Today, the autonomy package for Kashmir should be such as to prevent Muslim fundamentalist forces of the Taliban variety from coming to power. Indeed the precondition for the restoration of democratic political activity is that an end should be put to violence by militants both by sealing the border with Pakistan, as had been done a little earlier in Punjab, and by disarming those who hold weapons illegally along with punishing all those guilty of committing human rights violations, and initiating other steps leading to the formation of a South Asian Confederation.

Human Rights violations are indeed the theme of R.M. Pal's paper. His point is that human rights violations, whether committed by the terrorists or the Indian Security forces, are a violation of the rule of law and alienate the people from the state. Both need to be stopped.

Balraj Puri agrees with the contention that the people of Kashmir are alienated from the Central Government. According to him, the reasons behind the alienation was Farooq Abdullah's refusal to fight back when Indira Gandhi dismissed his government in 1983. When the Congress Party swept the parliamentary elections in India in 1984 after the assasination of Indira Gandhi, Farooq agreed to share power with the Congress then functioning under the leadership of Rajiv Gandhi, justifying the accord on the strength of his new found principle that "any one who wants to form a government in Kashmir cannot do so without sharing power with New Delhi." Next time around he joined the National Democratic Alliance even before it had formed the government at the Centre. As Balraj Puri puts it, "In 1999, in an intelligent anticipation of the results of the Lok Sabha election, he joined the Press Conference of the NDA uninvited as his party had not joined it formally, where its election mainfesto was to be released." Farooq has justified his stand, arguing that his backward state needs the special financial consideration of the centre which only a central government of a friendly party can ensure.

Ghulam Mohammad Shah insists on a regional analysis of the Kashmir issue. According to him, Jammu and Kashmir consists of several distinct sub-regions ranging from the plains of Jammu to the mountainous areas of Ladakh and the valley of Kashmir each with its own topographical and climatic variations. He postulates that these regions also have different political characteristics and demands. Accordingly, he identifies the following political sub-regions (i) a Pro-India Jammu Region of 10,000 square kilometres with a population of 25 lakhs (ii) a Pro-India Ladakh region of 92,000 square kilometres out of which an uninhabited area of 37,555 square kilometres is under Chinese control since 1962 with 2 lakh persons (iii) Pro-Pakistan Jammu Region with 20 lakh people (iv) Pro-Independence Kashmir region of 16,000 square kilometres with 50 lakh people as also the Muzaffarabad region on the Pakistan side, etc. These political classifications differ from both the way the Jammu and Kashmir Liberation Front and the National Conference who view the entire region as an entity and a unified state.

Hari Om proposes the strategy of trifurcation in which Jammu, Ladakh and the Valley would be given separate statehood within the Indian Constitution. He bases his contention on the fact that according to him, 46 of 87 members in the J&K Assembly are Sunni Muslims — an unfair representnation as they are only 45 per cent of the State's population. This ensures that the Chief Minister will always be from the Valley and discriminates against other regions in matters of job recruitment and resource sharing as was being done now. He, therefore, proposes a new demarcation of the State's constituencies.

The remaining papers as distinct from the earlier ones which seek to delineate the outlines of the Kashmir problem attempt to put forward proposals which can help to resolve the issue.

Dost Mohammad and A.S. Bhat have zeroed in on the central developmental concern of Jammu and Kashmir — the supply of adequate electricity, which as they emphasize, has hampered the growth of agriculture, industry and commerce in the State. The planning for power development has concentrated on the imports rather than on the creation of additional capacity. No new power project was commissioned during the past twenty years. At present the State of Jammu and Kashmir imports power worth Rs. 400 crores, especially in the winter season when, due to the inadequacy or shortage of water supply most hydro electric power stations do not function except on a very low level. The demand for electricity is high as, by 1996, about 6,000 villages (96.5 per cent of all villages) had been electrified in the State. The projects sanctioned so far are huge and will take a long time to be readied for the generation of electricity. While these are being constructed, the problem can be overcome by developing mini power stations at low cost in short periods of time. These plants are especially suitable for Kashmir, as they use renewable resources and cause no air and water pollution.

M.S. Bhat in his paper discusses the need to revive and further democratize the Panchayats. These have a long history of legal and institutional existence since Maharaja Hari Singh first promulgated the "Jammu and Kashmir village Panchayat Regulation No.1 in 1935." Several additional legislative measures in 1951, 1958 and 1975 helped to reform, reorganize and extend the reach and role of the Panchayats. At present, Panchayats function alongside District Boards and Development Commissioners. However, since all Acts so far enacted concerning Panchayats give powers to the ruling parties to dissolve, supersede and suspend the Panchayats and nominate members, elections have often not been held on a regular basis. The ineffectiveness of the Panchayats is to be seen in the poor quality of the existing meagre social infrastructure like schools, health services and bad roads in those areas where local rural governance has not existed either due to the campaiagn of terrorism by Pakistan instigated and trained militants, or due to the inactivity of the government. The need of the hour is to create a peaceful atmosphere for regular elections to the Panchayats, generate resources, as well as grant authority to promote rural development.

Everyone agrees that peace is a categorical imperative in Jammu and Kashmir, and that an end to violence alone will create the right conditions for the functionining of the electoral mechanism and the democratic system. According to Aijaz Ahmad, peace is contingent upon reconciliation and autonomy, and these will come through democratic negotiations. Peace as he argues, will open the doors for the demilitarization of the Indo-Pakistan Border and for civilian traffic between the two parts of Jammu and Kashmir in India and Pakistan.

G.M. Wani delineates the fact that, for the National Conference under the leadership of Farooq Abdullah, autonomy means a restoration of the pre-1953 situation wherein the Election Commission and the Supreme Court of India had no jurisdiction in Jammu and Kashmir. The 42 administrative applications orders enacted by the Central Government since 1952 need to be withdrawn as per the terms of the Autonomy Committee Report. Perhaps, a more detailed discussion of what these orders were would clarify the issue better. The option of the Central Government finding a middle ground between the old autonomy package and retaining all the 42 Administative Applications has not been ruled out.

How to achieve peace in Kashmir? A security expert's answer is not necessarily the same as that of an academician. Kshitij Prabha a Researcher from the Institute of Defence Studies and Analysis, believes that her strategy would need five to ten years to implement. Her proposed strategy is rooted in raising the efficacy and efficiency of the security forces to undertake counter terrorist operations by: (a) increasing their numbers (b) improving the quality of their equipment to match those of the terrorists (c) improving the intelligence system to collect information about the plans, movements and targets of the terrorists. Direct talks should be held with militant groups to win them over to an agenda for peace. Steps should be taken to stop drug trafficking and the transfer of money from the drug trade to terrorist organizations. The declaration of a ceasefire by the Hizbul Mujahideen and then its withdrawal at the behest of Pakistan shows the close control exercised by Pakistani government agencies over the terrorists in Kashmir.

Ashgar Ali Engineer has emphasized that Prime Minister Vajpayee's declaration of a ceasefire just before the holy month of Ramzan had brought him much domestic and international support. The stepping up of violence by Pakistan supported militants, as in the killing of innocent Sikh truck drivers, illustrates the lack of faith in negotiations on the part of the terrorists. The peace process must, however, be persisted with since it has broad support amongst the people. The moral bankruptcy of terror has no sanction in the *Quran* which defines *Jihad* to mean 'the utmost efforts to promote justice, goodness, benevolence and controlling base desires'. This does not bear the slightest resemblance to the politics of hate and murder being perpetrated and perpetuated by terrorists in the name of Islam.

Since these words were written, the ongoing Peace Process has highlighted the difficulties in arriving at a consensus over the Kashmir issue. Renewal of the ceasefire and then the holding of the Agra Summit between the President of Pakistan, General Pervez Musharraf, and Prime Minister Vajpayee without producing even a joint statement and the gory tale of daily killings of innocent men, women and children to create communal hatred shows the long course that peace has still to travel to reign supreme in Jammu and Kashmir. The central question today in Jammu and Kashmir is whether the Indian State can provide adequate security, democratic governance and socio-economic development to the people of Jammu and Kashmir who had democratically acceeded to India. In this respect the Kashmir issue is not very different from the Bihar or the Assam issue where again violence against the ruling social groups and government agencies has taken an endemic form in the absence of adequate and satisfactory governance. Can the present Indian State provide satisfactory governance in Jammu and Kashmir? This is the central question posed by the present volume to which it also provides numerous answers.

One

Geographical Setting of Kashmir Valley

Majid Husain

The Valley of Kashmir, nestled in north-western folds of the Himalayas is a transverse valley, surrounded on all sides by high mountain ranges and characterized by snow covered lofty peaks. The surrounding mountain ranges, rising to a height of 5,500 m on the north-east, where the Banihal-Pass provides an exit from the valley. The only outlet for the rivers is the Baramulla-gorge, where the placid Jhelum river leaves the smooth grassy banks and hurries headlong down its rocky course to the great plains of the south.

In the opinion of Lydekker, the Kashmir Valley is distinctly basin-shaped. It has a length of about 140 kms and a width varying from 53 to 55 kms. The lowest point in the Valley has an elevation of 1,600 m and the mean elevation is 1,840 m above the sea level.

The oval shaped Valley of Kashmir is filled with thick deposits of alluvium which have covered even the lower slopes of the surrounding ranges. On the borders of the Kashmir Valley and even in the Valley floor occur extensive elevated plateaus of alluvial and lacustrine material. These deposits are known as *karewas*. Owing to their elevated position these *karewas* cannot generally be brought under irrigation.

Side Valleys

Within the Valley of Kashmir, there are three important side valleys, namely: (i) The Liddar Valley (ii) The Sind Valley, and (iii) The Lalab Valley. A brief description of these valleys has been given below:

Liddar Valley

The Liddar valley extends from Anantnag to Pahalgam, including the Paraganas of Dachinpora and Khaurpora. At Pahalagam, the valley divides itself into two branches which stretch obliquely, one towards the north-east, leading up to the Sheshnag and the cave of Amarnath. At its lower end the valley is about 5 to 8 kms wide but at its upper end it is only a few hundred metres in width. On both sides, it is bounded by lofty mountains covered with dense forests. Cultivation of crops does not extend beyond about a mile north of Pahalgam. There is a road along the left bank of the river upto the Amarnath Caves. This path is traversed yearly by lakhs of Hindu pilgrims, in the months of July and August.

The river Liddar is fed with streams arising out of the *Kolhai* and Sheshnag glaciers. Towards *Kolhai* is a small valley covered with grass where glades are used by graziers. The steep sides of this valley show marred ice action with several waterfalls till the Kolahai glacier at an altitude of about 5,470 m.

Sind Valley

It is one of the most beautiful valleys of Kashmir. It owes its name to the river Sind-Lar which is fed by glaciers and streams. It extends from Ganderbal to the Zoji-La Pass, covering a distance of about 100 kms. Sonamarg is a beautiful meadow near the Thajwas Glacier in this valley.

The Sind valley widens after Shadipur. On either side of the valley are the lovely snow covered peaks. The valley abounds in large forests of pine, and other fruit trees. The famous lakes of Vishansar, Krishnsar and Gangabal are within the catchment of Sind river which attracts a large number of tourists every year.

Lalab Valley

This fertile oval shaped valley is situated in the north-western side of Kashmir. It is about 25 kms long and 5 kms wide. It is traversed by the Lahwal stream which flows down from the surrounding hills. The valley is covered by thick forests of deodar. The extensive pasture lands in the valley are the excellent grazing grounds. It is also famous for apple, cherry, peach and walnut.

Drainage System

The arrangement and disposition of streams which a drainage system etches into the land surface and which may reflect the sum total of factors which influence the number, size and frequency of streams in a particular area is known as a drainage system. The pattern of streams in a region are influenced by: (i) initial slope, (ii) lithology, (iii) structure, (iv) the geological and geomorphological history of the area, and (v) the climate and rainfall regime.

The Jhelum

Known as the Hydaspes to the ancient (Greeks and Romans), the Vedasta to the Hindus, the Jhelum is known to the Kashmiris as the Veth. When it leaves Kashmir at Baramulla it is called the Kashur - Darya and after joining the Kishnganga it is referred to as the Jhelum river. Though Verinag is considered as its source, the local people maintain that a spring, a little below Verinag known as Vethvatru, is the source of the Jhelum. The river Jhelum in fact, rises from the Pir Panjal Ranges about one km ahead of Verinag. Initially the river flows in a north-westerly direction and after passing through the city of Srinagar merges into the Wular Lake. Emerging from the Wular, it takes a south-westerly direction which it pursues upto Baramulla. It finally passes into Pakistan through the Baramulla gorge. The Jhelum flood plain is about 1,575m above the sea level.

The Jhelum river is navigable from Khanabal to Baramulla, a distance of about 170 kms. The great Wular Lake may be regarded as the delta of the Jhelum in Kashmir. In December, when the river is at its lowest, the average breadth is about 35 m and its mean depth only about 3 m.

In India, the river Jhelum flows for about 400 kms. and it drains about 28,500 kms. The maximum and the minimum discharges of the Jhelum river recorded near the Indo-Pak border are 29,600 m^3 and 112 m^3 respectively.

The Kishanganga

The river of Kishanganga is an important tributary of the Jhelum river. It has its origin in Kishansar Lake and consequently been named Kishanganga. It drains the Tilail, Burzha-Bal, Gurez and their surrounding region. Kishanganga merges into the Jhelum river near the city of Muzaffarabad.

Lakes

The Wular, the Dal, the Anchar and the Manasbal are some of the most beautiful lakes of Kashmir. These lakes are surrounded by the steep slopes of the mountains.

The Wular Lake

Most probably, the Wular has its origin from the Sanskrit would 'Ullola' meaning the lake with high waves. In the Kashmiri language Wular means 'cave'. It is said that at the place of the lake there was a city which was destroyed by an earthquake.

Wular is the largest fresh water lake in India, being about 80 sq. kms in area. It is almost surrounded by the lofty mountains which tower over the north and north-east of the valley. The Bohnar, Madhumati, and Erin rivers discharge their waters into the lake, while from the south the Jhelum seeks a passage through the Wular to Baramulla. The lands around the Wular are never safe when the floods come down and torrential rain in the surrounding areas with melting snow will spread the lake over several kilometres of the country.

Climate

Climate has been defined as the average weather conditions at a specific place over a lengthy period of time, i.e. more than 30 years, while the conditions of the atmosphere at any place at a specific time or for a short time is known as weather.

The weather and climate of the Kashmir Division are intrinsically linked with the weather in the subcontinent in general. The location of the Kashmir Valley at a high altitude (about 1600m) in the north-western corner of the subcontinent, surrounded by high mountains on all sides, give it a unique geographical character with distinctive climatic characteristics. In general, the distinctive features of the climate of Kashmir are: (i) mild summers, (ii) vigorous and severe winters with snowing and rain, (iii) a muggy and oppressive weather in July and August, and (iv) the most exquisitely pleasant spring (April and May).

On the basis of temperature precipitation per year in the valley of Kashmir may be divided into the following four seasons:

1. Winter (November to February)
2. Spring (March to mid-May)
3. Summer (mid-May to mid-September)
4. Autumn (mid-September to October)

The mean maximum, and the mean minimum temperatures as well as the average monthly rainfall of Srinagar have been given in Table 1.

Table 1
Srinagar: Mean Maximum and Mean Minimum Temperatures and Mean Monthly Rainfall (1965-99).

	Mean Maximum Temp. °C	*Mean Minimum Temp. °C*	*Rainfall in mm*
January	5.8	-1.6	102
February	8.1	-0.5	183
March	12.1	3.00	202
April	20.1	8.1	180
May	24.9	11.2	86
June	29.4	15.0	35
July	29.6	18.2	113
August	28.9	17.5	37
September	27.1	10.8	13
October	22.1	5.6	15
November	14.4	1.5	08
December	8.2	-1.4	10
Mean/Total	19.27	7.29	984

Source: Meteorological Department, Srinagar.

Winter Season

In the Valley of Kashmir, the winter lasts from November to February. The mean maximum and the mean minimum temperature in November at Srinagar reads about 14°C and 1.5°C respectively. The temperature substantially declines in December, the mean maximum and the mean minimum being about 8°C and 1.4°C respectively. In exceptional years of severe cold, e.g. the last week of December 1985, 1986, 1987, 1988 and 1994 in Srinagar, the temperature dipped below -15°C. Consequently, most of the lakes of the valley floor (Dal, Wular, Anchar, Manasbal) were frozen and became the playgrounds for the adventurous youths and sportsmen of Srinagar and its environs.

January is the coldest month in Kashmir which is locally known as the period of Chilla-Kalan (40 days of intense cold). Occurrence of heavy snow in this month in Kashmir is a common phenomenon. The non-occurrence of snow and rainfall in January is considered as a 'bad omen', leading to numerous epidemic diseases and scarcity of water in the rivers and springs during the subsequent seasons. The winter season receives about 120 cms of snow, the maximum snowing being in the month of January, i.e. about 42 per cent of the total snowfall. The greater calamity in the winter is the occurrence of Kot-Kushu (frost) which seems to freeze the damp moisture of the air and destroys trees and even congeals eggs. In the winter there is an acute shortage of fresh vegetables and at the occurrence of landslides in the Nashri area (between Batote and Ramban) the vehicular traffic between Jammu and Srinagar remains suspended for days together as a result of which the supply of sheep, goats and poultry gets disrupted. Consequently, vegetables and meat prices in the valley soar and the people of the valley face great difficulties in this period. Moreover, the Balan (fuelwood) prices go up, the outdoor activities remain suspended and the life of the ordinary people becomes miserable.

In the winter, the rains may be either partial or may be what the Kashmiris call Alamgir (widespread). It is believed that when the clouds gather over the Kausarnag Lake on the south-west mountains and over the Wular Lake in the north, the Kashmiris can predict with some degree of certainty that there will be general rain over the valley and 24 hours of rain will cause heavy floods in the river. The local adage based on the empirical experience of the people about the different types of clouds and their occurrence at different parts of the day have been expressed in the following adage.

'Red in the night the shepherd's delight
Red in the morning the shepherd's warning'.

If the clouds (Abras Hetun Nar) have caught fire (become red in colour) in the evening, it is a sure prelude to fine, sunny weather, Nihadu, which is red in the morning, presages (warning) rain. The Kashmiri folk have a strong conviction about the colour and nature of clouds. In their opinion white clouds (cirrus) are certain to bring heavy rain; dark clouds mean no rain or light showers.

In the winter, rainfall occurs from the western disturbances (temperate cyclones). These disturbances have their origin in the Mediterranean Sea. The rainfall generated by these cyclones is fairly widespread.

Spring Season

March to Mid-May is the season of spring locally known as Sonth: At the advent of March the weather starts improving and the mercury rises steadily. In March, the day temperature fluctuates between 10°C to 16°C. The mean minimum temperature remains around 3°C as a result of which nights are cold. There are, however, wide variations in the day and night temperatures at various altitudes. Although snow starts melting with the increase in temperature and many of the streams inundate, yet one or two snowfalls occur this month. In fact, March is the wettest month, having a high frequency of western disturbances and recording about 200mm average rainfall.

The day temperature shoots up abruptly in the month of April. The night temperature also registers a steady increase, the mean maximum and the mean minimum in this month being about 21°C and 8°C respectively.

In the spring, with the steady increase in temperatures, lush green grasses develop in the Margs (alpine pastures). April and May are the months when the Valley is in full bloom and the flowers of almond, apple, peach, pears and cherry (glass) add more fragrance to the fresh and salubrious air of the Valley. Agricultural activities which remained suspended during the long winters are again started in the ending parts of April or in the first week of May. The seeds of vegetables are germinated in the house to be planted in the Radhs (floating gardens) of the Dal Lake. Ploughing of paddy fields and preparation of rice nurseries also commence in the early part of May.

The Summer Season

June to September is the period of summer in the Valley of Kashmir. The mean monthly temperature in May at Srinagar reads about 22°C, the mean maximum and the mean minimum being about 29.4°C and 15°C respectively. July is the hottest month in which the maximum temperature on a particular day may shoot upto 35°C at Srinagar. Under the prevailing clear weather, blue skies and rarefied atmosphere this is the muggy, oppressive, unpleasant season in which mosquitoes swarm. July and August are the months when electric fans are needed and the rich residents of Srinagar plan their outings to Gulmarg, Pahalgam and other neighbouring hill resorts.

In September, the temperature begins to fall, the nights become cool and by the end of this month the evenings are almost cold. The mean maximum and the mean minimum temperatures in this month at Srinagar reads as 27°C and 11°C respectively. The average monthly rainfall in September is only 13mm.

Kashmiris

'Kashmiri' is a wider term. It consists of numerous ethnic and cultural groups. Though living and scattered in different parts of the state, their major concentration lies in the Valley of Kashmir, and Bhadarwah, Doda, Kishtwar, Banihal, and Ramban Tehsils of Jammu Division. They are also found in Kargil, Leh (Ladakh), Rajouri, Poonch, and Udhampur districts of the Jammu Division.

The word 'Kashmiri' has been loosely applied for several streams of immigrants, mainly from Afghanistan, Iran, Turkey and Central Asia. There is a close bearing of the Indo-Aryan culture on the ethnic composition of Kashmiris. In fact, the Kashmiri language has its origin from the Proto-Indo-European family, also known as the Kurgan language. Moreover, Kashmir has also received racial impulses from the Indo-Greeks which have influenced the ethnic structure of Kashmiris significantly. The influence of Dards, Ladakhis, Punjabis, Sikhs, Rajputs, Gujjars has also moulded the cultural ethos of the Kashmiris.

About 95 per cent of the total population of Kashmir consists of Muslims. Every Kashmiri Hindu, with the exception of Khatri shopkeepers of Srinagar, who are known as Bohras, is called a

Pandit or learned Brahman. Though not all are learned, they are all Brahmins, and chiefly the followers of Shiva, the Lord of the Mountain and the god of the hill people.

Population Characteristics

The spatial distribution of population in the Kashmir Division is highly uneven. The distribution and density of population vary from district to district and from meso to micro regions. The physical factors like terrain, topography, slope, climate, drainage, soil, natural vegetation and accessibility have largely influenced the distribution and density of population in the Valley of Kashmir. In general, about 85 per cent of the total population of the Kashmir Division occupy the Jhelum floor and 14 per cent live in the Kandi areas (lower hilly slopes), while the remaining one per cent is sprinkled in the high attitudinal zones of the Himalayas.

Population Density

The number of people in relation to the space occupied by them is known as population density. The simplest measure, crude density of population, is the number of people per sq. kilometre or per unit area and is most useful for small units such as districts and blocks rather than national states or continents, where internal environmental conditions vary markedly.

The density of population districtwise has been given in Table 2.

Table 2
Kashmir Division - Density of Population 1981

Unit	*Density of Population per sq. km.*
All India	216
Jammu and Kashmir	59
Srinagar	318
Pulwama	289
Budgam	268
Anantnag	165
Baramulla	146

Source: *Digest of Statistics, Directorate of Economics and Statistics, J&K,* 1994.

An examination of Table 2 shows that there are three districts, namely Srinagar, Pulwama, and Badgam in which the average density of population is much higher to that of the national average of 216. The highest density is found in the district of Srinagar being over 318 persons per sq. km followed by Pulwama (289) and Budgam (268). The districts of Anantnag and Baramulla having a density of 165 and 146 persons per sq. km are relatively less densely populated.

Sex Composition

The composition of a population according to sex is known as sex composition. The sex composition of population of a given region helps in understanding the workforce and the dependency ratio. The sex ratio in the Valley of Kashmir according to the projected figure is about 878 females per 1,000 males as against 927 for the national average (1991). The low sex ratio in the Valley is mainly because of the high mortality rate among the females and their low social status.

Literacy Rate

Literacy has been defined as the ability to read and write with understanding. Literacy reflects the socio-economic and cultural milieu of an ethnic group or community. The Indian Census has adopted this definition and now many of the countries too are shifting to this definition.

The districtwise literacy rate of the Valley of Kashmir has been given in Table 3.

Table 3
Kashmir Division - Literacy Rate 1981.

	District/State	*Persons*	*Literacy %*
1.	Anantnag	656351	22.93
2.	Pulwama	404078	20.47
3.	Srinagar	708328	33.90
4.	Budgam	367262	17.86
5.	Baramulla	670142	20.62
6.	Kupwara	328743	16.82

Source: *Census of India*, 1981.

It may be observed from Table 3 that except the District of Srinagar, the literacy rate in the remaining districts was around 20 per cent. The literacy rate, however, varies from rural to urban areas. The female literacy rate was only 15 per cent (1981) which was around 10 per cent in the rural females.

Religious Composition

Religion has been defined as the "feeling of absolute dependence". Religion is a symbol of group identity and a cultural rallying point. All societies have value systems, i.e. common beliefs, understandings, expectations, and controls that unite their members, and set them off from other different cultural groups. Such a value system is termed as religion when it involves a system of formal or informal worship and faith in the sacred and divine (God).

All religions are concerned with the well-being of mankind on earth. All religions have left an imprint on the customs, traditions, fine arts and overall gamut of life of the society. The basic needs like food, clothing, shelter, occupations and political aspirations of people are closely influenced by the religious values. Religion has been a divisive as well as unifying force. The religious composition of the Valley of Kashmir has been given in Table 4.

Table 4
Kashmir Division: Religious composition (1981)

Division	*Muslims*	*Hindus*	*Sikhs*	*Buddhists*	*Others*
Kashmir	94.00	4.42	1.20	0.05	0.33

Source: *Digest of Statistics, Jammu & Kashnmir*, 1994.

It may be noted from Table 4 that Muslims constitute over 94 per cent of the total population of the Kashmir Division and the proportion of Hindus and Sikhs is 4.42 and 1.20 per cent respectively. There are, however, variations in the concentration of the various religious groups in the different districts (Table 5).

Table 5
Valley of Kashmir - Districtwise Distribution of Religious Groups 1981

District	*Total Population*	*Percentage*			
		Muslims	*Hindu*	*Sikhs*	*Others*
Anantnag	656351	95.63	3.76	0.59	0.02
Budgam	361262	95.94	2.63	1.40	0.03
Baramulla	670142	96.50	2.02	1.46	0.02
Kupwara	326743	98.12	2.03	0.44	
Pulwama	404078	95.87	1.54	1.62	0.07
Srinagar	708328	90.65	8.38	0.89	0.08

Source: Census of India, 1981.

An examination of Table 5 shows that Muslims have an overwhelming majority in Baramulla (96.5 per cent), Anantnag, Budgam and Pulwama about 96 per cent each. Contrary to this, the proportion of Hindus is about 8 per cent in Srinagar and about 4 per cent in Anantnag, while in the remaining districts Hindus constitute less than 3 per cent of the total population. Nearly one per cent of the total population in each district constitutes Sikhs.

References

Bamzai, P.N.K., 1962, *History of Kashmir*, Delhi.
Bales, C.E. 1974, *Gazetteer of Kashmir*, Delhi.
Census of India, 1981-1991.
Drew, F., 1971, *The Territories of Jammu and Kashmir*, Delhi.
Husain, M., 2000, *Geography of Jammu & Kashmir*, Jaipur, Rawat Pub.
Lawrence, W.R. 1996, *The Valley of Kashmir*, Delhi, Navbharat Press.
Raza. M. et. al., 1978, *The Valley of Kashmir*, Delhi, Vikas Pub., House.
Wadia, D.N., 1994, *Geology of India*, 4th ed. Tata McGraw Hill.

Two

Reflections on Kashmiri Nationalism

Mohammad Ishaq Khan

The Kashmir problem has loomed large on the political horizon of the subcontinent ever since India appealed to the United Nations against the invasion of Kashmir by the tribals in October 1947. What prompted the Indian leadership to seek the help of the U N against the invader was not merely the invasion but the idea of delegating to itself the role of the champion of Kashmiri nationalism and secularism as against the ideology of the newly created state of Pakistan. This role was thoughtfully chosen by Pandit Jawaharlal Nehru to counter the influence of the two nation theory on the Kashmiri Muslims during the heyday of their struggle against the Dogra oligarchy. That Kashmiris were considered to be a distinct nationality by Nehru in the pre-Partition days is evident from his several writings. So enamoured was Nehru with the idea of Kashmiri identity that he even urged Kashmiri Muslims to feel proud of their Kashmiri origin in the manner of their compatriots, the Kashmiri Pandits.[1] Little wonder, then, that proponents of Kashmiri nationalism often invoked the past in order to bolster up their faith in the concept of *Kashmiriyat*.

It must, however, be borne in mind that Kashmiriyat is a vague appellation and is of recent origin. As a matter of fact, the term found currency in the early 1970s and particularly in the wake of the developments taking place in Kashmir following the Indira-Sheikh accord of 1975. Kashmiriyat was coined to discover the roots of Kashmir's ideological ties with the secular Indian nationalism, based on religious co-existence and cultural pluralism. Whatever the nuances of the term in a broader context of national integration from the Indian standpoint and also in a regional context of preserving Kashmiri identity from the Kashmiri view point. *Kashmiriyat* served the purpose of both the central and the Kashmiri leadership. At least, from 1975 to the early 1980s, conditions in Kashmir remained peaceful and stable in a certain relative sense. For the first time in contemporary history, during this decade, Kashmiri Muslims as a whole did not remain cut off from the Indian national mainstream. The conversion of the Plebiscite Front into the National Conference was no mean achievement in terms of the relevance of *Kashmiriyat* in the subcontinental post-political scenario of the break-up of East Pakistan. If on the one hand, the emergence of Bangladesh gave a vital blow to the two-nation theory, on the other Kashmiri Muslims' voluntary participation in the Assembly and Parliament elections was apparently a good augury for the future of Indian democracy, secularism and pluralism. No less significant is the fact that long before the Plebiscite Front had decided to give up its struggle for the right of self-determination for Kashmiris, the Jam'at-i Islami had taken the bold decision of contesting the elections in defiance of the former's boycott call. We, therefore, need to ask why in the post-militancy period the Jam'at-i Islami has altogether played a role contrary to the interests of the Indian State.

Nothing better explains the role of the Jam'at in the politics of Kashmir than the challenges posed to Kashmiri nationalism by the Indian State itself in the post 1953 era. Before an attempt is made to promote an objective understanding of such challenges, it is pertinent to ask whether the Jam'at, though ostensibly espousing a politico-religious ideology, has thrived on the National Conference's failure in securing a place of honour for the Kashmiri Muslims in the comity of nations.

Nationalism was not an active factor in the politics of Kashmir until the 1930s. True, Kashmiri Muslims were 'dumb driven cattle' as a result of the centuries of misrule and tyranny under the later Mughals, Afghans, Sikhs and Dogra rule; but it was after the sale of Kashmir to the Raja of Jammu in 1846 and the creation of Jammu and Kashmir state that the first signs of organized protest appeared in the valley. Apart from the political factor, at the root of the simmering discontent in the Valley wele the vexatious taxes to which the artisans of the Shawl industry were subject to the tyrannical system of forced labour (begar) tied the peasant to the land and the master. The shawl weavers' recurrent protests, the agrarian discontent of 1877 and the labour unrest in the Sikh factory of Srinagar in the 1920s—all point to the emergence of the rudiments of national consciousness in Kashmir. It was not until the foundation of the All Jammu and Kashmir Muslim Conference in 1932 that Kashmiri nationalism began to take a definite shape.[2]

The aims and objectives of the Muslim Conference were undoubtedly secular from the very beginning. Far from raising the cry of Islam in danger under the Hindu rule, Kashmiri Muslim leadership focussed its attention on the problems of peasants, artisans and working class groaning under the weight of oppressive taxes. Of course there were certain issues of a religious nature such as ban on cow slaughter, closure of the Pather Masjid and the alleged sacrilege caused to the Quran in Jammu. But these issues were raised mainly to mobilize the support of the commoners who were under the spell of the two religious heads of Srinagar—the Mir Waiz of Jama Masjid and the Mir Waiz of Shah Hamadan mosque. Initially, both the religious leaders played a significant role in enlisting the support of their followers for Sheikh Mohammad Abdullah, the emerging champion of Muslim sentiment. But when Sheikh Abdullah himself used the readymade platforms of the mosque and the shrines for bestirring his people into political action against the Dogra oligarchy, the role of two religious heads gradually receded into the background. While Mir Waiz Mohammad Yusuf Shah of the Jama Masjid remained at loggerheads with Abdullah mainly because of having been eclipsed by the charismatic leadership of the latter, the Mir Waiz of Shah Hamadan mosque remained loyal to Abdullah throughout his chequered career. Realizing that Kashmiri Muslims were wedded to the shrines, Abdullah in due course succeeded in exercising a virtual control over the most important shrines through Auqaf-i-Islamia.[3] Thus, was forged a symbiotic relationship between Islam and politics in Kashmir without, indeed, directing the struggle against the Dogra rule on politico-religious grounds.

Little wonder, then, that as early as 1932, Sheikh Abdullah criticized the Muslim press of Punjab for giving a communal colour to the Kashmir movement. Although he did not belittle the contribution of the outside Muslim press to the ferment of the early 1930s, nevertheless, he did not approve of the Punjabi Muslim and Punjabi Hindu attempts at creating communal divide in Kashmir. Having succeeded in undermining the influence of the politics of the Muslims of Punjab on Kashmir, Abdullah now addressed himself to the task of winning over Kashmiri Pandits against the Dogra oligarchy. This task was avowedly accomplished by the conversion of the Muslim Conference into National Conference in 1938 despite the strong opposition of the leader of the Jammu Muslims, Chaudri Ghulam Abbas. Although Abdullah ultimately convinced a diehard like Chaudri Abbas of the need for rechristening the Muslim Conference into National Conference in order to enthuse the spirit of the nationalism among the minorities, the Jammu leader later parted company with the National Conference.[4] He revived the Muslim Conference and both he and Mir Waiz Mohammad Yusuf Shah supported the two-nation theory. However, being the product of the masses, Abdullah not only proved himself to be the ardent champion of Kashmiri nationalism, but, also as a force to be reckoned with in the politics of Kashmiri Muslims.

But long before the National Conference stood forth as the champion of Kashmiri rights the Kashmiri Pandits had contributed their mite to such consciousness, thanks to the spread of modern education first among them. Tension between Kashmiri Pandits and the Punjabis began to express itself in the former's agitation of 'Kashmir for Kashmiris'. Although the Pandit agitation was actuated by the influx of the Punjabis into Kashmir for jobs, nevertheless, it forced the Maharaja's government to define the integrity of his state vis-a-vis its subjects. Henceforth, not only were state-subjects preferrred in government jobs but the state also imposed a ban on the sale of land to persons other than the state-subjects.[5] The state-subject ordinance thus provided the historic opportunity to stimulate the Kashmiri nationals as well as the regional interest.

The Dogra government had its own specific objectives in placating the Kashmiri Pandits. The Maharaja saw his state not only in terms of a separate entity but also as a large estate in which common people were tied both to the land and the master.

Nonetheless, in terms of his long-term project of enhancing the prestige, economic development and sovereign political character of the state, it was also necessary to woo Muslims who were the deprived lot from every standpoint. However, the state could not maintain social and political order efficiently with the emergence of national consciousness among them characterized by strong ties of religion, language, culture or even attachment to the land. What also provided a meaning and basis to the formation of a national identity in the conditions of crisis was the emerging sense of the Kashmiris' will to exist as masters rather than slaves of their natural and rightful destiny. This fact is superbly reflected in the Kashmiri poetic literature of the 1930s-1940s. We may quote only one of the greatest Kashmiri poets, Ghulam Ahmad Mahjoor, whose compositions are full of ideas about human freedom, the brotherhood of man, religious tolerance and respect for manual labour.[6]

> "Hindus will keep the helm and Muslims ply the oars;
> Let us together row ashore the boat of this country."

It should not be supposed that the nationalist struggle in Kashmir from its very beginning was necessarily born out of a collective will of its people to carve out an independent Kashmir. The aim of the struggle was the attainment of some constitutional recognition as a nation in order to achieve more autonomy within the existing State of J&K. Far from achieving complete national independence, the leaders of the Muslim Conference aimed at retaining a separate sense of national identity within the context of cultural or ethno-nationalism that existed in tension with strong opposition to the state created as a result of British imperialism. Based upon a strong ethno-national potential going back to 1846 when Kashmir was sold to Gulab Singh, it was intrinsically rooted in a distinct written language and cultural tradition. Not the least, it was sustained by strong support from the two religious heads of Srinagar and commoners, especially peasants and artisans.

But Kashmiri Pandits' reaction to the ebullient political emergence of Kashmiri Muslims from the centuries-long torpor of oppression, however, was symptomatic of the crisis of emerging Kashmiri national identity. Of several dimensions of this crisis we may focus on the threat felt by the Kashmiri Pandits in respect of the government jobs hitherto monopolized by them. But more important than this was the threat of what they termed revival of the 'Muslim rule' with the emergence of Kashmiri Muslims as a political force. This fact is particularly reflected in several editiorial comments and articles of the daily *Martand,* always claiming to represent the minority viewpoint in Kashmir. Pandit Prem Nath Bazar was the only Pandit who saw eye to eye with the secular politics of the Muslim Conference and played a significant role in paving the ground for its conversion into the National Conference in order to win over his community to the cause of Kashmiri nationalism. Notwithstanding the fact that a few educated Pandits joined the National Conference, their community as a whole generally opposed its political ideology. This is evident from Jawaharlal Nehru's warning to his "own people" not to fall into what he called "the trap into which minorities so easily fell." He, therefore, urged them to join the National Conference, which under Sheikh Abdullah's leadership had steered the mass movement "out of the narrow waters of communalism into the broad sea of nationalism."[7]

Notwithstanding Pandit Nehru's advice to Kashmiri Pandits to join the mainstream of nationalist politics in Kashmir, their reactionary role reinforced a sense of the existence of dual identities in Kashmir, not to speak of multidimensionality of national identity of Kashmir vis-a-vis the Buddhist and Hindus of Ladakh and Jammu regions respectively. At the root of the Kashmir problem, therefore, lies a lack of consensus over the aspirations of the great majority of Muslims of J&K comprising the three regions of Kashmir, Jammu and Ladakh. Such a phenomenon has always shown a tendency for these identities to fragment and for Muslim, Hindu and Buddhist identities to polarize.

Little wonder, then, that Kashmiri nationalism, in spite of cutting across religious local, regional and sub-national sentiments and identities, could neither reinforce national identity of the Valley nor that of the state in the strictest terms. This marked feature of Kashmiri nationalism naturally defines the role of even a towering leader like Sheikh Abdullah in contradictory terms.

It must be stressed that Sheikh Abdullah's historic struggle against the Dogra regime was intrinsically inspired by the Treaty of Amritsar that resulted not merely in the sale of Kashmir to Gulab Singh but also in the annexation of Kashmir to the newly created state of J&K . While the Quit Kashmir movement of 1946 was launched by the National Conference against the background of the Dogra occupation of Kashmir, one sees a blatant contradiction in NC's decision to assume the reins of the government of J&K state following the tribal invasion. Worse still, the National Conference's ratification of the accession of J&K certainly impinged on the right of self-determination of the people of J&K for obvious reasons of giving a certain degree of legitimacy to the Indian rule in Kashmir rather than creating favourable conditions for the holding of a plebiscite under the auspices of the U.N. Wasn't the National Conference's main objective behind ratifying the accession motivated by considerations of preserving Kashmiri national identity in the larger pluralistic framework of the Indian State? True, ideologically, the National Conference was closer to the aims and objectives of the Indian National Congress, but, then it would be a grave error to suppose that the National Conference's acquiescence in the sovereignty of India cemented closer ideological ties of Kashmir with the Indian State. What is of significance to emphasize, and so far least demonstrated in any analysis of the Kashmir problem, is a very different kind of political ambience created by the National Conference's ratification of the accession. That there were certain inherent contradictions in the National Conference's grotesque approval of the accession to India is amply demonstrated by the turn of events after August 9, 1953 when for nearly a quarter of the century Sheikh Abdullah challenged the very foundations of accession. That Kashmir acceded to India under very compelling circumstances cannot be denied. There was not merely a certain degree of compulsion but even what may be called historical inevitability in the Maharaja's choice of surrendering the sovereignty of his state to India considering his desire of maintaining cordial relations with both the independent states of India and Pakistan. The tribal invasion certainly afforded an opportunity to Delhi to act as the champion of the cause of the right to self-determination for the people of J&K as against Pakistan's claims to territoriality on the basis of religion is an undisputed fact of history.

However, the invasion brought to the surface not merely the question of the security of J&K against its neighbours but also roused a strange mixture of feelings against the past invaders. Thus, Sheikh Abdullah, until his death, never failed to criticize the Mughals, the Afghans, the Sikhs and the Dogras for subjugating Kashmir. One of the worst consequences of the tribal invasion, therefore, was the fatal blow struck by it to a new-found self-confidence of J&K as an independent state. Little wonder, then, that any organized movement worth the name in Kashmir against India did not mark the period between 1947 and 1952 or so. The common perception of the Indian armed forces stationed in J&K then was that of defenders of Kashmir's national identity and integrity rather than that of the army of occupation. To a large extent the National Conference government was successful in projecting the image of Kashmir in terms of efficiency and modernity. The radical land reforms inaugurated by it marked a great step forward in Kashmir's transition from 'feudalism'. However, such a development, though in consonance with the spirit of economic nationalism, does not seem to have evoked an encouraging or a positive response from Delhi. Sheikh Abdullah's government was dismissed on August 9, 1953. Whether the vested interest among the Pandits influenced the mind of Delhi against Sheikh Abdullah or not remains a moot point.[8] However, it cannot be denied that, before Sheikh Abdullah's removal from power, the political atmosphere had become surcharged with emotions of every kind in J&K. The Praja Parishad had already started an agitation in Jammu on communalist lines for the merger of J&K with the Indian Union. Consequently, far-reaching implications of the Maharaja's accession to India and its ratification by the National Conference for the Muslims of the State in terms of the assimilation of their historical identity in the synthetic and unitary model of the Indian state had begun to be visualized by even Sheikh Abdullah as detrimental to the interests of the Kashmiri Muslims. In his fiery speeches, he lashed at the communalist and even integrative forces in Indian Policies, notwithstanding a certain degree of validity given to accession by the Delhi Agreement and the incorporation of Article 370. Delhi itself was, therefore, responsible for giving birth to separatist form of nationalism in Kashmir following the expulsion of Sheikh Abdullah in 1953.

There was yet another critical dimension to the Kashmir Assembly's ratification of accession. The essential point quite often ignored in almost all analyses of the Kashmir problem is that none of the members of the Assembly who are said to have ratified the accession were elected representatives of the people of J&K. The first elections held in Kashmir under the National Conference's government were a sham and fraud in that, members of the Assembly were government nominees rather than elected representatives of the people. Even if one considers such members to be representatives of the people, the question that assumes crucial significance and relevance is whether a half-hearted constitutional decision on an issue of both international and national importance can be regarded as valid in the absence of opportunity denied to the supposed 25 representatives of "Azad Kashmir" whose seats are still reserved in the Kashmir Assembly. The point is that the question of the ratification of the Maharaja's accession to India by the State Assembly is still as vulnerable as Jammu and Kashmir itself in the face of Pakistan's claim to it.

It is no surprise, therefore, that from 1953 to 1975 Kashmiri Muslims under the leadership of Sheikh Abdullah articulated a distinct sense of separatist identity and sentiment as against their national identity within the broader framework of the Indian pluralistic national mainstream. What forced the Plebiscite Front, founded in 1955 by Mirza Afzal Beg to take an exclusive form was the idea of separation of J&K from India. This antagonism was based on the Indian State's brutal subversion of Kashmiriyat on August 9, 1953. Until the early 1970s, August 9 was observed as the Black Day in Kashmir under the direction of the Plebiscite Front. Now, since 1989, we have been witnessing January 25 and August 15 being observed in such terms by the people of Kashmir. What adds insult to the injury is a series of crackdowns enforced in various parts of Srinagar for about a week before such auspicious occasions.[9]

Patronised by Delhi, Bakshi Ghulam Mohammad, the one time close associate of Sheikh Abdullah, after becoming the Prime Minister of J&K unleashed a reign of terror in the Valley notwithstanding the razzmatazz and glitter that characterized his attempts at seeking integration of Kashmiri Muslims with India through the organization of annual cultural shows like the Jashan-i-Kashmir. In spite of Bakshi's role, Kashmiri Muslims continued to remain alienated. Most of the leaders and workers of the Plebiscite Front remained interned. Sheikh Abdullah was released in 1958. The heroic welcome given by the people to him after his release should have served as an eye-opener to Delhi for its ill-fated enterprise of suppressing the will of the people. Reacting to this Delhi banked upon the Bakshis for serving the interests of India in Kashmir.

Jawaharlal Nehru, the architect of the Kashmir problem from every standpoint, realized the futility of winning over the Kashmiris to India through Bakshi's repressive and corrupt regime only in the wake of the sacred relic agitation. As B.N. Mullick records Nehru's conversations in a meeting of the members of the Emergency Cabinet Committee in which Kashmir affairs were discussed.

> The Prime Minister started by saying that, even after fifteen years of association, if Kashmir still remained in such an unstable state that even on a simple issue like the *Muy-i Muqaddas* the people could be so provoked as to rise in defiance of the government, then in his opinion a new approach had to be made and a radical change in our thinking about Kashmir was called for. He said that he felt disappointed that after all that had been done for the people of Kashmir they were apparently still [unprovoked] by a certain amount of mis-government. He also felt that Sheikh Abdullah still had a strong hold on the people of Kashmir and in the changed circumstances, no political settlement in the Valley could be thought of without bringing him in. It was therefore, desirable that he should be released.[10]

Sheikh Abdullah was released in 1964. For the first time a genuine attempt was made by Delhi to resolve the issue of Kashmir through a tripartite dialogue. Nehru sent Abdullah on a political mission to Pakistan. Unfortunately, with Nehru's death, a positive and meaningful process for resolving the Kashmir issue came to a halt.

With Indira Gandhi at the helm of affairs, earlier attempts at seeking J&K's merger with India assumed acute dimensions. Delhi sought to accentuate the process of national integration through the extension of central laws to J&K. Whatever their merit, the regional public opinion against them or in their favour began to be moulded within the changing contexts of Kashmiri national identity and national integration. The antipathy among certain sections of the population to the Centre's policy of achieving national integration at the cost of Kashmiri nationalism is not so much reflected in the guarded response of the Srinagar press as in *Azan*, the official organ of the Jamat-i Islami. The Jamat which remained politically backward so long as Delhi did not extend the central laws to the state now gradually sought to mould the Kashmiri public opinion not only in favour of its crusade against social atrophy but also against what was called the Brahmanic attempts at seeking the assimilation of both Islam and its cultural values in the synthetic Indian model of national integration or cultural synthesis. No other group was so sensitive to the perceived threat of what was termed the cultural onslaught of Brahman imperialism of Kashmiri Muslims as was the Jamat-i Islami. The Jamat's decision to contest the Assembly elections despite the boycott call of the Plebiscite Front needs to be viewed in a wider context of its attempt at differentiating itself in terms of a distinct Muslim identity and set of interests within the framework of both the Indian and State constitutions. That the Jamat was careful to emphasize constantly that its concern was more for preserving the distinct Muslim character of J&K is reflected in several sources.

The emergence of Bangladesh had a far-reaching impact on the developments in Kashmir. Pakistan which had morally and materially supported the Front since 1955 was now a weak nation in terms of the cessation of East Pakistan and also as a result of a serious jolt received by the ideology of religious separatism. Such developments eventually convinced Sheikh Abdullah of the futility of banking on the support of Pakistan for the cause of Kashmir. They also reconfirmed his belief in *Kashmiriyat* as against the two-nation theory. What prompted him to ask for more autonomy within the Indian constitution was his pre-1953 belief in a genuinely pluralist democracy of India envisaged to foster the sense of tolerance of different regional and national identities and interests.

He did not now deem it proper to open up past wounds considering a certain degree of tolerance shown by Delhi towards sensibilities and interests of Kashmiri nationalism. Since, in the changed circumstances, Kashmiri nationalism was not perceived to threaten the integrity of the Indian State, an accord with Sheikh Abdullah was perceived as an achievement for the whole of India and not just for J&K. The presence of dual national identities was also perceived to be a stabilizing factor which would contribute both to the strengthening of the consciousness of Kashmiriness and Indianness. Such an arrangement was also a timely reminder that a unitary, visualized as one dimensional national identity, was not a prerequisite for the viability of states.

Notwithstanding the significance of the Indira-Sheikh Accord in establishing closer economic integration of Kashmir with India, it could not withstand the strains put upon it by the tension between the Kashmiri nationalists and the Indian centrist forces. What is of crucial significance to stress is the mobilization of Kashmiri nationalist sentiments for two diametrically opposed goals by the National Conference and the Jamat-i Islami. Whereas in the districts of Doda and Poonch, the National Conference undoubtedly pandered to the communal sentiments of Muslim inhabitants, in the Valley, however, the National Conference's historic role in liberating the peasant from the chains of chakdars and jagirdars was invoked. Not the least, the dream of making the Naya Kashmir Manifesto a reality was, indeed, an important election plank that, by and large, kept the hopes of *Kashmiriyat* alive.

The Jam'at-i Islami, on the other hand, had a different election agenda. It did not proceed on the authority of *Kashmiriyat* but what may be termed Muslim *Kashmiryat*. For the Jam'at its decision to contest elections was not designed to acquiesce in the sovereignty of India but to create favourable conditions for the cause of Islam and Muslims of J&K by capturing political power.

We may take political party membership and voting behaviour as key indicators for measuring the role of Jam'at and the National Confrence in the post-Accord days of Kashmir. However, in spite of their organizational strength and influence, the political role of both the parties proved to be a destabilizing factor in the Muslim politics of Kashmir in the long run. Neither

Kashmiryat, espoused by the National Conference, nor the politico-religious ideology invoked by the Jamat for seeking radically different objectives could serve the interests of the Kashmiris. True, both the parties showed concern about the continuity and development of a threatened Kashmiri identity at the time of elections; but their slogan-mongering was insufficient as a programme for political action. Despite this failure, both the National Conference and the Jam'at sought to elevate themselves above mediocrity. While the National Conference aroused deep feelings for *Kashmiriyat* by glorifying historical symbols like Lal Ded, Shaikh Nuruddin Rishi, Yusuf Shah Chak, etc.,[11] through the Jammu and Kashmir Cultural Academy, the Jam'at and particularly later its breakaway student wing, Islami Jamiat-i Tulaba, devised counter-strategies to oppose the power of the Brahmanical state.[12] Long before the onset of militancy in Kashmir, the youth under the influence of the Jamiat were gradually perceiving themselves as valuable and capable of self-sacrifice for saving Islam against the onslaught of what was termed Hindu communalist and chauvinistic forces. Despite this development, it must be stressed that the J&K Cultural Academy had admirably succeeded in uniting Kashmiri Muslim and Pandit writers on one platform for lending support to the somewhat vague concept of *Kashmiriyat*. Kashmiri writers undoubtedly stimulated the love for Kashmir by the identification of individuals with a set of symbols. Kashmiri culture was glorified to the extent of giving birth to the conviction that the Kashmiri nation is a trasncendent entity. True, many Kashmiri Muslim and Pandit writers emphasized the synthesis of Hindu mysticism and Sufism in Kashmir to support the cause of the Kashmiri identity as well as secular Indian state. But cultivation of national language and culture proved to be insufficient to inform political developments in Kashmir. Although the right to the autonomy of J&K was recognized by the Indira-Sheikh Accord, the process towards the fulfilment of that objective could not begin in the right direction for two basic reasons. The National Conference was never serious about initiating the process towards greater autonomy beyond raising it as the main plank of its election campaign. That the party leadership, particularly after the death of Sheikh Abdullah, lacked both will and self-sacrifice to fight the

Centre on this issue is borne out by several statements of Farooq Abdullah. As a matter of fact, he did not feel shy of equating *Kashmiriyat* with regionalism and even parochialism in the aftermath of the Rajiv-Farooq Accord.

Little wonder, then, the Rajiv-Farooq Accord was denounced as a total sell-out in Kashmir. What, in fact, hurt the susceptibilities of Kashmiri Muslims was the attack made on the concept of their historic identity from the pulpit of the dargah of Hazratbal by the once flamboyant champion of "your country, my country! It is Kashmir, it is Kashmir." Kashmiri nationalism entered a very crucial stage when the concern for preserving the Muslim character of the state reached a crescendo in the unification of various religious and political groups as the Muslim United Front. In the changed political scenario in the Valley, the sole aim of the enthusiastic adherents of the rights of Muslims in J&K was to ensure the defeat of the National Conference at the next elections. However, the slogan mongering of MUF afforded an opportunity to the National Conference leadership to project the suppressed concern for Kashmiri identity as 'fundamentalism'. The Centre thus had no qualms about giving free license to the National Conference to rig the elections. The victory of the National Conference, however, proved to be a nightmare in that it served to confirm the widespread, though orchestrated, belief of Kashmiri Muslims about the insidious designs of the 'Brahmin imperialism' against them.[13]

Conclusion

Notwithstanding the role of the separatist forces in contemporary history, Kashmiri nationalism, in essence, does not contemplate trifurcation of J&K or the creation of an independent Kashmir on the grounds or religion. Given the politics of the Hindus of Jammu and the Buddhists of the Ladakh regions, the separatist movement represents only a considerable majority of the Muslims of the State. Viewed historically, however, the so-called Muslim separatism in the state is not separatism as such in the strictest sense. By legitimizing a discourse based on the specific secular and plural ideology, Kashmiri Muslim separatism, in my view, comes quite near the idea of sharing a national identity with both India and Pakistan on certain historical terms. True, the cry for *azadi* of J&K has been suppressed. But then one may ask: doesn't the continued observance of January 26 and August 15 in the Valley as 'Black Days' for the last 11 years call for a serious dialogue on the crisis in Kashmir?[14] One may also argue that since the concept of preserving the integrity of J&K as an independent historic entity is not totally in conflict with the secular and democratic principles of the state and the Indian Constitution, a meaningful tripartite dialogue on this issue cannot altogether prove a futile exercise like the one between India and Kashmir or between India and Pakistan. Seen in this perspective, in spite of all that has happened in the Valley, there is still an ample scope for the flowering of the idea of being a nationalist in J&K without indeed seeking the independence or division of the state on religious lines. However, such a dialogue can take place only within the framework of pluralism rather than within the bounds of the two-nation theory or the so-called one nation ideology of the Indian State. It, therefore, remains to be seen whether Delhi and Islamabad allow enough space for their nations in J&K to feel represented and cultivate their difference in symbiotic relationship or seek their assimilation in monolithic identities that do not exist at all in South Asia.

APPENDIX A: CONTEMPORARY HISTORY

Kashmiriyat at the Crossroads

Mohammad Ishaq Khan

Two events have, unfortunately, assumed a certain degree of sinister significance in the social consciousness characterizing the inhabitants of the areas around the Bakshi Stadium, Srinagar during the last ten years. "Why do January 26 and the August 15 continue to be celebrated by the champions of *Kashmiriyat* while being indifferent to our untold sufferings?" This question is asked to me by certain educated gentlemen who had gathered at Magarmal Chowk on August 13, 2000.

The security forces resort to a series of crackdowns and search operations from house to house a week before such historic events. Paradoxically, during such operations no distinction is made between an Indian and an anti-Indian or between what a senior citizen remarks pathetically, "a friend and a foe." Interestingly enough, at the time of a recent crackdown in Magarmal Bagh, an old worker of Shah Sahib in his characteristic ironical style complains: "Why doesn't Mohiuddin Shah, our elected representative and the senior most cabinet minister, arrange an excursion for us to Pahalgam on the eve of such auspicious occasions? Has he taken our support for granted?"

"No male should stay indoors during the crackdown," thunders the Border Security Force personnel. Fortunately, over the years, I have learnt to be patient and calm in such situations, notwithstanding my dying habit of exchanging heated arguments or even jokes with the somewhat disciplined army personnel in the early 1990s. What has, however, gradually dawned upon me after experiencing dozens of such traumas is the sad fact about the total annihilation of my identity as a Kashmiri. True, at least, on paper, I may be an Indian citizen. But, judged by the so-called progressive, liberal and democratic standards of our time, the consciousness of being treated as slightly better than a slave of the Roman Empire condemns me to believe that I have no identity of my own or an identity to be really proud of.

More than seventy-one years have passed since Sir Albion Bannerji, disgusted with the unimaginative mind of the ruler of Kashmir, resigned the post of the Foreign and Political Minister which he had held for over two years in Maharaja Hari Singh's regime. He was very critical of the Dogra oligarchy for practically governing the Kashmiris like what he called "the dumb driven cattle." I cannot really say whether Mr. Banerji's remarks are still relevant to the contemporary situation in the Valley. But the question that has continued to trouble my mind since my recent historical experience at Magarmal Chowk is whether the crackdowns of the sort cut at the root of our human identity and dignity or not. The answer is in the affirmative.

True, crackdowns may be inevitable in a situation like ours. But the manner in which such operations are conducted without the slightest regard for the rights of citizenship or cherished norms of decency and culture makes a mockery of *Kashmiriyat*—a concept that has given an unlimited authority to the National Conference to rule the oppressed humanity called Kashmiris. My observations, both as a Social Scientist and what we call in historiography, an insider of the event are based on two reasons. Before writing this article, I was writhing in a great deal of mental agony whether to place on record certain unnoticed facts about crackdowns or not. Unimportant, as they may appear to some, but from the standpoint of social history, such trivialities contribute a great deal to the making of the history of humankind. Also, there is a professional factor involved in that a contemporary historian under such circumstances is bound to invoke the past not so much for glorification as for edification. Shouldn't a social historian make sense of even nonsense?

Magarmal Bagh is the only locality in Kashmir which has evolved a true secular environment over the decades past, notwithstanding its physical and environmental degradation in terms of its transformation from a once posh residential area into a breeding ground for outside transport agencies — thanks, indeed, to the inspiring example set by Mr. Mohiuddin Shah. Significantly, however, a Catholic church, a mosque, two temples and a gurdwara that adorn this locality of a few hundred people have since educated its residents to live in perfect harmony and peaceful co-existence. Despite this fact, one may nauseatingly recall the scenes of the residents of this locality being forced to sit in abject conditions on the road for hours together. One may show one's identity card to the security forces, but they don't care to have a look at it. "Let the Sahib (Commandant) come..." And the Sahib arrives in a gypsy. When one is about to approach him, he gives a disdainful look; and a jawan shouts "O! why don't you sit? Unless you receive two or three slaps you will not sit down." The Sahib watches every one of us. What an irony of history! He treats us all with his strange and suspicious looks for nearly an hour or so. However, I thank him for allowing me to sit on the concrete step of a nearby shop. Old memories connected with the deceased owner of this shop. Ghulam Rasool, remind me of the wonder that was Magarmal Bagh in the good old days. Rasool could speak Nepali and Punjabi fluently, thanks to his social intercourse with the Gurkha army officers and servants of the Dogra period.

While I am brooding on the past, I hear the hullabaloo caused by an autorickshaw. Four passengers are asked to come down and join us. Their moans and entreaties fail to excite the pity of the gun-wielding gentlemen in uniform. The mourners belong to a bereaved family. Living in Shaikh Hamza colony behind the Police Lines, they are desperate to collect the dead body of their dear one from Rajbagh. On the contrary, the somewhat - VIP treatment meted out to an influential and rich goldsmith of our locality presents a sad contrast. Sardar Sahib is allowed to leave his home for an unknown destination in a Zen car driven by a Kashmiri Muslim just before the residents had begun to assemble at the Chowk. To our consternation, Mr. Santokh Singh returns home after two hours in the same car, just five or ten minutes before we are commanded to disperse.

The assembly of four to five hundred people sitting in Magarmal Chowk is composed of diverse elements. Two of our Kashmiri Pandit neighbours are conspicuously present, besides about a hundred non-State subjects, both Muslims and non-Muslims. The non-State subjects are segregated from us. From a certain distance, I can see an old man in his late seventies, a

Muslim from UP with his long grey beard. I cannot understand the logic or wisdom behind taking such an innocuous person, a virtual prisoner for two hours. But then I see some eyes focused on a Sardarji. He is Mr. Bali, an Engineer in the Public Works Department, Mr. Zaffar, ex-Conservator of the State Forest Department, who has always kept us in good humour during the periods of such trials and tribulations, unexpectedly, looks pretty glum. He feels extremely sorry for Mr. Bali on account of the tragedy that has befallen the latter. Mr. Bali lost his mother three days ago. The proverbial human concern of the Kashmiris over the death of a neighbour is reflected in deep-felt sentiments expressed by the people sitting around me. "It is a pity that even the grief-stricken soul has not been spared..." observes one of my old neighbours in rage.

Whatever the significance of the crackdowns, I see a certain ugliness about the manner in which we are forced to sit on the road side on "auspicious" occasions. In fact, when I contemplate such ugliness. I shudder to put my painful experiences in black and white. Is it that we, Kashmiris as a whole, have collapsed into worse than pariahs in the caste-ridden Indian society? The question of human rights is not merely an affair of random brutality. What is more appalling is our experience in terms of continued psychological genocide of unimaginable proportions.

Notwithstanding the claims of the state power in restoring a certain kind of "normalcy" stranger than fiction — Kashmir. It is not an unusual sight to see innocent people being paraded in the markets and on the roadside every day. Often, we are pushed from side to side with sneering remarks. True, in moments of introspection I had always been secure enough to think of my Kashmiri identity as something unique yet dynamic, something though exposed to grave dangers and bruised, yet not cut off from my sense of a glorious past or rich cultural heritage. But alas! today, the past that I had always felt seems to be lost. Contemporary Kashmir, to say the least, knows only the gun-wielding masters all around. Doesn't the Valley of Sufis and Rishis today look anarchic, shallower and frightfully vulnerable?

Published in the Greater Kashmir, August 19, 2000.

References

1. Ishaq Khan, *Perspectives on Kashmir: Historical Dimensions* (Srinagar, 1983).
2. Ishaq Khan, *History of Srinagar: A Study in Socio-cultural Change* (2 ed . Srinagar 1999; distributor, Manohar, New Delhi).
3. Ishaq Khan, "The Significance of the Dargah of Hazratbal in the socio-religious and political life of the Muslims of Kashmir", *Muslim Shrines in India,* ed. Christian W. Troll (Oxford University Press, New Delhi, 1989).
4. Chaudhari Ghulam Abbas, *Kashmakash* (2nd ed. Islamabad, n.d.)
5. Prem Nath Bazaz, *Inside Kashmir.*
6. *History of Srinagar.*
7. *Perspective on Kashmir.*
8. Both Sheikh Abdullah (*Aatish-i Chinar*) and S. Mir Qasim (*My Life and Times*, Allied, New Delhi, 1992) suspect the hand of a vested interest among the Pandits behind the former's deposition from power.
9. Ishaq Khan, "Kashmiriyat at the Crossroads", *Greater Kashmir,* August 19, 1999.
10. Mullick, *My Years with Nehru* (New Delhi: Allied, 1971).
11. For the historical role of the Rishi movement in Kashmir, see Ishaq Khan, *Kashmir's Transition to Islam: The Role of Muslim Rishis* (2nd impression, 1997, Manohar, New Delhi).
12. *Perspective on Kashmir.*
13. Ishaq Khan, "Kashmiri Muslims Social and Identity Consciousness", in *Islam Communities and the Nation: Muslim Identities in South Asia and Beyond.* ed. Mushirul Hasan (Manohar, New Delhi, 1998) Earlier published in *Comparative Studies of South Asia. Africa and the Middle East,* Vol. XVI No. 2 (Duke University 1996).
14. See an eye-witness account of the author: "Kashmiriyat at the Crossroads" (Appendix A).

Three

Origins and Dimensions of Crisis in Kashmir

Noor Ahmad Baba

The crisis in Kashmir has been the outcome of the deep-rooted discontent accumulated over the past several decades. The source of all protests is some sort of serious disaffection with the existing political arrangement.[1] It takes a violent form only when the normal and peaceful channels of the expression of dissent get blocked and constrain the disgruntled to revolt in a violent form. The disaffection in Kashmir has very deep roots, going back even beyond its accession with the Indian Union. After the accession, the political arrangement that evolved in the State has suffered a serious crisis of legitimacy. This problem has never been addressed so seriously in its different dimensions. In fact, the successive governments, both at the level of the State and the Centre, have only aggravated the situation to the extent that the accumulated discontent has burst in a violent manner[2].

The State of Jammu and Kashmir in its geo-ethnic structure has been of a heterogeneous character. It comprises different regionally identifiable groups with divergent political orientations and aspirations. Within its population, there were different types of forces operating for discordant political ends during the crucial years preceding 1947[3]. There were forces active for the State's merger with Pakistan and the forces that wanted Kashmir to accede to India. In addition, there has always been a strong opinion in favour of Kashmir remaining independent. However, none of the forces had an easy choice because of the various checks and balances operating from within and without. Even Maharaja Hari

Singh failed to take a prompt decision about the future shape of his State. It is only after being confronted by a compelling situation created as a result of the tribal entry into the State that he acceeded to the Indian dominion. But his belated decision did not settle the problem of the future alignment of the State in its different dimensions, as from the very beginning various powerful forces who were opposed to it, from within and without, remained active against it. The result of the entry of the Indian forces into the State was that it practically got divided into two parts. Some areas came under the control of Pakistan, while as the larger and most important part came under the control of the Indian Union[4]. It included the Valley of Kashmir, which has been central to all political upheavals that followed for its relatively greater ethno-cultural uniformity. In actuality more than the legal niceties of the accession, it was the physical force that made the real decision about the actual control of the area.

Leaving aside the question of its legal validity, Maharaja Hari Singh's accession did not substantially contribute to the legitimacy of the Indian Union's hold on Kashmir as his own legitimacy to rule the State had been questioned by the predominant majority of his subjects. In political terms, his decision had validity in the areas of his personal and primordial linkages and influences, i.e. Dogri dominated areas of Jammu region[5]. It was for this non-representative character of the Maharaja, that the government of India offered to refer the final decision about the issue of accession to the people of the State. However, on its part to strengthen its claim, the Government of India was very particular to get the endorsement from the National Conference leadership, which was supposed to have a dominant position particularly in the Valley of Kashmir. Part of the explanation for not thrusting into the areas of the State beyond what came to be known as the cease-fire line was the lack of a mechanism that could help to legitimize the Indian hold in those areas. These were known for more explicit pro-Pak sentiments. It is a voluntary popular consent that transforms a purely legal proposition into a substantive political reality.

There is some evidence to suggest that Sheikh Abdullah supported accession to India in the hope of securing a meaningful autonomous status for the State, which he considered necessary for translating his vision of Naya Kashmir into actual practice[6]. He probably thought that he would not be able to secure such a position within Pakistan. He was, in fact, able to secure this position for the State through protracted negotiations, which resulted in an understanding that became the basis for the incorporation of Article 370 into the Indian Constitution. This granted distinctly a special position to the State in the context of the quasi-federal character of the Indian Union. The position thus granted to the State was in no way more than the position that each constituent state of the United States of America enjoys under its federal constitution. However, eventually the people of Kashmir were disappointed on both the commitments that Indian leadership made with them. Those commitments are:

1. To refer the issue of a final decision about the future alignment of the State to its people.
2. To secure and safeguard their special autonomous status within the Union of India.

The Indian leadership went back on its promise of the right to self-determination for the people of Kashmir around the middle of the 1950s on the pretext that Pakistan had entered into an alliance with the United States. To an ordinary Kashmiri this could not be a satisactory explanation. He was deprived of his right for an act of a third party and for none of his own fault. This feeling of betrayal has gone deep into the psychology of the people of Kashmir. The eventual erosion of the special position that Kashmir had secured further intensified their sense of betrayal. The pressure for this erosion started shortly after the adoption of the Indian Constitution in 1950. As a result of this, the cordiality between the governments headed by Sheikh Abdullah and Pandit Nehru was being replaced by anger, open bitterness and frustration vis-a-vis each other. The political events of 1953, that led to the dismissal of Sheikh Abdullah, the most potent advocate of the State's autonomy started casting their shadow on the State's special position. This facilitated the process of greater legal merger of the State within the Indian Union beginning with the presidential order of 1954. This further undermined the legitimacy of the Indian hold vis-a-vis the people of Kashmir. That is why, in spite of greater legal integration, the State had to be increasingly dependent on coercive agencies creating a situation of strangulation for the people. Corruption and nepotism became rampant among the political elite and the common man had to face severe kind of repression and organized *goondaism*[7].

This is why, in spite of greater legal integration carried out during 1953-1975, the State's political future within the Indian Union remained most fragile and uncertain. Democracy became the first victim of this uncertain relationship. This had to be supported by elections that necessarily had to be a farcical exercise more particularly in the Valley. State authority rested on continuous repression leaving very little of elementary civil and political rights to its people[8].

Sheikh Abdullah's assumption of power in 1975 was a welcome development more because it carried (along) the promise of restoring the original special position of the State not only as a result of the Beig-Parthasarthy Accord, but more for its associated rhetoric. His impressive electoral victory in 1977 in what has been considered to be the most fair elections in the State was largely an outcome of the National Conference's use of symbolism for playing the imaginations of the people with respect to the restoration of the original shape of the State's autonomy and opening of the Srinagar-Rawalpindi Road, etc.[9]

Farooq's impressive electoral performance in the Valley in 1983 was not only an outcome of the same legacy (Resettlement Bill) but also had added dimensions of an open hostility with Mrs. Gandhi's Government in the Centre. The roots of the present crisis in the State can be safely traced back to Farooq's unjustified dismissal in July, 1984 and the installation of a regime which for its survival had to impose a curfew for about 70 days of its initial 90 days existence to pre-empt protest demonstration in the Valley. This further exposed the hollowness of the Accord that had brought the National Conference back to power with the promise of regaining the special position to the State that had been lost since 1953[10].

It was during the subsequent Governor's/President's Rule in 1986-87 that extremist trends in Kashmir politics started emerging and gaining strength. Parties with proven secular, Nationalist credentials like the National Conference started losing ground and new forces with a more radical non-secular tinge started gaining ground in the Valley. These forces later re-grouped together under the name of the Muslim United Front (MUF).

From his earlier dismissal as Chief Minister, Farooq Abdullah had drawn a wrong lesson that, in order to be in power it is necessary to secure and enjoy the goodwill of the government at the Centre and that the popular mandate was immaterial. This prompted him to enter into an alliance with the Congress Party that was in power at Delhi. This alliance totally undermined him and his capacity of representing the distinctive Kashmiri sentiments and the identity urges of the people there. In other words, it blocked the normal and moderate channels of expression of Kashmiri sentiments, thereby paving the way for extremists forces to replace them as vanguards of the people and their interests in the State. This situation helped in strengthening the Muslim United Front (MUF) to make it a major force in Kashmir politics. So much so, that the NC-Congress alliance had to resort to large-scale rigging in order to secure a clear majority in the State Assembly and prevented the MUF from winning a respectable number of seats in the State Assembly. By doing this, a golden opportunity of exercising an influence of moderation on the MUF was missed by denying it an opportunity of participation in the democratic process and thereby co-opting it into the system. Instead, this exposed the NC-Congress alliance further and people got completely alienated. They lost faith in democracy and the younger elements felt that in order to get justice the only alternative left to them was to resort to armed violence. More significantly it marked the resurgence of a separatist movement in the Valley with the vigour never witnessed earlier.

Groups of young men who took to violence comprised mostly those who had actually worked during the 1987 Elections on the side of the MUF. These people were subjected to severe torture for their association with the opposition alliance. The objective situation thus created provided a good opportunity to Pakistan to get involved in Kashmir as never before[11]. Initially the militancy in Kashmir was confined to a committed group of young men dedicated to the cause of independence for the State of Jammu and Kashmir. They got spontaneous approval and enthusiastic support from the people of the Kashmir Valley. This created a situation of euphoria and a lot of optimism for gaining independence was generated. In this situation a number of groups with divergent political objectives emerged. The only thing common among them was their opposition to the Indian hold on Kashmir. Thus, the movement broadly got divided into pro-independence and pro-accession (to Pakistan) groups. This situation resulted in a series of group clashes. However, in spite of this premature division in the militant ranks, they continued to receive popular support and approval. The gun in hand raised the social position of even those who otherwise belonged to very humble backgrounds. As a result more and more young men started joining the militancy. Many of them hardly shared any commitment to the cause for which the militancy had earlier been initiated. Many lumpen elements found militancy a profitable venture to attain personal aggrandisement and got involved in a series of criminal activities. But, the greater pressure from the security forces made many such elements change their side to what came to be known as the pro-government/renegade militants. These so called reformed militants operating in liaison with or on behalf of the army and the paramilitary forces "emerged as a major menance in many areas of the Valley" by getting involved in a number of criminal activities. They did help to weaken and contain the militancy for some time. But in the process they further alienated the people. Their success against militancy was also temporary as it re-emerged with greater vengeance and sophistication. In the changed situation we saw the militancy getting confined to people with a higher degree of motivation, dedication and skill drawn both from within and without. In the process, the militancy also gained the pan-Islamic dimension.

The continued repression of the State agencies and with growing criminal elements among the militants forced many people previously sympathetic to militancy to a position of neutrality. However, this common man's distancing from the militancy should not be construed as the change of heart on the basic issues of the movement. In fact, the greater repression by the State agencies and indiscriminate violation of human rights of the common man, further alienated the people from the existing political set-up. In this situation, the present elected government in the State, working under a number of constraints has not been able to deliver any thing worthwhile that could help to change the ground situation in Kashmir in any meaningful way.

Moreover, in spite of the elimination of various committed militants, and changing of sides by many less committed militants, the militancy is not dead. In fact, what has changed is only its character. As against the past, today's militants comprise hard core, committed elements with better training and methodology to confront the security forces. It is for this reason that in spite of the decreasing number of the militants, the casualty figure of the security agencies has been growing. Militancy is not likely to vanish and therefore, the resultant violence is likely to continue. In spite of the very difficult situation the militants are still finding the recruits from within in addition to contingents of support that they are drawing from outside. This and more particularly the continued alienation of the common man in Kashmir suggests that the problem needs to be addressed, in all its vital dimensions. The security apparatus alone cannot sustain any political arrangement that is bereft of legitimacy. The challenge is much greater today and cannot be met by simple patchwork. The casualty figure of those who lost their lives in the turmoil ranges between forty to seventy thousand people. This is in addition to the tremendous economic, social, psychological and material loss that the people had to suffer in the process. There is probably no family left in Kashmir, which has not been adversely affected by the situation. The external agencies have got engaged and entrenched into the State affairs as never before. State authority that had completely collapsed in the initial years of militancy has not recovered significantly in spite of some improvement in the situation. The State authority in Kashmir is still largely dependent on coercive and repressive agencies. It is a major reflection of its weakness rather than strength. The situation of anarchy with all its attributes of in-security and uncertainty is likely to prevail. Recently the present army chief, Mr. S. Padmanabhan and the Defence Minister of India, Mr. Fernandes echoed the considered view of the Indian army that Kashmir is fundamentally a political problem and requires a political settlement[12]. So the problem needs to be addressed more boldly and with a greater sense of urgency. This has to be done through a dialogue at different levels involving all parties to the dispute.

We the people of Kashmir have undergone the traumas associated with violence. So it is the people of this place who realize the value of peace and have a deep yearning for the same. But it is the people here who know what the realistic contours of peace are. Simple wishing does not give you peace, especially when there are powerful agencies interested in undoing it. We cannot simply wish them away. Quest for peace must mean taking cognisance of different dimensions of the problem and then addressing them in the manner they deserve.

First and foremost, Kashmir is basically the people of Kashmir. Meeting their aspirations is fundamental to creating peace. Coercing them into silence cannot bring peace. The people of Kashmir aspire for peace, but that has to be peace with dignity and honour. This should also include provisions that address the plural character of the State.

Second, that Kashmir is also a dispute between India and Pakistan. We the people of Kashmir in particular have always faced the brunt of it.

The peace is not possible unless both the dimensions of the issue are addressed. By addressing one, we cannot wish away the other and cannot ensure the peace that we are longing for. Some of us may not like it but this is the reality. At the face of it, the problem looks quite complex. But dialogue opens up the way to peace. Peace building comes through the process of give and take. Through peace we see countries opening up the world over. Once that process picks up, many problems will get resolved automatically. Many physical and psychological barriers are broken. The world is moving towards that direction. South Asia cannot escape it for long. Lahore was a good beginning. Forces that could not see the imperatives for the change scuttled the process. But the costs of the misadventure are going to be extremely heavy. The two countries may find it difficult to sustain the Kargil tempo for long. Sooner or later the two will have to return to the Lahore process. The Indian leadership sometimes seems to be tempted to address the problem only internally as it looks feasible to bypass Pakistan in view of the difficulties that country is confronted with both on the internal and the external front. But in the light of our ground experience it is going to be futile. It was under similar circumstances, that the 1975

Accord between Sheikh Abdullah and Mrs. Gandhi was reached. That did not solve the problem. As we have seen, it has re-emerged with greater vengeance getting Pakistan involved much more directly along with forces (Pan-Islamic) drawn from outside Pakistan. Apprehensions are that the problem if allowed to continue for longer, these forces are likely to get involved much more extensively. The reports are that with greater opening up of the Muslim societies, Kashmir is attracting much more attention of the press and public opinion within the Muslim world. But building peace in the situation of complexity like Kashmir is also a difficult task. It involves the difficult task of promoting a right atmosphere at different levels by different agencies of civil society that may be operating independent of but in complementarity with each other. Two important developments of the contemporary world should help in arriving at a rapprochement between India, Pakistan and the people and the leadership in Kashmir. One of these is that nationalism in its aggressive form is gradually losing its vigour and scope. Secondly, there are greater imperatives for regional co-operation. Working out of more cordial relations between the two most important countries of the region, i.e. India and Pakistan will contribute to the greater effectiveness of the SAARC as a framework for regional cooperation. In today's context, confederation arrangements are substituted by regional organizations serving the same purpose. The European Union is the best example of the same.

References

1. See Ved Marwah, *Uncivil Wars: Pathology of Terrorism in India*, (New Delhi, Indus, 1995), p. 72.
2. *Ibid.*, pp. 55-56. For a more comprehensive background to the rise of militancy in Kashmir see *ibid.* pp. 32-151. Balraj Puri, *Kashmir Towards Insurgency* (New Delhi: Orient Longman, 1995). Historically speaking, Kashmiris have been known in the State. This is not to suggest that, in recent years the entire population has taken re-recourse to violence as a means of attaining political objectives. In fact, it is a small fraction of the society that has taken to the gun. But the overwhelming majority of Kashmiri society, at least in its initial phase, did directly or indirectly approve and appreciate the use of violence against the established political front with all its internal and external linkages. This has been the view of most of

the prominent authorities/writers on Kashmir, like Walter R. Lawrence, G.M.D. Sofi, Premnath Bazaz, Balraj Puri, etc.

3. The princely State of Jammu and Kashmir was the largest State of the British Indian Empire. It had an area of 222,236 square kms and comprised four broad natural divisions with immense religious, cultural, linguistic, ethnic, and geographical diversity. For more details, see Census of India: Volume XXII: Jammu and Kashmir State, Part I. (Jammu, The Ranbir Government Press, 1943) For a discourse on diversity in the State and its political ramifications, see Balraj Puri, *Jammu and Kashmir: Triumph and Tragedy of Indian Federalism* (New Delhi: Sterling, 1981, pp. 10-21).
4. Out of the total area of 2,22,236 sq. kms. of what constituted the Jammu and Kashmir, 35.15 per cent, i.e. 78,114 sq. kms. is presently under the control of Pakistan, 2.29 per cent, i.e. 5180 sq. kms. has been ceded by Pakistan to China, 16.92 per cent (3755 sq. CMS.) has been occupied by China) and 45.64 per cent (1,01387 sq. kms.) remain with India. (*Some Facts and Figures about Jammu and Kashmir*, Manthan, New Delhi, October 1991).
5. The princely order of the Maharaja was ethno-culturally rooted in the Dogra segments of the Jammu population. Numerically speaking this segment constituted less than 20 per cent of the total population of the state. His ancestors had got Kashmir as a sort of reward for their services to the British during their campaign against the Sikhs. They did very little to win over the people of Kashmir, particularly its predominant Muslim segment. In 1931 the Kashmiris launched an organized uprising for the establishment of a popular order culminating in the quit Kashmir agitation in 1946.
6. See Ram Hari, Special Status in Indian Federalism: A Case Study of Jammu and Kashmir. (Dissertation submitted to the Centre for Political Studies, Jawaharlal Nehru University, 1978, pp. 58-59). For details see M.K. Teng and Santosh Kaul, *Kashmir Special Status* (Delhi: Orient Publications, 1975).
7. For a lucid and comprehensive account of these developments, see Sumantra Bose, *The Challenge in Kashmir* (New Delhi, Sage, 1997), pp. 23-54 and Puri, N.[2].
8. Puri N2. Particularly chapters 10 and 11.
9. *Ibid*. P.S. and Noor Ahmad Baba. "Indian Union and the Problem of Ethno-Regionalism" in Gopal Singh (ed.) *South Asia: Democracy, Discontent and Societal Conflicts* (Delhi: Anamica, 1998).
10. Bose, N7, pp. 42-43. And Baba, *Ibid*.
11. *Ibid*. And Puri, n.2, pp.54-70.
12. See "Fernandes echoes Padmanabhan" *Greater Kashmir* (Srinagar), October 24, 2000.

Four

Kashmir: At Perennial Crossroads

Nayana Bose*

"Gunfire reverberates in the rugged mountains from two other positions to their left and right. A minute later, a stout burly man shouts, "Allah-o-Akbar". Three youngsters charge towards the wooden boxes, while the rest hold on to their positions. One of them quickly plants an explosive and sets it off. The guerillas scramble back to their positions—they have barely 40 seconds to be out of the blast range.

The mountains echo with the mighty explosion while the sound of gunfire is heard from a new direction. "The mujahideen guarding our backs are blocking Indian reinforcements," says an instructor, explaining the exercise aimed at destroying Indian military convoys."

— Routine drill at a training camp in "Azad Kashmir.[1]

Something must have led to this. Thousands of committed *jihadi* fighters are being trained in Pakistan to fight against the Indian security forces in Kashmir. For every *jihadi* killed in Kashmir, there are a hundred more waiting to replace him. Picked up largely from the NWFP and Punjab and increasingly from Karachi too, young indoctrinated Pakistanis flock in droves to the Islamic training camps. "I pray to Allah that my turn to go to Kashmir comes soon," says Abu Mohammad, a volunteer of a guerilla organization in Muzaffarabad. "I have only one dream—to be a martyr".[2]

At the time of writing (month four of the Vajpayee ceasefire), the only commodity being "martyred" is peace. While much of the current crisis is external what with *jihad* factories working overtime, there is a tremendous amount that India and the government in Kashmir is responsible for.

This paper focuses on the recent past, tracing factors responsible for the rise of the insurgency explaining why Kashmiris took to the streets, demanding justice. The latter part of the paper will spotlight the current crisis: the ceasefire, the relentless killings of security forces, the increasing targeting of minorities. Where is this all leading to? A blind alley or a tunnel with light at the end?

The Recent Past

The first free and fair elections in Kashmir were held in 1977, under the Janata regime. Sheikh Abdullah and the National Conference were swept to power. The Congress limped far behind. The Jamaat-i-Islami, the pro-Islam, pro-Pakistan party managed to win just one seat.

It is an unfortunate commentary that it took 30 long years for the first "fair" elections to be held in Kashmir. Sheikh Abdullah, who personified Nehru's faith in Kashmir, spent nearly twenty of these thirty years under house arrest, as Kashmir went from one unrepresentative government to another. Beginning with Bakshi in 1953 who was Chief Minister for a decade, followed by Shamsuddin, followed by Sadiq. Elections were so obviously rigged during Bakshi's time, that Nehru wrote him a note in March 1962: "In fact, it would strengthen your position much more if you lost a few seats to *bona fide* opponents."[3] But throughout this time, Kashmir was peaceful. Except for the Moe-e-muqqadas unrest in 1963, followed two years later, by war with Pakistan in 1965. Democracy though denied in its entirety, did not obfuscate overall economic and social development. And Kashmiris who had ample opportunity to rise in revolt against the Indian State during the war with Pakistan, chose instead, to demonstrate their loyalty. Perhaps because of Sheikh Abdullah and the hope he inspired in his people. In the faith they had in him and his decision to opt for India. The belief that this was in their best interests.

Betrayal. The one word verdict on the Sheikh and the Kashmir Accord of 1975, signed with Indira Gandhi. Pakistan and those hankering for *azaadi* condemned Abdullah. He had been tempted by power and had sold his soul, his people. Betrayed them. But whom did he betray? Not those who lived in Kashmir, who benefited from his tenure as Chief Minister. Not those who welcomed the Accord with open arms. Not those, who realize that independence was a forlorn hope, that India would have to do. And certainly not those, who remained aloof from the wars of 1947 and 1965.

Sheikh Abdullah died of a heart attack in 1983. "The grief as the cortege passed burst out like an uncontrollable wave. The salutation—our lion—was on everyone's lips. People wept, they chanted *dirges* and mouthed melancholy slogans... for that day, the man Kashmir remembered was not the Sheikh who had been Chief Minister for five years, but the man, who, for nearly thirty years, had symbolized Kashmir's identity."[4]

And there began another chapter in Kashmir.

Kashmir's one man show came to a halt. His legacy left to Farooq Abdullah, his son. Then politically naive, Farooq was a pawn in India's intricate games of power politics. He inherited a peaceful population, an overwhelming amount of goodwill: in short the opportunity of a lifetime. Within five years the gains of four decades were recklessly squandered. Irrevocably?

The Drift

Farooq Abdullah began well. Young and enthusiastic, he contested the 1983 elections against Indira Gandhi, who campaigned personally for the Congress. The 1983 elections were fought on clear communal lines with the Congress reminding Jammu that it was part of Hindu India and had been neglected by Muslim Kashmir and Farooq Abdullah aligning with Mirwaiz Farooq's Awami Action Committee, a pro -Islam party though it campaigned for preserving Kashmiri identity. The National Conference won overwhelmingly in the Valley and the Congress won substantial seats from Jammu. Interestingly, the BJP in Jammu and the Jamaat in the Valley were wiped out.

Prime Minister Indira Gandhi however wished to form a Congress government in Jammu and Kashmir. "The decision to topple the state government went ahead without much debate about how dangerous this could be in Kashmir where the people were, at the best of times, deeply sensitive about the way democracy had always been denied to them."[5] Capitalizing on the power struggle between Farooq and his brother-in-law, G.M. Shah, the Congress helped MPs shift loyalties to Shah. Jagmohan, the Governor of Kashmir dismissed Farooq Abdullah, on the pretext that he had lost his majority. Shah was sworn in as Chief Minister, incurring the wrath of the public. This was a mockery of an election.

Farooq Abdullah did not have his father's tenacity. "In Kashmir, if I want to run a government, I have to stay on the right side of the Centre. That is a hard political reality I have come to accept...If I had continued to sit on the fence I would have to watch the destruction of everything for which my father worked and did."[6]

If in 1985, Kashmiris were sympathetic and supportive, in 1987 they lost the last vestiges of respect for him. Farooq aligned himself with Rajiv Gandhi and for the first time in history, the National Conference and the Congress contested an election together. When a similar proposal was in the offing in 1983, Farooq had "discussed the matter with senior colleagues...it became clear to us that if we agreed to an alliance with the Congress, the National Conference would gradually be wiped out."[7] His words were prophetic.

The 1987 elections were a watershed for Kashmir, the catalyst for the insurgency which erupted two years later. Syed Salahuddin the supreme commander of the *Hizbul Mujahideen* contested those elections as Yusuf Shah, candidate for the Muslim United Front (MUF). He "lost", As Maulana Abbas Ansari of the MUF succinctly said "But for the 87 elections, which were rigged, the youth would not have picked up guns nor even known that Nehru had promised a plebiscite."[8]

The MUF a motley collection of parties opposed to Farooq and Rajiv, was doing rather well. In hindsight, not well enough to win the polls, but well enough to give a close fight. The results were so obviously rigged, that it seemed the work of amateurs. The following eyewitness report confirms this: "At the Dooru station, the presiding officer declared an NC (National Conference) candidate elected as soon as he took a 300-vote lead even though one ballot box with 1100 votes had still to be counted. The MUF coordinator Quasi Nissar, who was present there, pleaded with the officer to be fair, but in vain."[9] In spite of which, the MUF did manage to corner 32 per cent of the votes.

In 1966, Jayaprakash Narayan an opposition leader had poignantly remarked:" We profess democracy, but rule by force in Kashmir... Kashmir has distorted India's image for the world as nothing has done... the problem exists not because Pakistan wants to grab Kashmir, but because there is deep and widespread political discontent among the people..."[10] The irony is that nothing has changed. Kashmiri militants, those who spearheaded the insurgency in 1989, were young men, in their early twenties. A generation alien to the Sheikh. By the same token, a generation alien to their parents and grandparents who did not support this violent movement, who still voted National Conference. Syed Salahuddin is a dramatic product of those elections. Thousands like him, less prolific perhaps, also turned to an alternative source of power: arms.

To compensate for the victory, the Centre pumped vast amounts of financial assistance into Kashmir. Ostensibly to be used for all round welfare schemes and development. Farooq had a slightly different angle on development; cable car resorts, luxurious villas, five star hotels and 'developing' the world's highest golf course at a cost of Rs. 2.5 crore were priorities. The common people, disgruntled and disconsolate, drifted further away.

In 1989 Rubaiya Sayeed, the daughter of the Home Minister of India, Mufti Mohammad Sayeed was kidnapped by the JKLF. The ransom: release four hard-core terrorists in lieu of Rubaiya. Farooq, typically was holidaying in London. He took the earliest flight out. And suggested that the Government hold firm. For "this was a game of nerves and if we had persisted with the first negotiator, Mr. Wani, the girl would have been released without the exchange of militants."[11] Other militant groups condemned the JKLF as it was considered `unIslamic' to have targeted a defenceless woman. The V.P. Singh Government at the Centre did not have the nerve to hold out. In a show of shocking weakness, which opened the floodgates for many more similar kidnappings, it released the militants two hours before Rubaiya was freed.

Jagmohan was brought back as Governor in 1990. To try and salvage a rapidly deteriorating situation. Kidnapping and killings had become routine.

With his *bete noire* back at the helm of power, Farooq resigned. Unrepenant. When questioned about the rigged polls, and the squandered funds, he was aggressive in his defence: "They said the same thing (i.e. the polls were rigged) in 1983. But they couldn't prove a damn thing. And now let them keep saying that again until kingdom come... The trouble in Kashmir is that they think everybody's a crook. Forty years ago these people had no clothes. Were they even owners of their own fields?... Today we've become masters of the land. They have tinned roofs and clean drinking water. Where the hell do you think these things came from?"[12]

They came from the success of Sheikh Abdullah's New Kashmir Plan of the 1940s.

The denial of political rights and, the high rate of unemployment leading to desperation and widespread corruption are perhaps the main reasons for the current insurgency. Other explanations include:

Firstly, Pakistan's active interference in Kashmir, its training and recruitment of militants, its indoctrination of young minds in the *madrassas* that have mushroomed in the Valley through the early 1980s: in short, "Pakistan's not so hidden hand," well documented by international analysts and justified by Pakistani writers.

Secondly, the Pakistani reason for the uprising: "*Intifada* in Kashmir is the indigenous uprising among Kashmiri Muslims to achieve their right of self-determination by force. The forces impelling insurgency include historical betrayals, constitutional despotism, negation of socio-cultural identity, economic deprivation and repression."[13] This is dramatic rhetoric. Kashmiris benefit from massive Central Government subsidies and are better off than their counterparts in the rest of the country; per capita household consumption is higher than the national average: Kashmiri families buy mutton twice a week; the infant mortality rate is 70/1,000 as opposed to 90/1,000 in the Hindi heartland.[14] As for "repression", it is the Pakistani supported Sunni—*Wahabi* militancy that is repressing Kashmiri culture, art and its Sufi way of life.

Thirdly, international inspiration. Independence from both India and Pakistan is the hope and dream of every Kashmiri. A tryst with destiny, if Nehru's words can be appropriated. The splintering of the Soviet Union into Islamic states, and the creation of a semi-autonomous Palestine, inspired Kashmiris. A more direct influence is the fall-out in Afghanistan. With the Soviet withdrawal in 1990, which in itself is seen as a victory for the *mujahideen*, a large number of armed and trained *mujahideen* have now crossed over to Kashmir, to wage the war against infidels.

However, a key factor in explaining the current insurgency is the level of political awareness of the rising middle-class in Kashmir. To a degree that was absent for most of Kashmir's history: during the Sheikh's time he dominated politics across party lines. But his policies of socio-economic reform laid the foundation for today's rebellion. A generation who grew up experiencing the form of democracy not the substance. Sumit Ganguly in his book, *The Crisis in Kashmir* argues that the insurgency in Kashmir is the result of a fundamental paradox of Indian democracy: Kashmir represents both the mobilizational success and, simultneously, the institutional failure of Indian democracy... And it is in this dichotomy—the increase in political mobilization against a background of institutional decay that best explains the origins of the secessionist insurgency."[15]

This generation of Kashmir is better educated and informed. They are therefore painfully aware of the denial of their political, civil and democratic rights. The mass media has played a catalytic role in creating a socially and politically aware society. Its growth has been phenomenal, not just in Kashmir, but throughout India.

Number of Newspapers Published in Jammu and Kashmir and in India as a Whole, 1965-1984[16]

	1965	*1970*	*1975*	*1984*
Jammu & Kashmir	46	102	135	203
All India	7906	11306	12423	21,784

Radio and television—particularly the growth of satellite television has allowed Kashmiris uncensored news from the globe. In the early days, Pakistan TV and Doordarshan would compete for an audience. Today, BBC, CNN are beamed directly into homes. When a population is made aware of its rights, when a population is able to articulate its grievances, when a population is informed about misdeeds—political and economic—it is then ready to voice its demands. Sometimes peacefully, sometimes not. Sometimes in one voice, sometimes in a chorus. "In transforming the socio-economic landscape of Kashmir and producing a generation of politically aware Kashmiris while also allowing the political institutions in Kashmir to be stunted and corroded, the national and state-level governments left open few institutional channels for the expression of political discontent and dissent...As secular and institutional pathways of expressing political dissent were curbed, political mobilization and activism increasingly proceeded along an ethno-religious dimension."[17]

The 1990s: Euphoria, Despair, Elections

"Some people consider that a Muslim majority area must necessarily belong to Pakistan. They wonder why we are in Kashmir. The answer is plain and simple. We are in Kashmir because the people of Kashmir want us to be there. The moment we realize that the people of Kashmir do not want us to be there, we shall not be there even for a minute."

—Sardar Vallabhbhai Patel addressing the
Bombay Provincial Congress Committee, 1948.[18]

Some would argue that the moment has long arrived. Along with the army, the BSF, CRPF, ITBP, and Rashtriya Rifles make up the bulk of the security forces (estimated to be 500,000 strong) stationed in Kashmir. Instead of tourists meandering down the picturesque alleyways of Srinagar, militants flee for their lives, with the security forces in close pursuit. Tourism, once the mainstay of the economy is a non-industry. The days of visitors thronging Lal Chowk, shopping or haggling over the price of a *shikara* ride at Dal, or trekking on the slopes of Gulmarg and Sonmarg were reduced to pleasant memories of the past and are now, hopes for the future. Mired in a decade of violence, Kashmir is struggling to break free.

The story began well. Young Kashmiris, fired by idealism and determination (and Kalashnikovs) challenged India. Trained in thousands across the LoC through the late 1980s, this was an insurgency with potential. For the first time, a Pakistani backed initiative showed signs of 'success.' "Shopkeepers and artisans talk freely about creating Pakistan or 'liberating' Kashmir," says Mushtaq, a shopkeeper... "We are not afraid. When you come here next year, you will have to bring your passport." And the crowd around him in chorus: "*Inshallah*."[19]

Kashmiris were led to believe that Pakistan, within six months of the uprising, would step in and "liberate" Kashmir from India. Except that intentions are seldom so noble. The script had a different ending which soon became apparent within the first two years of the insurgency. As early as 1991, support to the JKLF (financial and material) shifted to home grown pro-Pakistan groups like the Hizbul Mujhahideen and the Muslim Janbaz Force.

By 1993, the visible presence of mercenaries and *jihadis* increased. Within five years of its inception, the goal of *azaadi* was hijacked into a pro-Pakistan movement. Funding, men and material continued unabated for Kashmir's imported *intifada*. Initially welcomed by the people, foreign mercenaries and *jihadis* in time, began to dominate this now rather confused struggle for self-determination. The JKLF, arguably the most representative of Kashmiris, called for a ceasefire in 1994. By this time, Kashmiri involvement in the insurgency had declined appreciably and continued to decline. The increasing lawlessness of the *azaadi* movement "has unquestionably eroded the near universal public sympathy for 'our *mujahideen*' that existed in the 1990s and into 1991."[20] The leaders of the Hurriyat Conference supposedly representative of the Kashmiri people, came under increasing scrutiny. Their ostentatious lifestyles (the exception being Yasin Malik), and the forced recruitment to the "freedom" movement are resented tremendously. "Several people....allege that unlike their sons and brothers, who are forcibly being taken to Pakistan for training, the Hurriyat leaders have ensured that their children are comfortably settled in jobs and flourishing business. The common refrain is: "Why is it that our sons are the ones who should die"?[21]

Navnita Chadha Behera, in her recent work, *State Identity and Violence: Jammu, Kashmir and Ladakh*[22] categorized five distinct phases of the insurgency. The overwhelming support of Kashmiri Muslims was the key to its success in the early years but vehement opposition by more than half the population of the state (peoples of Jammu, Ladakh and Kashmiri Pandits) proved to be an obstacle that could not be overcome. Phase I (1988—1990) is divided in two parts, the underground militant movement (1988-89) and the mass political movement (1990). This was the most powerful period for the JKLF who led the armed rebellion. This was then, for most purposes, an indigenous uprising based on Kashmiri identity, defined much like the National Conference had in the 1940s, as a syncretic and unique identity, inclusive of Pandits, Muslims and Sikhs. But by 1990, the JKLF manifesto defined its goals as complete independence for Jammu and Kashmir with a system of "Islamic" democracy that would safeguard minority rights. The subtle shift from Kashmiri Islam to Islam, resulted in selective killing of Pandits in 1989 and the tragic exodus by early 1990. Phase II (1991—1993) is characterized by the rise of the Hizbul Mujahideen and the agenda for Islamicization. The strength of the Hizbul Mujahideen at this time was nearly 20,000 strong: "it was clearly the organization most patronized by Pakistan in arms training, logistics and funds."[23]

Phase III, (1993) marks the turnaround in the militancy, beginning with the Hazratbal siege and surrender by militants in April 1993. "Militants lost face and people felt angry for having undergone severe hardships for nothing."[24] This is the year that Pakistan took a conscious policy decision to infiltrate Pakistani and Afghani mercenaries to keep the movement alive. Kashmiris as early as 1993, had begun distancing themselves from active participation in the movement. "Afghan veterans were bringing back the larger battle of establishing "truly" Islamic governments and were pushed into the Valley to wage a new *jihad* lest they start creating trouble within Pakistan."[25] Groups such as the *Harkat ul Ansar, Harkat ul Jehad Islami, Harkat ul Mujahideen, Jamial ul Mujahideen* and *Lashkar e Taiba* mushroomed. Their members consisted of Pakistanis, Afghanis, Sudanese, Lebanese, Arabs and Central Asians who saw themselves as genuine "jihad Mussalmans."

Behera emphasizes the turning points as Phase IV (1994-1995) and Phase V (1995-1996). Popular resistance to militancy, and exploring political avenues (the Hurriyat Conference was formed in 1994) were the highlights of Phase IV. Yasin Malik (JKLF) and Shabir Shah (Peoples League), leaders with credibility with the militants and the public, were released from jail in 1994. The JKLF announced a unilateral ceasefire in 1994 to facilitate dialogue. Regaining Kashmiri control over a movement which was now dominated by outsiders was seen as critical. Phase V continued the decline of the militant movement, "specially the Kashmiri component." Voluntary repatriation, "peace with honour" and restoring the political process were the highlights of this phase. Again, redefining Kashmiri identity vs. an Islamic identity was critical.

Turning the corner: Elections, 1996

> *"Do they send the military to fetch voters in India too?"*
>
> —Mohammed Ameen Qureishi,
> an 80-year-old voter, in the Srinagar area.[26]

Conditions in 1996 were certainly not ideal to hold elections but restarting the political process was the most logical way, in keeping with India's democratic traditions, of trying to turn the situation around. Elections to parliament were held in May, and by most accounts, Kashmiris were "forced" to vote. Caught between death threats by terrorists and coercion by the State, many were "escorted" to polling booths. The international press had a field day, "commenting" on the elections. The British paper the *Guardian*, carried a photograph of a soldier watching warily over a line of disgruntled Kashmiris, waiting to vote. The piece, titled "Soldiers force Kashmir to polls", read: "Beaten and herded like cattle, Kashmiris were driven from their home at daybreak yesterday to cast their votes for the first time in seven years, in an exercise stripped of any pretence of choice or freedom." There were many other similar reports.

The Indian press without exception, highlighted the positive: that the voter turnout was high. And that the beginning of any sort of political process held much hope for the future. Being a traditionally free press, all the papers reported on the forced voter turnout. "On being accosted, a group from Haatiwara village in

Anantnag alleged: The Army came at 5 am and threatened us that if we did not vote, we would be killed and our houses burnt down.' The view was expressed by all who were approached by this correspondent."[27]

Unlike the international press, who had written off the elections as a farce, the Indian press, perhaps cognisant of the enormous complications in physically holding the elections, was less dismissive. Looking ahead, editorials while acknowledging that the voters were coerced to vote, commented on the possibility of Assembly elections soon to follow, building on the momentum of change. The mood: disillusioned but hopeful.

> "It is seven long years since elections were held in the troubled border State and even in the 1989 polls barely five per cent votes were cast in Baramulla and Anantnag. In sharp contrast, almost ten times the number were cast this time, a turnout which may be pointed out is larger than in some of the other states like Gujarat in the just concluded general election. Polling was also largely peaceful in the Valley despite stray demonstrations, bandhs and bomb blasts as well as firing by Pakistanis along the LoC.... The large turnout in the Valley and the relative calm that prevailed there on polling day must therefore be a setback to separatist groups and their sponsors across the border. However, the surprisingly high polling in the Valley would have been far more welcome had there not been widespread allegations of coercive voting."[28]

Three months down the road in September 1996, elections for the State Assembly were held. The Hurriyat Conference as usual, boycotted the polls, the National Conference contested and won. The mood in the Valley without any appreciable change in conditions seemed to have shifted again, defying political parameters. A despatch from the BBC read:

> "The village of Waripara near the Kashmir resort town of Gulmarg was in an excited mood when I visited last week. The local Congress Party candidate had come campaigning. More than half the village gathered to hear his election speech. The youngsters of the village clapped, cheered and chanted and when the speech was done, they

took the Congress party flag on a victory tour round the village. The Congress flag is in Indian national colours. The Indian tricolour flying unchallenged over a Muslim Kashmiri village is a sight rarely seen over the past seven years of separatist insurgency."[29]

The first phase—held in the rural areas—was, by all accounts, a success. Even the *Guardian* commented: "...Thousands voted on their own, saying that they were tired of living in the shadow of guns, whether wielded by the rebels or Indian soldiers."[30] A genuinely high voter turnout—close to 60 per cent indicated that the pendulum began swinging towards that elusive peace.

An existence that most of us take for granted. The second phase, held in Srinagar and areas considered to be rebel strongholds, was wrecked by separatist violence, claiming 3 lives and injuring nearly 50 people. Voter turn-out was significant—close to 29 per cent. An accepted political process emerged from the shadows of violence. Reported the BBC: "Parties opposed to India's control now have a major problem. Their success in boycotting parliamentary elections held in December 1989 marked a turning point in the history of Kashmir. The failure of their boycott call this time marks another turning point."[31]

The "Legacy" of the 1990s

Pandit Flight

The tragic fallout of the first two years was the flight of Pandits from the Valley. Almost 95 per cent left. In the initial euphoria of the insurgency, when slogans like *nizame mustafa* became the *mantra* of Kashmiris, when prominent Pandits were killed and the rest, justifiably felt insecure and threatened, when the Jagmohan government encouraged Pandits to leave promising that they could return in three months, that's when the legacy of division began. In the last ten years, an entire generation of Kashmiri Muslims and Pandits have grown up, independent of the other. In the Pandit camps, home is still an address in Srinagar. The desire to return is overwhelming. Contrary to popular misconception, Pandits have not assimilated into mainstream India. Most of those who left the Valley in 1990 continue to live in deplorable conditions in the camps. In Kashmir, people speak about the tragic flight of a community. Walking through areas that were once Pandit localities bring to mind an immense sense of loss. They would be welcome back, but who would guarantee their safety? For people like the *Lashkar e Taiba*, Pandits in the Valley would be a soft target. Kashmir though is incomplete without its Pandits, who have contributed much to art, education and literature. For any lasting peace they must return home.

There are straws in the wind. Even during the height of the insurgency, temples were safe. "Smaller temples, situated in villages which abound with militants, were not harmed right through the 1989 to 1991 period when militancy was at its peak..."[32] And there were many individual instances of Muslim families persuading Hindus to stay in the Valley. But, says Mohammad Sadiq: "We would get up in the morning and find that people had left in the dead of night. It hurt very much."[33] There is an overwhelming sense among the handful of Pandits who had the courage of conviction to stay behind, that they are much better off than those living in the squalor of refugee camps, uncertain of ever returning.

The legacy of division is now an unfortunate reality. Extremities of opinion are heard in Pandit camps, some like the Panun Kashmir movement who demand a created "homeland" in the Valley. A generation is growing up, oblivious of the other. Everyday interaction is becoming a thing of the past. Its imperative now, that leaders in the Pandit community and leaders from the Valley, take initiatives to bridge the gap. Otherwise a unique heritage is in danger of being forever lost.

Human Rights: Not Quite Cricket......

"....A fundamental democratic rule is that innocent civilians must never be made a target. Yet thousands of them have died in Kashmir and the Indian government must account for their deaths... India is a party to the International Covenant on Civil and Political Rights. It is under an obligation to put its house in order. At the very least, it must act in accordance with its own, admirable constitution. It insists that Kashmiris are Indian citizens. It cannot, therefore deny them their rights as citizens."[34]

More than 50,000 have been killed in the past decade—some victims of the Indian security forces, some victims of the militants. Human rights abuse, particularly in the early years of the insurgency by the security forces alienated Kashmiris. Innocent lives were lost, innocent people picked up for questioning never to return. The frustration of the security forces is evident. The conditions under which they operate are hardly conducive—unfamiliar terrain, an inhospitable climate, and a hostile local population. Though each soldier is now armed with a handbook on human rights signed by the army chief which warns of severe punishments, abuses do occur, which are more often than not, a result of prevailing circumstances.

Such as Pakistan's active involvement in attempting to bleed Indian resources. Such as the inevitably hard nature of the counter insurgency operations itself. Such as the widespread powers—TADA (Terrorist and Disruptive Activities Prevention Act), PSA (Jammu and Kashmir Public Safety Act) the security forces have, which "contravene some of the most important human rights stands laid down in international human rights instruments to which India is a party, notably the right to life and the right not to be subjected to torture or to arbitrary arrest and detention."[35]. But that cannot excuse the violent and in some cases, totally unjustified reactions of the Indian security forces. Three particular incidents come to mind: Bijbehara in October 1993 (37 killed, 57 injured); Sopore in November 1993 (15 killed, 129 commercial establishments burnt) and Kupwara in January 1994 (27 killed). In all three, unarmed civilians were fired upon, without provocation.

Counter insurgency measures by definition are hugely unpopular. Broadly divided, they include: 1. The creation and maintenance of secure zones; 2. Combing—cordon and search operations; and 3. Administering judicial and extra-judicial punishments. Of the three, the first is the least offensive. A secure zone is characterized by huge bunkers and intensive patrolling—its where the government offices and military installations are. The "insecure" zones are where most of the people live and militants roam the streets, freely. "It is the government's expectation, naturally, that this bifold arrangement of the Valley will end in due time and that the two zones will merge into one—secure—area."[36]

Cordon and search operations. The infamous crackdowns. Mainly conducted by the paramilitary forces, these are unannounced, pre-dawn raids in residential areas. The objective being to uncover hideouts of hard-core militants and their less conspicuous supporters. Residents are rounded up, and wait, sometimes for upto 6 hours, while the search continues. Hooded informers, "cats" identify suspects, who are then picked up by the forces. Crackdowns are immensely unpopular not so much for the inconvenience or the intrusion of privacy, but for the humiliation and abuse endured, which have been so well documented on film, "that most Indian officials do not even attempt to deny them."[37]

Torture, custodial deaths, disappearances. By far the most blatant and horrific violations occur within the last category: judicial and extra-judicial punishments. Because of laws such as TADA and PSA, suspects can be detained for weeks at interrogation centres. Officials deny torture, but documentation suggests otherwise. Amnesty International in its reports on Kashmir have focused on the extra-judicial methods in practice. Torture Nephropathy—dehydration during torture and breakdown of soft tissues—and the "roller"—where the muscles on the legs are crushed—seem to be common.

That's one side of a rather horrifying story. In the name of *azaadi*, militants terrorized, abused and violated the human rights of Kashmiris too. As the insurgency gathered momentum, targets became selective. In the latter half of the 1990s security forces were specific targets of the non-Kashmiri Kashmiri led militant groups. But throughout the insurgency, those who were suspected to be police or army informers (*mukhbirs*) were ruthlessly killed. Those few who had the courage to refuse food and shelter to militants were killed. Those who wanted to vote in elections were threatened, physically abused and some killed. With the recent rise of *jihadi* groups, Pandits and Hindus in Jammu district become soft targets. Local Kashmiris who wish to see an end to the cycle of violence who formed Village Defence Committees have been selectively massacred. Militants believe that their goals are noble and that they are not bound by international humanitarian law. Their methods are indiscriminate: an IED explosion, grenade or bomb may kill the soldier or policeman it was intended for, but they also kill hundreds of innocent Kashmiri bystanders who just happen to be there. Incidents of cross firing too between the security forces and militants, have orphaned many children, widowed many women, killed many innocent men. Table 1 shows the statistics on militant destruction.

Table 1
The "Fruits" of Militancy[38]

Year	*Incidents of Violence*	*Targeting and Killing Political Activists**	*Destruction of Property (Public) Buildings)*	*Destruction of Private Property*	*IED and RDX Attacks*	*Grenade Attacks*	*Incidents of Crossfiring*
1990	5153		129 schools, 172 bridges, 501 other public buildings		1280	242	475
1991			93				
1992	7315						
1993	7987						
1994	8784		337 (from '92 to '94)			821	
1995	8731						1891
1996	6633	61	122 (from '94-96)	602	358	444	1089
1997	4702	57	29	437	255	168	959
1998	4150	52	29	273	264	187	1126
1999	4326	47	18	284	293	201	1205

*157 out of a total of 217 killed were National Conference Members, all Kashmiri.

What a wonderful legacy of abuse, of scarred minds, of a brutalized society where children in schools are taught "B for Bomb, C for Curfew." What a legacy too of numbered and maimed soldiers, terrorized policeman and traumatized paramilitary men, stationed in Kashmir not out of volition, killed merely because they are in uniform. By those who fight a faceless war.

2000 and Beyond: the "Crises" of Ceasefires

The millenium brought with it a series of "ceasefires". Beginning with the hastily retracted Hizbul Mujahideen ceasefire in July/August 2000, followed by the unilateral ceasefire by the

Vajpayee government of November 2000 which despite much provocation, will be in place till March 31, 2001. The ceasefire brings Kashmir to yet another crossroads: will it become permanent? Or after May will the bunkers return, the crackdowns continue, the security forces reposition themselves in full strength?

If the answer lay in the hands of Kashmiris, there is no doubt that the current ceasefire would become permanent. Kashmiris, including its self appointed representatives such as the Hurriyat Conference are willing to enter into an unconditional dialogue with New Delhi. If the answer lay in the hands of the Central Government, there is also no doubt that the ceasefire would remain in place long after the May deadline. India believes in dialogue, its Chief of army staff has gone on record stating that Kashmir is a political problem, not a military one. There would be just one reason and one country responsible if the ceasefire is revoked: the unrelenting violence of the *jihadi* groups and its sympathizer, Pakistan, "the land of the pure."

1996-1999

The 1996 elections forced a brake to the mindless violence. Eager to resume a "normal" existence, Kashmiris tired of the senseless loss of life and painfully aware that violence will not bring any results, are resigned to their fate within India. Most long for the time when children could be sent to school secure in the knowledge that they will return. That there would be no curfews, no cordon and search operations, no disappearances. That the Pandits would return. That *Kashmiriyat* would triumph.

The first two years after the elections (1997-1998) saw an appreciable decline in the level of militant violence.[39] Life, after eight long years of uncertainty and terror, was slowly limping back to normal. The government stumbled along. Farooq Abdullah's impulsive style of governance, continued. Ratan Irani's film unit was gifted Rs. 10 lakhs for being the first film crew to return to the Valley. The First National Winter Games were held in January 1998 in Gulmarg, at a cost of Rs. 10 crore. While it was symbolic to project normalcy through holding the Games in Gulmarg, there was little need to import German snow beating machines, French engineers to operate the cable cars, or even spend the Rs. 70 lakh to refurbish the Gulmarg Golf Course. But that's Farooq: flamboyant. The National Conference did create 13,000 jobs out of the 26,000 it promised in its mandate. But recruitment for the jobs has been corrupt. The administration remains corrupt, even lethargic. Essential services—water, power, health—remain neglected. Despite which the summer of 1998 saw a return of tourists, particularly domestic tourists to the Valley. Kashmiris spent summer evenings picnicking on the shores of the Dal Lake. Bhat a *shikarawallah*, echoed many voices:: ""What *azaadi*, what militants? This is *azaadi*".[40]

Then Kargil happened. Followed by the infiltration of a large number of *jihadis* into Kashmir. Followed by the inevitable response of the security forces. But despite the presence and now dominance of well over 3000 foreign mercenaries, mainly veterans from the Afghan war working with *Lashkar-e-Taiba* and *Jaish-e-Mohammad* and *Harkat-ul-Ansar*, Kashmir as in the past, is resisting the clarion call of Taliban-type of Islam.

Ceasefire vs. Jihadis

"Islam does not allow a ceasefire. We believe in achieving our goal through jihad."

Maulana Masood Azhar, Chief Jaish e Mohammad.[41]

"We have no dearth of funds or volunteers. India is tired and wants to get out of the fighting, we won't let the Indian army rest until it is kicked out of Kashmir

Pakistan-based Kashmiri commander of a militant group.[42]

"Let this opportunity not be missed by all those that desire peace for our patience is not infinite".

Prime Minister Atal Bihari Vajpayee announcing the three-month extension of the ceasefire till May 31, 2001.[43]

The short-lived *Hizbul Mujahideen* ceasefire of July 2000 caught most people off-guard.Most of all, the *Jihadi* groups in Pakistan who denounced the move, reacting with anger and surprise. Seen as a betrayal to the Kashmir cause (ironically by non-Kashmiris) they rejected the *Hizbul* initiative, vowing instead to step up violence.

Syed Salahudddin expressed his disappointment openly:"Having worked with us for so many years, these organizations should have known that the *Hizb* would never compromise the freedom struggle. I am disappointed to see that other organizations have resorted to malicious propoganda against us".[44] There remains a great deal of speculation regarding Pakistan's role in this drama. Most analysts agree that Pakistan (the ISI) did call the shots behind the scenes.The *Hizb* demand that Pakistan be included in the talks from the very beginning was unnecessarily unreasonable given India's insistence that talks with Pakistan would be conditional on Pakistan withdrawing its support to *jihadi* groups. The ceasefire fell through in three weeks, but not before a 100 innocent people were massacred in what has been termed "Kashmir's Night of Terror" between August 2 and August 3, 2000. Those massacred included Hindu pilgrims on their way to the Amarnath *yatra*, migrant labour from Bihar, and as usual, innocent Kashmiris.

If this was intended to derail the fledgling ceasefire, to the credit of the Central government, it didn't succeed. Kashmiris watched in despair as the initial euphoria over the *Hizb* ceasefire turned into a bloodbath by those supposedly fighting for Kashmiri interests. Salahuddin, though unable to continue with the initiative spoke passionately in its defence: "Sitting in Pakistan or India, it is very easy to criticize the cease-fire decision because people in these two countries are not aware of the extent of the Kashmiri's sufferings. You should go to Kashmir and see how happy the Kashmiris are with our decision. For every Indian soldier we have killed, they have killed 10 innocent Kashmiris. We were engaged in an armed struggle because we had no other choice, but we sincerely believe that most conflicts are invariably resolved on the negotiating table and not in the battlefield."[45] He almost sounds like Yusuf Shah.

The year 2000 paradoxically may be referred to in the future as the one where the peace process in Kashmir began (if the ceasefire continues), but it was also one of the most violent in recent times. Thirty-four Sikhs in Chhattisinghpora were gunned down in March 2000, by 15 unidentified gun men, just before President Clinton's visit to India. Dressed in army fatigues, they separated the men from the women and shot the men in cold blood, near the Gurudwara. Their identity remains unknown: Pakistan says that the army killed the Sikhs (an absurd claim). India maintains that the terrorists did. Though human rights organizations—Amnesty and Indian organizations—conclude that the killers were renegades. Regardless of their identity, this was the first time that Sikhs, a sizeable minority were targeted in the insurgency. August saw the killings of hundred and more innocent people in the span of twenty-four hours. Reports confirm though that most of the Amarnath pilgrims in Pahalgam were killed in the crossfire between militants and security forces.

But the year 2000 also saw some welcome signs of "normalcy." The Indian NGO community took some tentative steps to work with NGOs in Kashmir, who for most of the decade were kept silent. Working with orphans, working with women who've been abused, working on counselling the victims of violence is being facilitated by Indian NGOs. On the political level, a number of track two initiatives have begun. People are being given a platform to speak. And many speak openly about the futility of violence, their opposition to militancy, their resentment against *jihadis*. And their disillusionment with Pakistan. They speak too of the human rights abuses committed by India's security forces, of the extreme humiliation that they, as innocent Kashmiris, have suffered. Most of all they speak of sons and brothers: killed, disappeared. The important point is that some sort of a dialogue between the people of Kashmir and the rest of us, has begun. The overwhelming sentiment of any dialogue is common: "*Hame aman chahiye* (we want peace). Peace with honour." Even Yasin Malik quotes Gandhi in his speeches.

Politically, Farooq lived upto his maverick image and pushed the Autonomy Bill through in August 2000, just when the *Hizb* ceasefire was on. The Central Government's summary rejection of the Bill was disappointing and many questioned Delhi's willingness to talk to *Hizb*, but ignore the National Conference, an ally of the NDA government. The NC is fast losing credibility with its inept and corrupt government but, despite what Hurriyat may claim, there really is no opposition. There are other players outside the APHC and the NC who have considerable constituencies and much to contribute if a prolonged peace process truly begins.

The first step towards which is the Vajpayee ceasefire. Announced at the end of November to mark the beginning of the holy month of Ramzan, this is an unprecedented step. A truly bold initiative, which was welcomed unreservedly by all shades of opinion in Kashmir. After decades, Kashmiris celebrated Ramzan late into the night without worrying about getting home before dark, as was common during the insurgency hit years. The *jihadis* too refrained from any major acts of violence, save the spectacular Red Fort shoot-out in Delhi, killing two, which was high on symbolism, nothing else. It is entirely to Vajpayee's credit that the ceasefire was extended for another month, till January 22. Refusing to bow down to sensationalism, India stuck to its peace mission. The Pakistani response has been a reduction in shelling across the LoC, little else.

The second month of the ceasefire began with death. On Christmas day, a fidayeen squad of the Jaish e Mohammad stormed the headquarters the 15 Corps, in Srinagar. Bilai Ahmed, aged 24 and a student from Birmingham, UK ran the explosives-laden car into the army camp. The *Lashkar-e-Taiba* celebrated the second month of the ceasefire by a suicide attempt by storming Srinagar airport on January 16, leaving fifteen dead, including women of the security forces and an innocent 16-year-old Kashmiri girl. These were just the spectacular strikes. On a routine basis, jawans, police and innocent bystanders were being selectively killed. Sikh truck drivers were killed by an IED blast on the Jammu-Srinagar highway. National Conference workers were targeted to such a degree that Farooq's reaction was a "to hell with the ceasefire."

In the mainstream press, concerns over the rise in *fidayeen* attacks were voiced. With bunkers and check posts having been dismantled, terrorists freely roamed the roads, walking into high security areas with guns hidden under phirans. In the rural areas, people were once again, terrorized into "helping" militants. "Javed Bi fled Surankote with her six children, the youngest of them less than a year old, after her husband Mishar, was executed by terrorists. Mishar was beheaded after he refused to help build shelters for the terrorists around his village, now free of army or police presence."[46] More than 3000 people, Hindus and Muslims, all Kashmiris have fled from their homes in the remote villages in

Rajouri and Poonch, preferring to live in makeshift camps near Jammu.

The second extension of the ceasefire, from January 22 to February 22 was made despite hardliners in India and the state government in Kashmir advocating the opposite. The statement issued by the Cabinet Committee for Security Affairs read: "The Government believes violence must be ended and peace—which has been welcomed by the people of J&K—given every chance. The present phase of peace is being extended in that hope by another month". Concerns remained: that militants had regrouped and were fired with the success of their suicide squads. That the state police were becoming increasingly demoralized. That the security forces would prefer to fight a war with their hands untied. But proponents of the ceasefire pointed to the relative inactivity of Kashmiri militants, such as the *Hizbul Mujahideen* as a sign of optimism. That with time, international pressure would force Pakistan to rein in the *jihadis*, which would eventually then pave the way for a sustainable peace. Most newspapers ran editorials supporting the extension:

> "From the very beginning, all those weeks ago in November when New Delhi announced its peace initiative, the ceasefire has been an enterprise fraught with risk. And never so far more than at this juncture. The overwhelming consensus evident just weeks ago on the initiative is now showing signs of fraying at the edges.... In fact with Pakistan—based *jihadi* groups attempting to outdo one another in executing heinous attacks, it is but a matter of time before the nation's patience wears out... Thankfully, the Cabinet Committee on Security has kept in focus another lot of protagonists in this entire drama: the people of Jammu and Kashmir. Civilian casualties may be up in the state but the longing for peace and for a determined peace process is more than audible. Surely that—in addition to the diplomatic imperative to run the extra mile in this extraordinary gesture—had to be a deciding factor behind the decision to extend the ceasefire."[47]

If the ceasefire was in any danger of falling apart, month

three would have been ideal. Lashkar ran amuck—expected; the security forces opened fire on demonstrations—unexpected. The first casualties were Sikhs. Soft targets, necessary in a dirty war. On the February 2, six Sikhs including a woman were gunned down by militants as they walked towards their homes. There are an estimated 75,000 Sikhs who live in the villages of Kashmir. The Sikh community is now debating migrating out of Kashmir, just like the Pandits did more than ten years ago. If they do, it would be one step closer towards physically at least, Islamicizing Kashmir.

Within a week of the Sikh killings, Lashkar militants massacred fifteen members of three Muslim families in Rajouri district. The dead included three women and seven children. Their crime: they were families of village defence committee members, the men also worked as porters for the army. The same night in Srinagar, a *Lashkar* suicide attack on the police control room, killed eight. A good night for *Lashkar*: twenty-three killed the cost of one dead militant, Abu Mauya. On February 23, militants fired grenades on the police in Kokernag, killing six.

Meanwhile, on February 15, the Army opened fire on a crowd of demonstrators on the Sopore—Kupwara road near Haigam, who were protesting the killing of Jaleel Ahmed Shah by the Kashmir police Special Operations Group. The police maintain that he was a militant killed in an encounter: the local people say he was a member of JKLF who had even donated blood for victims of the Gujarat earthquake. A crowd of over 800 people had gathered to receive his body. The army, frustrated at not being able to pass, opened fire, killing six, injuring 26. Signs of patience snapping? Squandering in the matter of seconds, immense gains of the ceasefire, which till then, had begun to prove that the relentless violence is one sided. Three days later in Maisuma, Srinagar, as a mob defined curfew to protest the Haigam firing, a military intelligence (MI) person in plain clothes, fired with his pistol. In the melee that followed a teenager was killed—unclear whether he was hit by the bullet or killed in the stampede that followed. The MI person was arrested immediately. Sign of an individual snapping?

That the ceasefire is taking its toll on lives, patience and sanity is stating the obvious.Kashmiris are now in small number beginning to mumble about the ceasefire being an eyewash for the international community. That though is patently unfair. India has invested with lives—young lives of its officers—for long-term peace. At great risk, bunkers and checkpoints have been dismantled. The daily frisking of civilians has stopped. And except for the Haigam firing, the ceasefire has by all accounts, been strictly adhered to by the Indian security forces. Certainly, the diplomatic gains are many: for one, Pakistan has been forced to mouth support for a peace initiative. Second: the world is watching, while India sincerely gives peace a chance.

Against the odds. "There can't be any peace while India remains intact. Cut them, cut them. Cut them so much that they kneel before you and ask for mercy. Only then can we think of any talks."[48] Hafeez Mohammed Saeed, chief of *Lashkar-e-Taiba* personifies the obstacles to peace. Fanatic in his anti-India tirade, his mission is clear: Kashmir becomes part of Islamic Pakistan, till such time, India continues to pay with blood. He has scant respect for a pluralistic society. For democracy. "Democracy is among the menaces we inherited from an alien government. These are all useless practices and part of the system we are fighting against. Many of our brothers feel that they will be able to establish an Islamic system while working within this system. This is trash and you just dirty your hands by dealing with it."[49]

Based on a sprawling campus of 190 acres of land, thirty miles north of Lahore, the *Markaz Dawa wal Irshad* is a centre for education, preaching and *jihad*. The *Lashkar-e-Taiba*—ironically translated "the army of peace"—is its militant wing of highly trained mercenaries. The *Markaz Dawa wal Irshad* was founded in 1987 by three university teachers, two from the University of Engineering and Technology, Lahore and the other from the International Islamic University. The campus includes the opulent Jamia mosque funded by a Saudi donor, a garment factory, an iron factory, a woodworks factory, a stable and swimming pool. The construction for the Dawa University is underway. The organization runs 30 schools, where 5,000 students are enrolled. With its impressive network of schools and social service groups, recruitment is guaranteed.

Its annual three-day jamboree is fertile recruitment ground for the *Lashkar-e-Taiba*. Close to 100,000 people, including relations of those who have been killed in Kashmir attend the largest religious congregation in Pakistan, where the virtues of *jihad* are preached to the common man. Emotional speeches, rhetoric and ideology win over thousands of converts, every year. It is difficult to remain aloof from graphic, though highly suspect accounts such as these: "I slaughtered five members of my family with my own hands because they were informers for the Indian army," relates Abdullah, from Srinagar. "I was a Hindu, yet I joined the path of *jihad*. What keeps you away from it?"[50] Speaker after speaker concludes that "*jihad* has become mandatory." Has it? On whose behalf? Deafened by the sound of martyrdom, who's listening?

The *Lashkar-e-Taiba's* operate exclusively in Kashmir. At any given time, the *Lashkar-e-Taiba* trains many more men than the number required to fight in Kashmir. The training is carried out in isolated parts of "Azad" Kashmir: a 21-day standard course, the *Daura-e-Aama*, followed by an intensive 3-month special programme, the Daura-e-Khasa on guerrilla warfare, the use of small arms, survival and ambush techniques. There are an estimated 18 jihadi groups in Pakistan with camps based in NWFP and Azad Kashmir, whose training courses are equally rigorous, whose rhetoric is equally shrill. Volunteers are many. Entire families have given up their lives for Kashmir. And the majority of recruits are from Punjab and the NWFP, not Azad Kashmir. As an Al Badr publication states, "Salahuddin should make it clear that it is not just the Kashmiris who shed their blood for Kashmir. There are thousands of Pakistani families whose boys have nurtured the Kashmir movement with their blood."[51] And will continue to do so. Mothers who wept at their son's deaths took solace and pride in the fact they had produced warriors who died fighting infidels.

Recruitment isn't confined to Pakistan alone. Maulana Masood Azhar's Jaish-e-Mohammad rumoured to be the "favourite" of the ISI, has international recruits. The Birmingham bomber was till the age of 18, an average British Asian who enjoyed clubbing. Till he saw the Prophet in his dreams and then became a devout Muslim. He was recruited in 1994 as a teenager in the UK in a mosque by AI Maddad a recruiting agency for young Britons. There are nearly 2000 recruits (*jihadis*) of Al Madal operating in Chechnya, Bosnia and Kashmir. Bilal joined the *Jaish-e-Mohammad* in 1995 and was trained in Northern Pakistan and Azad Kashmir. He wasn't the first Briton to die in Kashmir, reports say that there are hundreds of British *jihadis* fighting in Kashmir.

Most of the cadre for *Jaish-e-Mohammed* are drawn from the urban and rural lower middle class and the *madrassa*. *Jaish* has strong links with Taliban, which given its penchant for statute—bashing does not augur well for Kashmir's pluralistic society. Abdul Gani Lone, a senior member of Hurriyat voices caution: "Pakistani *mujahideen* come to Kashmir, and we thank them for their struggle and sacrifices. We expect that they should be part of our struggle and support it. But they should not have their own agenda. They are great sympathizers, but they should confine their role to support only."[52]

The ceasefire is being challenged by an irrational enemy, who see it as a sign of weakness on India's part. A sign that the Indian forces are backing down. That they, who fight a coward's war, are succeeding. Unable to think beyond narrow, selfish ends, unable to think of a civilised world without AK 47s, the *jihadis* have done their best to bait Vajpayee into abandoning this tentative beginning towards sustainable peace. The government, though refused to be baited. After a difficult meeting of all political parties the government announced that the ceasefire has been extended by three months till May 31, 2001. The enlightened *Lashkar* response: predictable.Fifteen policemen and two civilians were massacred in Rajouri district on March 2, when rockets and grenades hit their vehicle. Those trapped inside were torched to death; six managed to jump out of the vehicle and had to trudge 10 kms for help. Three days later, a *Lashkar* attack on an army camp in Baramullah, killed four and wounded four.

The outstanding failure (Haigam apart, which is inexcusable at so critical a juncture) of the ceasefire has been the government's inability to begin a political process. To follow up the cessation of violence with political initiatives. Without which the ceasefire is turning into a well-intentioned but poorly executed exercise. The seesaw over whether Hurriyat should go to Pakistan or not is becoming embarrassing. The deliberations over who should be part of the Hurriyat team is really not any of Delhi's business. The argument that if Hurriyat goes, they will be seen as representative of Kashmiris with official sanction, does not hold water. These are pointless excuses: Hurriyat should go, if only to prove that India has not left any stone unturned in its peace initiative. "When Vajpayee announced the ceasefire for the holy month of Ramzan the people of Kashmir saw a ray of hope in him. Most people developed a soft corner towards the Prime Minister and his efforts. The change in people's attitudes could have provided a breakthrough in changing the present situation had it been utilized properly."[53] But perhaps the government has other pressing engagements, such as countering the *Tehelka* tapes. The tragedy is that the *insaniyat* driven ceasefire instead of consolidating gains with political initiatives, is being allowed to be blasted always by those who have much to gain by perpetuating conflict: the *jihadis* and mercenaries, the *mehman mujahideen* who have long outlived their welcome.

A Lament

"Let there be a major earthquake in Kashmir so that we all die in peace.... never to see these miseries again. Never to see our loved ones die one byone"

Ghulam Hassan Wani, brother-in law of Abdul Majid,
constable killed in a Lashkar-e-Taiba bomb blast
in February 2001.[54].

Kashmiris voted for an end to violence. They had hopes, high hopes from the ceasefire.They had misplaced hope that their self-proclaimed saviours, the *jihadis* would respect their wishes and reciprocate the ceasefire. So that peace, after years of mindless violence, would be given a chance. Instead its been a disappointing game of how many killed and by whom. Pakistan's claim that it has no control over *jihadis* is pathetic. With a population brainwashed into supporting *jihad*, with collection boxes in the smallest of stores, with *madrassas* in·every mosque "which have been transformed into centres for *jihad*"[55] with Islamic political parties, present in all of Pakistan's 106 districts attracting recruits, this *jihad* cannot be wished away. It is too deeply entrenched in the psyche of Pakistan, with thousands waiting to be "lucky" enough to be martyred in Kashmir.

Kashmiri political leadership talks in terms of peace and dialogue, regardless of their different affiliations. The notable exception being Syed Ali Shah Geelani, who is beginning to sound like a mouthpiece for the *jihadi* groups. But the rest, who represent at least ninety-five per cent of the population speak of negotiations. Speak of peace. Including Syed Salahuddin. That is where hope lies. In the people who will have the courage of their conviction, the courage of tradition, the courage of *Kashmiriyat* to rise, unarmed against armed fanatics.

Or will Kashmir forever be at a crossroads of simmering violence and a compromised peace?

References

1. Siddiqui, Taimur. "The Soldiers of Allah", *Newsline*, Karachi, February 2001.
2. Hussain, Zahid, "Inside Jihad", *Newsline*, Karachi, February 2001.
3. Akbar, M.J., *Kashmir: Behind the Vale*, New Delhi, Viking, 1991.
4. Singh, Tavleen, *Kashmir: A Tragedy of Errors*, New Delhi, Viking 1995.
5. *Ibid.*
6. Interview with Inderjit Badhwar, *India Today*, New Delhi. Living Media Pvt. Ltd. November 30, 1986.
7. Varshney, Ashutosh. *Three Compromised Nationalisms: Why Kashmir has been a Problem.* Perspectives on Kashmir: The Roots of Conflict in South Asia. Boulder, Colorado,Westview Press, 1992.
8. Baweja, Harinder. Kashmir: A Calculated Gamble, *India Today*. April 30, 1992.
9. Badhwar. Tarnished Triumph, *India Today*, April 15, 1987.
10. Akbar, M.J. *Kashmir Behind the Vale.*
11. Ibid.
12. Badhwar. Farooq Under Fire, *India Today*. September 15, 1987.
13. Rahman, Mushtaq. *Divided Kashmir: Old Problems, New Opportunities for India, Pakistan and the Kashmiri People.* London Lynne Rineer Publishers, Inc. 1996.
14. Ray, Maj. Gen. Arjun. *Kashmir Diary: Psychology of Militancy*, New Delhi, Manas Publications. 1997.

15. Ganguly, Sumit. *The Crisis in Kashmir: Portents of War, Hopes of Peace*, Cambridge, Cambridge University Press, 1997.
16. Source: *Mass Media in India*, 1978 (New Delhi: Publications Division, Ministry of Information and Broadcasting, Government of India, 1978); *Mass Media in India*, 1986 (New Delhi: Publications Division, Ministry of Information and Broadcasting, Government of India 1987).
17. Ganguly, Sumit. *The Crisis in Kashmir*.
18. Primary source.
19. Badhwar, Kashmir: Valley of Tears, *India Today*. May 31, 1989.
20. Davis, Anthony. The Kashmir Conflict, *Jane's Intelligence Review*, Vol. 7, No. 1 Surrey, January 1995.
21. Baweja, New Disenchantment, *India Today*. December 12, 1995.
22. Behera, Navnita Chadha, *State, Identity and Violence: Jammu, Kashmir and Ladakh*. New Delhi, Manohar Publishers, 2000.
23. *Ibid*.
24. *Ibid*.
25. *Ibid*.
26. Reuters dispatch, *Kashmir Elections* by Naqvi, September 21, 1996.
27. Inderjit, Sabina *The Times of India*, New Delhi, May 24, 1996.
28. Editorial, *Pioneer*, New Delhi, May 25, 1996.
29. Whitehead, Andrew, *Kashmir Elections*, London, *BBC World Service*, September 3, 1996.
30. Kemp. *The Guardian*, London. September 8, 1996.
31. Lyon, David, BBC World Service, Delhi, September 9, 1996.
32. Baweja, Damaging Lies, *India Today*. February 28, 1993.
33. Baweja, Living on the Edge, *India Today*. July 15, 1992.
34. Editorial Comment, *The Times*, London, August 12, 1993.
35. Torture and Death in Custody in Jammu and Kashmir. *Amnesty International*, New York. January 1995.
36. Wirsing, Robert, *India, Pakistan and the Kashmir Dispute*. London, Macmillan Press Ltd. 1994.
37. *Ibid*.
38. Figures compiled from Dr. Kamal Mitra Chenoy's Report on Human Rights Violations presented at the conference in Srinagar on October 1, 2000 organized by the Kashmir Foundation for Peace and Development Studies, Srinagar. The report contains the findings of a working group of three persons formed to investigate human rights violations in Jammu and Kashmir, on the initiative of the Kashmir Foundation for Peace and Development. The report was published by the Foundation in its journal *New Hope*, but I have referred to the version published in Seminar: Frameworks for Peace, December 2000, New Delhi.

39. Refer to Table "Fruits of Violence"
40. Baweja Out of the Mists, *India Today.* December 1, 1997.
41. Hussain, Zahid, "Lethal Weapon", *Newsline*, Karachi, January 2001.
42. Siddiqui, Taimur, Soldiers of Allah, *Newsline.*
43. *Indian Express*, February 22, 2001.
44. Interview with Syed Salahuddin, *The Herald*, Karachi, August 2000.
45. *Ibid.*
46. Swami, Praveen Unceasing Fire, *Frontline*, Chennai, Messrs Kasturi and Sons Ltd., February 16, 2001.
47. Editorial, Two to Tango, *Indian Express*, New Delhi. January 24, 2001.
48. Hasnain, Ghulam. "Ready for Jehad" *Outlook*, New Delhi, September 25, 2000.
49. Khan, Zahid Allah's Army, *The Herald*, Annual Karachi: Herald Limited Press, January 1998.
50. *Ibid.*
51. Hasnain, Ready for Jehad, *Outlook.*
52. Interview with Abdul Ghani Lone, *Newsline*, January 2001.
53. Zahoor Malik, *The Kashmir Times*, Jammu February 22, 2001.
54. Oberoi, Surinder Singh, The New Targets, *India Today.* March 26, 2001.
55. Hussain, Zahid. Inside Jihad, *Newsline*, February 2001.

Five

Human Rights Violations: A Report

Kamal Mitra Chenoy

Introduction

An independent citizen's committee to inquire into human rights violations in Jammu and Kashmir comprising Dr. Kamal Mitra Chenoy, Associate Professor, School of International Studies, Jawaharlal Nehru University, New Delhi, as Convenor; Dr. Ambrose Pinto, S.J., Executive Director, Indian Social Institute, New Delhi, and Shri Zafar Iqbal Manhas, columnist and cultural activist, Srinagar, as members, was constituted at the request of the Kashmir Foundation for Peace and Development Studies, Srinagar in August 2000.

The committee visited Srinagar, Chittisingpora, Pahalgam, Jammu, Akhnoor, Rajouri, Surankote and Poonch, between August 26 and September 3, 2000. It met a wide cross-section of officials including those in the Army, paramilitary forces and police, citizens from various walks of life, and victims of the violence. We are deeply grateful to our informants who frankly shared their experiences and opinions with us, often despite the fear of the gun. But for them, this report could not have been written. We also record our appreciation of the Kashmir Foundation for Peace and Development Studies, Srinagar, which consistently gave unstinted support to our committee, while encouraging us to arrive at independent judgements at every stage. Hence, the views expressed herein are those of the committee, and the responsibility for all opinions as well as any shortcomings in the report is entirely our own.

For informed observers of Jammu and Kashmir, and many of its citizens, little of what this report contains is new. But much of what may seem common knowledge, particularly in the Valley, is not well known in the rest of India. We believe if the Indian public comes to realize the extent of human rights violations in the State, public pressure to curb such violations will mount. But this report is unusual on one specific count. Unlike most human rights reports, it also describes and indicts human rights violations by the militants. While the militants may reject the Indian Constitution and Indian law, they have no moral or legal right to violate the universally recognized canons of international humanitarian law. To the extent they do, they are also violators of human rights and must be criticized as such.

We dedicate this report to the long suffering people of Jammu and Kashmir, with the fervent hope that it may contribute its mite to the ending of this tragedy.

The Political Background

It is clear to any dispassionate observer, that the insurgency in Jammu and Kashmir is the result of the alienation of a substantial section of the population from the Indian state and from there own elected representatives, seen as agents of the former. As is well known, Jammu and Kashmir acceeded to the Indian Union under very special circumstances in 1948, with Maharaja Hari Singh's hands being forced by the Pakistani-backed invasion of tribal raiders, to fight whom the maharaja needed the services of the Indian army.

Despite the role of Sheikh Abdullah, in rallying the Kashmiri people to support the accession to India, a suspicious Indian government incarcerated him for most of the 1953 to 1975 period until the Indira-Sheikh Accord of 1975. In the interim period, making use of pliable governments elected in elections generally believed to have been rigged in favour of the ruling party, the greater part of the autonomy given to the State under Article 370 as enacted and as existing in 1952, was systematically taken away by successive Union governments. This deepened the alienation in the Valley and increased anti-Indian sentiments. Though Pakistan continued to support secessionist forces in Kashmir from

1948 onwards, the critical event that led to a major insurgency in the Valley from 1989, is widely believed to be the elections of 1987.

There was a major challenge to the ruling National Conference from a coalition of parties grouped under the Muslim United Front [MUF] in the Valley. Contrary to popular expectations and predictions, the MUF was routed in elections believed to have been massively rigged by the National Conference [NC]. This sharpened popular alienation from both the Union government as well as the major pro-Indian party: the NC, and thus reportedly created the political and social base for the bloody insurgency that persists even today.

The insurgency and counter-insurgency operations by the Army, para-military forces, police and surrendered militants have created a vicious circle of violence in which, according to some estimates, as many as 60,000 people have died. The record of human rights violations is a direct consequence of this bloody, and in part, fratricidal conflict.

Counter-Insurgency Laws: Some Legal Questions

The major Act that governs military action in Jammu & Kashmir is the Armed Forces (Special Powers) Act, 1958 [as amended in 1972]. Human rights activists have long argued that this Act is unconstitutional and violates international humanitarian law. The Supreme Court has, like in the earlier case of TADA, upheld the validity of the law, but in view of the potential abuse of human rights has laid down some detailed guidelines for its use. Nonetheless, we believe this is a "lawless law" which violates both the Constitution and international law.

The Act gives no precise definition of "disturbed area." The declaration of any area as 'disturbed' under Section 3 is the prerogative of the Governor of the State or the Central Government. The State legislature has absolutely no jurisdiction in the matter, though under the Constitution 'public order' is a State subject [Seventh Schedule, List II, Entry 1]. Under Section 4(a) of the Act, even a non-commissioned officer can order his men to shoot to kill "if he is of the opinion that it is necessary to do so for maintenance of public order...' This gives very wide discretion to even very junior officers. Similarly, Section 4(b) allows such military personnel to destroy any shelter from which in his opinion, armed attacks "are likely to be made" or which has been utilized as a hideout by absconders "wanted for any offence." This latitude has permitted the destruction of large numbers of dwellings and other buildings in the State, including in collateral damage when buildings adjoining the one targeted have been damaged or destroyed.

Section 4(c) of the Act permits the arrest without warrant, with whatever "force as may be necessary" of any person against whom " a reasonable suspicion exists that he is about to commit a cognizable offence." This has provided the basis of indiscriminate arrests,, and the use of brutal force including firing against innocent civilians. Section 4(d) authorizes the entry and search, without warrant, of any premises to make arrests as sanctioned under Section 4(c), or to recover any person "believed to be wrongfully restrained or confined," or any property "reasonably suspected' to be stolen property or any arms, ammunition or explosive substance "believed to be unlawfully kept in such premises..." For military personnel operating in a culturally alien terrain, 'beliefs' and 'reasonable suspicions' are often wholly unfounded leading to human rights abuses, as we shall see below.

Though Section 5 of the Act explicitly lays down that, "Any person arrested and taken into custody under this Act shall be made over to the office in charge of the nearest police station with the least possible delay...," this has been repeatedly violated. Section 6 exempts Army personnel from prosecution, stating, "No prosecution, suit or legal proceeding shall be instituted, except with the previous sanction of the Central Government, against any person in respect of anything done or purported to be done in exercise of powers conferred by this Act." The exemption from prosecution is not only for what is done under this Act, but also for what is "purported to be done."

Experts in the UN Human Rights Committee, which met in Geneva in March 1991, were categorical that this Act is violative of several Articles of the International Covenant on Civil and Political Rights to which India is a signatory. Article 2(3) directs the state to ensure that any person whose rights have been violated "shall have an effective remedy, notwithstanding that the violation has been committed in an official capacity." While Article 4(1) permits State Parties to take measures derogating from their obligations in the time of national emergency. Article 4(3) lays down that any such derogation must be reported to other State Parties through the UN Secretary-General. The Indian government has made no such communication. In any case, as an expert in the UN Human Rights Committee pointed out, such an emergency must be a temporary measure, and cannot be in operation for decades, as this Act has been in various parts of India.

Further, Article 4(2) stipulates that no derogation from certain key Articles, including Article 6 [right to life], may be made under this provision. But Section 4 of the Act, as we have seen above, empowers firing, which may result in death, merely based on a relatively junior officer's opinion or suspicion. This violates Article 6(1) of the Covenant which inter alia states that, "No one shall be arbitrarily deprived of his life." Under international law, once India has signed this Covenant, its provisions can even supersede the Constitution. In other words, the Armed Forces [Special Powers] Act cannot be upheld as legal and valid on the ground that it is consistent with the Constitution, even if it violates the Covenant.

In any case, human rights activists have consistently held that the Act is also violative of the Constitution. It, like TADA, violates Articles 14 and 21 of the Fundamental Rights, and is derogation from Entry 1, list II of the Seventh Schedule. Article 13 which voids all laws inconsistent with the Fundamental Rights is infringed. Article 19, which protects freedoms of speech and expression, of peaceful assembly, and the right to form associations and unions, is also violated. Though the Supreme Court has upheld the Act, after laying down detailed guidelines to curb misuse, it should be remembered that the apex court also upheld TADA, to be overruled later by parliament.

The Committee is of the firm opinion that the continued misuse of this law, and the exemption from prosecution it provides to military personnel, is a major source of human rights violations by army formations in the State.

Blood and Death in Jammu & Kashmir

Human rights activists and others often argue, that since the militants do not accept either the Indian Constitution or Indian law, these do not apply to them, and as such their human rights violations, as it were, cannot be criticized, as violations as such, since they have not violated anything they themselves have accepted as law, or as a valid standard. In this vein, it is argued that violations by the militants, or individual terrorism, should not be the subject of study, since Indian law applies only to security forces and the Indian State, who are instead guilty of state terrorism. This betrays an ignorance of international humanitarian law all of which applies to all combatants, militants or statists. The international legal instruments including the Universal Declaration of Human Rights, International Covenant on Civil and Political Rights, Geneva Conventions, etc., which India has signed, apply to both the Indian forces as well as to the militants.

Militants, and the Pakistan government, have argued that in the Kashmir case, the special concept of '*jihad*' or holy war applies, which supersedes all international humanitarian law, not to speak of Indian law. Pakistan, an Islamic state, does not itself govern its own international relations on the basis of such a controversial reading of Islamic law, but on the basis of internationally accepted secular international law. Islamic scholars have also argued, that this interpretation of '*jihad*' itself is not in consonance with either Prophet Mohammed's own life or preachings. The Prophet's life was marked by a reverence for peace and mercy towards His enemies. Be that as it may, in a world of myriad religions and ways of life, no one religious interpretation can substitute for internationally accepted standards and law. The Indian state may argue, as it does, that its own excesses are justified or at least excusable, because it fights foreign 'terrorists'. This argument too is specious, and is a violation of international humanitarian law. State terrorism is neither a legal nor humane response to religiously fundamentalist individual terrorism.

Thus, in this report, as indicated at the outset, the committee has criticized human rights violations by both sides, security forces and militants alike. This is, unfortunately, unusual, but for the reasons cited above, in keeping with the core, internationally accepted precepts of human rights and impartial judgement.

Since 1990, there has been substantial militant activity in the State. According to police sources, there were 5,153 incidents of violence and other militant activities in that year. These rose sharply to 7,315 incidents in 1992, and amounted to 7,987, 8,784, 8,731 and 6,633 incidents in 1993, 1994, 1995 and 1996 respectively. After this, with an elected National Conference government taking office in October 1996, militant activity declined to 4,702, 4,150, and 4,326 incidents in 1997, 1998 and 1999 respectively. In the 10 year period involving the militants, signifying a high level of activity, which was however, significantly reduced after 1996.

The militants also targeted political activists. In 1996, as many as 61 were killed, of which 36 were from the NC, and 19 from the Congress. In 1997, 1998, and 1999, 57, 52, and 47 political activists, of which 121 were from the NC, and 18 were from the Congress, were killed by militants. The plan by the militants was obviously to discourage 'over-ground' political activity, particularly by the major parties: the NC and the Congress which bore the brunt of the killings. But the killing of 217 political activists over a period of just 4 years, is a premeditated assault on legitimate political activity and is as such a clearly politically motivated human rights atrocity, allegedly planned by the ISI and other agencies across the border.

The pattern of destruction of property by militants was similar to the total incidents of militant activity. For instance, in 1990, according to official sources, as many as 802 public buildings including 129 schools, 172 bridges and 501 other buildings, were destroyed or extensively damaged allegedly by militants. By 1991, this total plummeted to 93, going up by 1994 to 337. By 1996, public buildings destroyed came down to 122, falling further to only 29 in both 1997 and 1998, to as low as 18 in 1999. In 1996, 602 private buildings were destroyed, of which 432 were stated to belong to the majority community, and 170 to the minority community. By 1997, this came down to a total of 437 private buildings of which 303 and 134 were owned by the majority and minority communities, respectively. In 1998, the total dropped to 273, of which 189 and 84 were majority and minority community owned, respectively. There was a slight increase in 1998, the total going up to 284, of which 233 and 51 were buildings belonging to the majority and minority communities respectively.

Human rights activists question these figures arguing that some of this damage is collateral damage, caused by the security forces in the course of their counter insurgency operations. Even if this was so, and these would be human rights violations, systematically deflated figures would still indicate the widespread damage to public and private property by militant activity, causing great damage and grief to the civilian population.

Other attacks by militants include the use of explosions through mines, IEDs using RDX, and so on. There were as many as 1280 such attacks in 1990, reduced to 358 in 1996, 255 in 1997, 264 in 1998, and 293 in 1999. Between 1990 and 1999, i.e. in a period of 10 years, there have been 4,013 such attacks. In this case, this particular form of militant activity is unfocused in its choice of victims. Apart from the security forces which often, though not always, appear to be the main target, innocent civilians, including hapless women and children, are also killed. Since these explosions are often set off by remote control, this form of militant activity is the most violative of the human rights of innocents, whose only fault was that they were in the wrong place at the wrong time, even if that place was their home, and the assailant was a foreigner.

Another form of militant activity has been through grenade attacks, which from 242 in 1990, rose to 821 in 1994, going down to 444, 168, 187, and 201 in 1996, 1997, 1998, and 1999 respectively. In the 10-year period of January 1990 to December 1999, there have been a total of 4,231 such attacks. In these attacks also, both security forces and innocent civilians are killed. Often such attacks are followed by indiscriminate firing and even arson by security forces, in violation of both international and Indian humanitarian law, according to media and human rights reports. But such attacks themselves, while an act of terror directed against the Indian state, are also a violation by the militants of the human rights of innocent civilians.

By far the largest violation of human rights are in so-called 'cross firings' between militants and security forces, in which a very large number of innocent civilians are killed and wounded. In 1990, there were only 475 such incidents. These peaked at 1891 in 1995. In 1996, 1997, 1998 and 1999, there were 1089, 959, 1126, and 1205 such incidents. In other words, these have increased since 1997. In all, between 1990 and 1999, there were as many as

13,129 such incidents. While it is true that in many such incidents, the firing is initiated by the militants, a large proportion of the casualities are caused by indiscriminate and often panic-stricken firing by the security forces.

To cite only one recent instance, in the August 1, 2000 cross firing between two alleged foreign militants and the CRPF guarding the Amarnath pilgrims in Pahalgam, 35 civilians, apart from the two alleged militants, were killed. Media reports as well as the CRPF personnel we interviewed in Pahalgam concede, that a large proportion of the Amarnath yatris and local porters who were killed, were killed not by the two militants who were killed in the first 10 minutes of the firefight, but by the panic stricken CRPF jawans who continued firing for another 20 minutes. Despite the national furore over the episode, no judicial enquiry has been ordered. Almost all analysis we interviewed claim that up to 80 per cent of the civilians killed in cross firing are killed by the very same security forces who are supposed to protect them.

Civilians are also killed in random firing, which increased from 744 incidents in 1990 to peak at 1428 in 1996. In 1997, 1998 and 1999, there were 950, 795 and 838 such incidents, respectively. There were a total of 9,829 such incidents in the 10-year period from 1990 to 1999. Civilian loss of life and limb in such instances of militant firing are also a human rights violation.

We could get no authentic figure of disappearances. According to official figures, abductions increased from 169 in 1990, to a peak of 666 in 1996, before tapering off to 448, 298 and 241 in 1997, 1998 and 1999, respectively. The total number of abductions in the 10-year period from January 1990 to December 1999 amounted to 3,658. Despite official claims to the contrary, not all these are abductions by militants but include kidnappings by counter insurgency forces including surrendered militants. Because of their very nature, the agency behind these abductions is very difficult to prove, but there is no doubt that apart from the abductions by militants, a significant number of kidnappings can be attributed to counter insurgency forces. These consolidated figures are not available from unofficial sources. The official figures are discussed below. Of course, when the kidnapped are found dead, the blame is apportioned to the militants though this is, not the case on a significant number of occasions.

State Recorded Allegations of Human Rights Violations

On the basis of official figures from the complaints made to the National Human Rights Commission [NHRC] and to the Jammu & Kashmir State Human Rights Commission [SHRC], a total of 708 allegations of human rights violations were received between 1996 and 1999. But these figures exclude the security forces apart from the police, since neither the NHRC nor the SHRC is empowered to investigate either the Army or the paramilitary forces, who have their own courts and internal corrective mechanisms which are not open to public scrutiny. Thus, since alleged human rights violations committed by the Army, and in particular the Rashtriya Rifles[RR], the BSF and the CRPF, i.e. by the bulk of the forces in action in the State, are not included in these figures, these must be a very substantial underestimate of the total number of serious allegations made.

The largest number of violations, 256 relate to custodial killings, of which 61, 115, 45 and 35 were allegedly committed in 1996, 1997, 1998 and 1999, respectively. Killings of innocents totalled 157 in this 4 year period with 25, 40, 83 and 9 killings alleged in 1996, 1997, 1998 and 1999, respectively. Allegations of disappearances totalled 103, of which 27, 43, 18 and 15 were reported in 1996, 1997, 1998 and 1999, respectively. Cases of rape and molestation amounted to 75, with 16, 30, 13 and 16 cases reported in 1996., 1997, 1998 and 1999, respectively. Fifty-four cases of torture were alleged of which 7, 37, 6 and 4 were reported in 1996, 1997, 1998 and 1999, respectively. Allegations of beating/ harassment totalled 63, of which 14, 18, 14, and 17 were made in 1996, 1997, 1998 and 1999.

From all accounts in the media and by human rights investigators, these are gross underestimates of the actual incidence of these human rights violations. A very large number of cases do not even reach the stage of investigation, on the basis of which the above official figures were compiled.

Security Forces and Human Rights Violations

The Indian security forces have little training in counter insurgency, even less on human rights, especially in the lower ranks. Officers have been specifically instructed to minimize their casualties, with their future prospects depending on low casualty rates. This leads to officers and non-commissioned officers using maximum fire power to reduce losses, leading to excessive use of force and unnecessary collateral damage. Report after report of firefights with militants shows that houses neighbouring the ones where militants fire from are also damaged, if not destroyed by Army and paramilitary fire. Often, innocent civilians are also killed or maimed in this so-called crossfire. The protection provided by the Armed Forces [Special Powers] Act, insulates Army personnel from action in these cases of violations BSF, CRPF and ITBP personnel are also not subject to the scrutiny of the NHRC or SHRC.

Very senior Army officers have gone on record to say that they would not capture foreign militants alive. The argument presumably being that foreigners were mercenaries and thus not entitled to the protection of Indian law or even the Geneva Convention. It is indeed deplorable that no action was taken against such officers for such outrageous and illegal statements. On occasions when the Army has suffered casualties including from *fidayeen* strikes they have even misbehaved with the police forces suspecting them of collusion. There are repeated complaints of arson against the army and paramilitary forces, particularly after the latter have suffered casualties after a firefight. In very few cases has any action been known to have even been initiated.

The natural tendency in all the security forces is to to play down allegations against them. Of course, to maintain some discipline within their ranks and some public credibility, some action is taken within the service through their own internal mechanisms, including court martial. But this information is confidential, and not available for public scrutiny. Under the circumstances, it is hardly surprising that the overwhelming public sentiment is that human rights violators in the RR, BSF and CRPF get away unchecked and unpunished. Since counter insurgency critically involves winning over public sentiment, in purely military terms, such a public perception is a major victory for the militants, the 'enemy'.

In the J&K police, the special operations group [SOG] better known as the special task force [STF] is particularly notorious for human rights violations. Modelled on the Punjab pattern, the J&K STF suffers from the same ills as its predecessor. The Punjab SOG was found guilty of repeated human rights violations and civil courts are still investigating unaccounted for deaths and disapperances. Like in Punjab, STF officers and ranks are given out of turn promotions and large financial rewards proportionate to the number of militants they kill, force to surrender, and the arms they recover. In such an environment, fake encounters, the killing of civilians, including petty criminals claiming that they are militants, are bound to occur, and even be rewarded. The committee repeatedly heard allegations that seized arms and explosives had actually been purchased from the blackmarket, in order to further career prospects and to obtain financial rewards.

Sometimes the incentives policy coupled with pressure to show quick results can have devastating implications for human rights. To cite just the latest instance, the joint STF-Army operation after the Chittisingpora massacre, after which five innocent civilians were allegedly picked up and butchered, is a case in point. It is significant that the Justice Pandian Commission has been set up only to investigate the firing on the protest demonstration that followed, not the killing of the five civilians.

The most notorious counter insurgency force is the surrendered militants backed by the Army. Popularly known as 'renegades', they are widely believed to be guilty of every conceivable human rights violation. Some believe they were behind the massacre at Chittisingpora. The surrendered militants have never been given human rights education. In their earlier role as militants they had shown scant respect for human rights. Now when their unlicensed weapon is replaced by a licensed one, what is there to ensure that they will respect human rights including of their former comrades, as a retired police officer asked the Committee?

Human Rights Restrictions and Harassment

What is perhaps most humiliating and galling to the local citizenry is the regular harassment and mistreatment they regularly face in the course of ordinary, non-violent checking and enforcement by the security forces and police. Roadblocks, road patrols and other checks result in brusque even rude questioning, frisking, and in the case of women, even physical humiliation when, for instance, their veils are lifted to ensure that they are actually women and not men in disguise. Any protest under such circumstances leads only to aggravated behaviour, even to violence. Is this how the world's largest democracy treats its citizens, many anguished Kashmiris ask?

In some rural areas a 'lights out' is enforced at 10 pm sharp. This is particularly damaging for students who need to burn the midnight oil, but can only do so at the risk of the lives of the entire household. In Poonch town, the Committee was told of the case of the owner of a rice mill, who was tortured and harassed by the Army in 1999 for operating his mill at night. The Army claimed he did so, to give the milled rice to the militant under cover of darkness. His pleas that he worked at night because of regular power supply, that was not available during the day, fell on deaf ears. He later committed suicide, blaming Army torture and harassment for his death.

The Valley of Fear

What is most striking and depressing in what is, arguably, the most beautiful State in India is the atmosphere of fear and despair. Intellectuals, including journalists and faculty in Kashmir University, are wary and scared of speaking openly, particularly against the militants and the Army. While some general statements may be permissible, any specific comment has had, on occasion, serious consequences.

This fear coupled with rampant alienation perhaps leads to a special kind of 'political correctness'. For instance, several local people and a J&K police constable on duty during the massacre on August 1, 2000, who were interviewed by members of the Committee, insisted that the CRPF firing was caused by a panic reaction to the sound of a back fire, and that the two alleged militants who were killed were innocent civilians. About Chittisingpora, there is a widespread belief that the massacre of 35 Sikhs was carried out by the Army itself. The Committee interviewed several survivors in Chittisingpora and though the witnesses were extremely wary, their statement indicated that they suspected militants of being responsible. But the very fact that contrary perceptions are widespread, shows how much the security forces have alienated themselves from the very people they are supposed to protect.

Recommendations

The only real solution to human rights atrocities is the cessation of hostilities. But for this to occur, and last, a political solution is imperative. Failing that some measures are possible that will reduce, but not eliminate, human rights violations. Some of the most important measures are briefly listed below:

1. Withdraw the Armed Forces [Special Powers] Act from operation in the State. The armed forces have sufficient powers under other laws to function adequately.
2. Amend the Acts under which the NHRC and SHRC function to enable them to inquire into allegations against the Army and paramilitary forces. The NHRC and SHRC must be provided with sufficient investigative staff to inquire into such complaints.
3. All such NHRC and SHRC reports and recommendations should be binding on the concerned governments and forces, subject only to judicial review. These should be public documents.
4. Since amendments to these Acts will not be retrospective, action taken by the Army and paramilitary forces on earlier complaints should be made public. An enabling law should be passed facilitating judicial review of these earlier decisions/actions.
5. All incentive schemes in the security forces and police that reward the killing of militants, must be withdrawn. Under both international and Indian law, militants should be captured alive if possible. Financial rewards for killing tantamount to 'blood money' are repugnant to civilized values and societies.
6. Peace committees must be set up in all localities in the insurgency affected areas. Counter insurgency forces must cordinate with these committees when carrying out their operations in these areas.

7. Counter insurgency forces and the civil administration must coordinate to reduce harassment to civilians in the course of 'normal' everyday patrolling and checking. A coordination committee should be set up to examine complaints and take remedial action.
8. All counter insurgency forces must be trained on human rights and gender sensitivity. They must be aware of the requirements of international humanitarian law. Consequently, ranks must be instructed that orders that violate these laws are illegal.
9. Surrendered militants should be removed from counter insurgency operations. If absolutely necessary, they may be used as 'spotters' but should not be deployed in armed formations.

Six

The Kashmir Issue Today and During the Formative Years of the Indian States System

Shri Prakash

Problems Posed by the Present Context

The history of the Jammu and Kashmir issue both as a domestic political one within the ambit of Centre-State relations and as a foreign policy issue between India and Pakistan is as old as the post 1947 Indian Federal System or the Indian Union whichever term we may prefer to use. The causes, course of and confabulations to resolve the domestic as well as the bilateral dimensions of the issue are not only well known, they have been much written about. The need for a new intellectual examination of and incursion into this theme arises precisely from the fact that these efforts in the past have failed to bring about any lasting solution to the conflicts in and about Kashmir.

It is necessary to state the premises of the dispute over Kashmir clearly in order to realize that as it stands, a resolution is clearly ruled out unless the basic positions of one or the other side change. So long as Pakistan continues to take an unalterable stand as it does today, that the part of Jammu & Kashmir which is in India is under Indian occupation through armed force; that India's policy on Kashmir is a clear case of denying the Kashmiri people their basic rights of self-determination; that the issue in Kashmir is holding a plebiscite as envisaged in the original UN Security Council Resolution of August 13, 1948, it does so on the assumption that sooner or later it can muster enough international support to push India into accepting international mediation. Another interpretation of the same Pakistani approach can be that its insistence on holding up an intractable and intransigent position ensures a permanent conflict with India and hence a permanent threat from India becomes credible. Such a situation to Pakistani strategists only reinforces their claims about Muslims and Hindus being two separate nations. A long-term conflict situation with India also provides a rational justification for Pakistan to seek support from other Muslim states and seek to benefit from international support for smaller states against the hegemony of "bigger dominating neighbours". An added political spin off for Pakistan is the justification it provides itself to maintain a large standing Army, which has grown three times since 1972 and now uses up almost 30 per cent of the annual Central Government Expenditure. Presuming India to be the aggressor seeking to dismantle Pakistan would also explain the constant search by Pakistani leaders for extending their "strategic depth" by acquiring new allies like the Taliban in Afghanistan or promoting various forms of religious extremism.

A proper analysis of the different interpretations or explanations of the underlying reasons for Pakistan's Policy on Kashmir is a precondition for trying to evolve an approach to negotiations with it and/or formulating a commonly accepted Agenda, without which no talks can take place. If it transpires and this is certainly the case on the basis of historical experience—the latest proof being provided by the timing and manner of starting the Kargil War, which even USA's satellite intelligence confirmed was done by Pakistani troops not in uniforms crossing the Line of Control — then every time an effort has been made to negotiate with Pakistan, it has either been sabotaged by the start of a war or resulted in inconclusive settlements as at Tashkent and or Shimla. These Agreements have brought partial peace but no definitive resolution of demarcating the Line of Control and/or settling an international border in Kashmir, without which the bilateral or the Indo-Pakistan dimension of the problem cannot be resolved.

The domestic aspect of the Kashmir issue concerns both the crucible of Centre - State relations, i.e. the definition, crafting and evolution of federalism in India and the project of building a pluralistic, secular and democratic society, especially in the vast spaces covered by the interaction between Islam and Hinduism as well as the continuing use of religious idioms, images, slogans and issues to mobilize Muslims and Hindus on political platforms. The notion of a 'pure' secular society in which religion, which is eminently a personal and social, i.e. public activity, will remain totally excluded from civil politics much in the manner envisaged not only by many liberal thinkers but also by Marx will take long to realize, if ever it comes about, not only in South Asia but all over the world. The degree and intensity of the involvement of the Roman Catholic and the Protestant churches in politics, their control over state and property have certainly declined. However, Christian Democratic politics continues to be a species not only in Germany, France and Italy but also within the broad rubric of Tory politics in Britain and Republican politics in USA. The church continues to influence its followers within the households as well as in public life through issues like abortion, marriage laws and practices, and the observance of religious rites as well as festivals.

However, the real change between medieval and modern civil society is the notion of pluralism long accepted in the Indian cultural ethos which now houses in small or big measure virtually all religions of the world and has actually done so for several hundred years. The problem arises when a conscious political effort is made to change from a liberal practice of religious pluralism to an aggressive revanchism based on promoting an active hostility to other religions in the name of setting right preconceived or misconceived historical wrongs but basically to build what is visualized as a permanent and stable political or electoral constituency. The domestic dimension of the Kashmir issue has to be viewed in terms of the various trends or strains of national and local politics.

In order to locate the domestic dimension of the Kashmir issue as a political problem one has to understand the contrast between Muslim politics in the rest of the country and the form it has sought to be given by some groups in Kashmir who preach secessionism through a plebiscite. Today there are over 120 million Muslims in India, only 4 per cent of whom live in Jammu and Kashmir. It is interesting to note that Muslims live in more than one hundred districts virtually all over the country. It is also worth emphasizing that their numbers have been growing in absolute terms through marriage or migration. The Indian State through all the different shades of governments it has been ruled over and they cover virtually all parts of the political spectrum—has in law stuck to its position of according equality to all religions and non-interference in the personal laws of different religious communities. Indeed, it is difficult to argue that the Indian State puts any deliberate obstacles in the way either of the practice of Islam by its followers or that it discriminates against them in matters of job recruitment, education or political rights. Despite all the shortcomings of implementation and practice and these are innumerable, the intention to build a secular, democratic system is undeniable. That it has not been able to root out communal riots or violence or indeed provide avenues for faster upward mobility to Muslims speaks for its ineffectiveness in implementing its own goals, lack of resources in providing modern education and adequate number of jobs and its inability in a constitutional democratic set-up to ban groups based on extremist religious programmes both among Hindus as well as Muslims. One cannot also forget the weaker position most Muslims started from economically and socially in post-partition India where the most propertied and the better educated among them often migrated to Pakistan in the hope of a bright and brilliant future.

When the complex nuances of the comparative analysis between extremist secessionist politics in Jammu and Kashmir and Muslim constitutional politics in the rest of the country is taken into account, one can begin to appreciate that to assume any inherent relationship between a Muslim majority area and its tendency towards political independence is fallacious. The All India Muslim League or the All India Muslim Conference are Muslim majority organizations but they are perfectly well prepared to function within the Indian constitutional framework as are the National Conference of Jammu and Kashmir which has been running the State Government for most of the time after 1947. Indeed, it is noteworthy that not only did the National Conference representatives participate in the All India Constituent Assembly, they led the proceedings in the Jammu and Kashmir Constituent Assembly which made J & K the only Princely State whose accession to the Indian Union was ratified twice.[1] That the accession and its ratification were not a one man show was to be seen when because of his tendency to question the accession, Sheikh Abdullah was arrested. His Second-in-command, Bakshi Ghulam Mohammad immediately took over as Chief Minister and the group around the Sheikh continued to function with his successor. Finally, neither finding external nor internal support and in the aftermath of the break up of Pakistan due to the formation of Bangladesh even the Sheikh entered into the 1975 Agreement with the then Prime Minister Indira Gandhi.

It is not only the case that there never has been a real dearth of local leaders with a group to form and run the government in Jammu and Kashmir. It is also the case that militant groups are often drawn from individuals who could not get to power either because they fell out with those in government or could not win elections on their own. A lack of strong mass-based opposition political parties has meant that the opposition gravitates to extra-constitutional terrorist methods, especially when funds and arms can be procured from across the border. One of the steps needed in such a situation is to enhance the defences near and patrolling of an admittedly difficult mountainous border to prevent infiltration into India. China has done this relatively successfully with its own borders in Sinkiang. Inability to do this so far represents a failure of military strategy in manning border defences rather than a demonstration of deliberate lack of concern towards J&K.

There can be no denying that soldiers in fighting or chasing terrorists can kill or hurt innocent civilians in J&K against which the Army Courts and National Human Rights Commission, etc., can take appropriate action. There can also be no denying that official statistics in this regard may not be fully accurate at a given point of time. However, from these observations to jump to the conclusion that the Indian Armed Forces whose record in saving Muslim women from horrific brutalities inflicted on them by the Pakistani Army in the erstwhile East Pakistan is well known are only in Jammu and Kashmir conducting a 'genocidal' like campaign against an unarmed civilian population defies reason as well as experience. To define terrorism in J&K as an insurgency when a government elected by the people is in place is an overstatement. Low voter turnouts can in fact be explained by the fear of terrorist attacks as well as dissatisfaction with the performance of the government in question. However, low voter turnouts take place even in elections in Delhi and other states and can be explained by a host of reasons.

One of the preconditions for involving more people in democratic politics is to restore peace and security by disarming the militants, who carry weapons illegally and appeal to them to do so voluntarily since neither poverty, unemployment or inequality can be mitigated or cured by terrorist politics. Those who seek power through covert military means in J&K stand a better chance if they campaign constitutionally through elections about the people's grievances. Indeed even low levels of militancy and terrorism provide a justification for posting a large number of troops in J&K with sensitive and disputed borders both with Pakistan as well as China. The state of nuclear deterrence between India and Pakistan while preventing all out wars are no guarantee against the latter launching limited wars in the hope of getting international support against India and demanding international mediation.

Post-Cold War Global Situation

The global situation after the end of the Cold War has evolved in a way that the Big Powers no longer stand to benefit directly from an India - Pakistan rivalry. Pakistan has little money to buy expensive weapons systems from USA. Its nuclear tests as with India have automatically excluded military sales from USA to these two countries. Russia does not sell weapons directly to Pakistan in deference to Indian wishes. China is Pakistan's main weapons supplier but at the same time publicly supports a bilateral dialogue between India and Pakistan. Pakistan gets some military supplies from intermediate powers like France. India buys its military supplies from many countries but mainly from Russia. Given its sheer size it would have to spend 3 to 4 per cent of its

GDP in order to maintain a credible defense system which is still lower than Pakistan's 6-7 per cent of GDP. For this to happen it does not actually have to be involved in conflicts. In the post-Cold War period USA's appreciation of the Indian effort to build a multicultural democracy has encouraged it to take a more balanced view of South Asia. After India has continued with its policy of liberalization, USA now suggests like others do, bilateral negotiations for India and Pakistan to solve their problems. Such an international situation is not conducive for Pakistan to attract international attention to Kashmir. The issues it wants to raise about plebiscite and the like are not acceptable to India as a basis for negotiations since Pakistan has not vacated the area occupied by it in Kashmir which was a precondition laid down by the UN resolution of 1948.

Given the stalemate between India and Pakistan in the foreseeable future on the bilaeral front, India while looking for a mutually acceptable Agenda for talks with Pakistan will be well advised to seal its own borders with Pakistan as it has done in Punjab. It should also seek to create an international consensus about the democratic and durable nature of Kashmir's accession to India. India's ability to hold the Peace and a gradual change in international opinion about Jammu & Kashmir being a "disputed territory" will also help to alter the perceptions of the Pakistani elites about their conflict with India and move them towards accepting the Line of Control in J&K as an international border. This seems to be one viable and feasible option.

The Autonomy Resolution and the Domestic Dimensions of the Kashmir Issue

Only recently the Jammu & Kashmir Assembly passed a resolution asking the Central Government to return to the 1952 Agreement between Sheikh Abdullah and Prime Minister Nehru. Drafted on the lines of the Anandpur Sahib Resolution of the Akalis it envisages that the Central Government will look after only Defence, Telecommunications, Currency and Foreign Affairs. The Supreme Court and the Election Commission will have no jurisdiction in Jammu & Kashmir.

As it stands such a decision, even if a government is willing to consider it, will require the approval of Parliament, if not, a Constitutional Amendment. As only a handful of states have asked for such changes the overwhelming majority of states stand committed to the basic division of powers laid down by the Constituent Assembly in the Union List, State List and Concurrent List. It has to be remembered that any administrative changes which have been introduced since 1952 have had the willing consent of the J&K Government.

There is a tendency to compare the Indian Federal system with the US or the Canadian Federal Systems. Although this is not the occasion to go into this issue in any detail two differences in the historical situation in which the Indian and the American Systems came into being should be remembered. First of all the various provinces which became states and an integral part of the Indian Constitutional System had earlier on numerous occasion in the long duration of Indian history also been integral parts of many All India Political Systems. They were not like the 13 American Colonies for the first time surrendering their sovereignty to each other who also decided to preserve their existing constitutional structures. This is one principal reason why the demand for self-determination or the right to secede was never included in the Indian Constitution which could learn from other existing systems and lay down uniform laws for the entire country. It seems quite clear that in order to get the necessary support for its Autonomy resolution, the Jammu & Kashmir Assembly will have to mobilize countrywide support in Parliament since no one has asked for convening a new Constituent Assembly.

At this stage of India's nation building process there will be many who would want to know why one must go to a Confederal regime within India as distinct from a Confederation between India and the other South Asian States. The issue of having a separate Supreme Court for only one state in fact goes against the sort of progressive reforms about women's rights which All India Muslim Organizations want to introduce within Islamic legal practices on a uniform basis as opposed to the draconian anti-Human Rights legislation introduced by the Taliban in Afghanistan in the name of Islam. Similarly, withdrawing the jurisdiction of the Election Commission from J & K will tend to put the weak constitutional democratic opposition parties there at a further disadvantage reducing the prospects of building a level playing field for democratic politics, which is the crying need of the hour and the way forward for nation building in India.

While discussing the issue of autonomy for Jammu and Kashmir, the question that needs to be asked is whether closer Central Government involvement in the administration of Jammu and Kashmir has helped the people of the State or not. As far as financial assistance goes, Jammu and Kashmir has under the Gadgil Formula used by the Finance Commission and the Planning Commission fared much better than several other states. For example, according to the Reserve Bank of India Bulletin of December 1995, Appendix I and II, per capita Central assistance for 1994-95 was Rs. 3,010 for Jammu and Kashmir as against Rs. 190 for Bihar, Rs. 305 for Tamil Nadu, Rs. 385 for Rajasthan and Rs. 341 for Uttar Pradesh. In the case of Jammu and Kashmir, 90 per cent of Central Assistance is now in the shape of grants and 10 per cent as loans; while for the four states mentioned above it is 30 per cent grants and 70 per cent loans. Likewise per capita non-plan grants in 1993 for Jammu and Kashmir was Rs. 720 while it was Rs. 72 for Bihar, Rs. 23 for Tamil Nadu, Rs. 81 for Rajasthan and Rs. 23 for Uttar Pradesh.[2] Table 1 shows data concerning the financing of Jammu and Kashmir's Annual Plans for the last three years underlines a trend which has become typical of the state's finances; the Central Assistance is invariably three times or more as compared to the resources raised by the State Government:

Table 1
Financing of Annual Plans in Jammu and Kashmir

Actual's *Figures in Rs. Crores*

	1997-98	*1998-99*	*1999-2000*
Central Assistance	2332	2459	3040
State's Resources	728	636	995

Source: Data supplied by State Plans Division, Planning Commission, New Delhi.

Central Assistance has definitely helped Jammu and Kashmir to do better on the front of Socio-Economic Development than several other states and this fact is borne out by the data compiled in Tables 2 to 7. At Rs. 9,116, J & K's per capita income in 1997-98 was higher than that of Uttar Pradesh, Bihar, Assam, and Orissa (Table 2). Its population growth rate was lower than that of Assam, Tripura, Maharashtra, Rajasthan, Gujarat and West Bengal: (Table 3). Its literacy rate was higher than that of Bihar and Rajasthan (Table 4). The share of urban population in total population was considerably larger than in Assam, Bihar, Uttar Pradesh, Tripura, Orissa and Meghalaya (Table 5). Availability of doctors, expenditures on water, sanitation and education was also higher in J & K compared to several other states (Tables 6 and 7). The rate of unemployment was 39 per cent in the rural sector in 1997 when compared with 22.7 per cent in Kerala; 15.3 per cent in Assam, 37.9 per cent in Orissa and 37.7 per cent in West Bengal.[3]

Considering the better comparative socio-economic profile of Jammu and Kashmir, it is obvious that the politics of violence being perpetrated there in the name of *Jihad* is a deliberate terrorism meant to cow down the people and the elected government. Hence, the first precondition for the restoration of peace is that all those having illegal weapons should surrender them failing which these should be seized by the authorities. Only licensed firearms should be held by the civilian population. Unauthorized crossing of the Indo-Pak Border should be prevented by all possible means and talks held with Pakistan for this purpose. Simultaneously, elections to the Panchayats, Municipalities and the Assembly and in the Parliamentary Constituencies should be held on schedule. More financial powers should be given to Panchayats to speed up rural development creating more jobs. Voluntary citizens committees can act as observers to ensure a free and fair poll.

Discussions should be held with the elected representatives about the scope of the Autonomy being asked for in order to arrive at a mutually satisfactory solution between the Central and the State Governments, without compromising the need for All India Coordination and local requirements as well as aspirations.

Table 2
Per Capita NSDP (State Income) at Currrent Prices of Selected States (Position as on July 25,2000)

(In Indian Rupees)

State	*1993-94*	*1994-95*	*1995-96*	*1996-97*	*1997-98*
1. Jammu & Kashmir	6521	6581	7551	8311	9116
2. Assam	5715	6493	7001	7394	8026
3. Bihar	3955	4418	4323	5431	5531
4. Uttar Pradesh	5287	6064	6605	7637	8273
5. Tripura	5300	5443	6480	7704	8166
6. Andhra Pradesh	7494	8830	10039	11242	11701
7. Maharashtra	12705	14200	16993	18488	20521
8. Meghalaya	7331	7772	8641	9401	10287
9. Orissa	4877	5800	6978	6685	8103
10. Rajasthan	6251	7628	8361	9876	10189
11. Tamil Nadu	9073	10743	12096	13985	15798
12. Gujarat	9997	13100	14248	16366	16998
13. West Bengal	6702	7643	8947	9827	11464
14. Punjab	12991	14253	15558	17948	19497
15. All India	7698	8845	10103	11554	12729

Source: Economic Survey Government of India, 2000-2001

Table 3
Rates of Growth of Population

States	*Population '000*					*Annual Rate of growth % between*				
	1951	*1961*	*1971*	*1981*	*1991*	*1951 and 1961*	*1961 and 1971*	*1971 and 1981*	*1981 and 1991*	*1951 and 1991*
1. J&K	3254	3561	4617	5987	7719	0.9	2.6	2.6	2.6	2.2
2. Assam	8029	10837	14625	18041	22414	3.0	3.0	2.1	2.2	2.6
3. Bihar	86374	69915	56353	46447	38782	1.8	2.0	2.2	2.1	2.0
4. Uttar Pradesh	63220	73755	88341	110863	139112	1.6	1.8	2.3	2.3	2.0
5. Tripura	639	1142	1556	2053	2757	6.0	3.1	2.8	3.0	3.7
6. Andhra Pradesh	31115	35983	43503	53551	66508	1.5	1.9	2.1	2.2	1.9
7. Maharashtra	32002	39554	50412	62783	78937	2.1	2.5	2.2	2.3	2.3
8. Meghalaya	606	769	1012	1336	1775	2.4	2.8	2.8	2.9	2.7
9. Orissa	14646	17549	21945	26370	31660	1.8	2.3	1.9	1.8	1.9
10. Rajasthan	15971	20156	25766	34262	44006	2.4	2.5	2.9	2.5	2.6
11. Tamil Nadu	30119	33687	41199	48408	55859	1.1	2.0	1.6	1.4	1.6
12. Gujarat	16263	20633	26698	34086	41310	2.4	2.6	2.5	1.9	2.4
13. West Bengal	26300	34926	44312	54581	68078	2.9	2.4	2.1	2.2	2.4
14. Punjab	9160	11135	13551	16789	20282	2.0	2.0	2.2	1.9	2.0
15. All India	361088	439235	548160	684329	846302	2.0	2.2	2.1	2.1	2.2

Source: *Basic Statistics Relating to the Indian Economy States*, September 1993. Centre for Monitoring Indian Economy, Mumbai.

Table 4
Rates of Literacy

	States	Total Literacy as %age of Population above the age of 4 years		
		1971 (%)	1981 (%)	1991 (%)
1.	Jammu and Kashmir	18.6	32.7	NA
2.	Assam	28.7	NA	52.9
3.	Bihar	19.9	32	38.5
4.	Uttar Pradesh	21.8	33.3	41.6
5.	Tripura		50.1	60.4
6.	Andhra Pradesh	24.6	35.7	44.1
7.	Maharashtra	39.2	55.8	64.9
8.	Meghalaya	29.5	42	49.1
9.	Orissa	26.2	41	49.1
10.	Rajasthan	19.1	30.1	38.6
11.	Tamil Nadu	39.5	54.4	54.6
12.	Gujarat	35.8	52.2	61.3
13.	West Bengal	33.2	48.6	57.7
14.	Punjab	33.7	48.1	58.5
15.	All India	29.5	43.7	52.1

Sources: Basic Statistics Relating to Indian Economy, States, 1976, 1993 CMIE.

Table 5
Rates of Urbanization

	States	%age of Urban Population		
		1971	1981	1991
1.	Jammu and Kashmir	18.6	21.1	23.8
2.	Assam	8.8	9.9	11.1
3.	Bihar	10	12.5	13.1
4.	Uttar Pradesh	14	17.9	19.8
5.	Tripura	—	11.0	15.3
6.	Andhra Pradesh	19.3	23.6	26.9
7.	Orissa	8.4	11.8	13.4
8.	Maharashtra	31.2	35.0	38.7
9.	Meghalaya	14.5	18.1	18.6
10.	Rajasthan	17.6	21.0	22.9
11.	Tamil Nadu	30.3	33.0	34.2
12.	Gujarat	28.1	31.1	34.5
13.	West Bengal	24.7	26.5	27.5
14.	Punjab	23.7	27.7	29.5
15.	All India	19.9	23.3	25.7

Sources: Basic Statistics Relating to the Indian Economy States, 1976 and 1993 CMIE, Mumbai.

Table 6
Selected Indicators of Government Expenditure on Social Sector and Available Facilities

States	*Persons Per Doctor*			*Per Capita Government Expenditure on Water Supply and Sanitation in Rs.*		
	1971	*1980*	*1987*	*1970-71*	*1980-81*	*1991-92*
1. Jammu & Kashmir	6.21	2.43	1.93	2.07	32.70	77.10
2. Assam	3.37	2.52	2.24	2.12	4.33	28.15
3. Bihar	5.39	4.10	3.38	0.37	3.78	8.55
4. Uttar Pradesh	6.86	4.90	4.32	0.96	3.18	13.67
5. Tripura	N A	N A	N A			
6. Andhra Pradesh	4.51	2.49	2.08	0.11	4.89	16.11
7. Maharashtra	2.31	1.61	1.75	0.59	7.83	26.45
8. Meghalaya	N A	N A	N A	12.49	49.41	87.79
9. Orissa	5.08	3.42	2.97	0.09	4.90	20.66
10. Rajasthan	7.72	4.22	3.42	0.49	11.40	32.54
11. Tamil Nadu	2.20	1.60	1.31	0.12	2.40	31.55
12. Gujarat	3.87	2.46	1.99	0.55	4.91	13.07
13. West Bengal	1.73	1.73	1.61	0.72	7.53	9.12
14. Punjab	1.10	0.84	0.76	3.25	7.04	26.66
15. All India	6.57	4.41	4.05	0.27	5.60	20.35

Source: *Basic Statistics Relating to the Indian Economy States*, September 1993. Centre for Monitoring Indian Economy, Mumbai.

Table 7
State Government's Expenditure on Education

States	*Per Capita Expenditure (Rs.)*		
	1975-76	*1980-81*	*1991-92*
1. Jammu & Kashmir	34.50	73.5	314.80
2. Assam	26.80	53.8	250.10
3. Bihar	14.30	33.8	149.70
4. Orissa	19.60	41.0	183.60
5. Uttar Pradesh	17.20	31.70	149.60
6. Tripura	43.40	82.80	439.0
7. Andhra Pradesh	19.60	43.10	179.10
8. Maharashtra	29.10	60.80	270.50
9. Meghalaya	31.70	74.90	436.80
10. Rajasthan	23.20	42.60	213.60
11. Tamil Nadu	26.10	50.00	241.50
12. Gujarat	24.70	53.10	256.00
13. West Bengal	21.60	45.30	203.40
14. Punjab	36.60	82.80	439.00
15. All India	23.00	46.10	207.90

Source: *Basic Statistics Relating to the Indian Economy States*, September 1993. Centre for Monitoring Indian Economy, Mumbai.

References

1. For a discussion of the Jammu and Kashmir Constituent Assembly see Justice J.S. Anand, *The Constitution of Jammu and Kashmir: Its Development and Comments*, Universal Book Traders, Delhi 110054, 1994; Granville Austin, *The Indian Constitution, Cornerstone of a Nation*. OUP New Delhi, 2001, Hamid Khan, *Constitutional and Political History of Pakistan*, OUP, Oxford, UK, 2001.
2. Sekhar Basu Roy ed., *New Approach, Kashmir Violence in Paradise*, Calcutta, 1999, p. 43.
3. G.A. Parthasarthy and K.A. Nirmala, Employment and Unemployment of Youth, *The Indian Journal of Labour Economics*, Vol. 43, No. 4 (October-December, 2000), p. 700.

Seven

Kashmir Made an Intractable Problem by Our Successive Governments

R.M. Pal

In the 1950s I happened to discuss Kashmir with a Kashmiri Pandit in the context of partition of India of which I was a victim. I migrated to India from the then East Pakistan. The Pandit (who was a faculty member of the college when I was a student there) was emphataic that Pandit Nehru's leadership, acknowledged all across the world, would ensure that Kashmir's accession to India was not questioned by any one and added that whoever questioned it he was a *gaddar* (a traitor)—he had in mind Pandit Prem Nath Bajaj and his leader M.N. Roy. While on the subject, I said that Pandit Nehru's internationalism was at stake because of Kashmir—the Pandit got so furious (how dare one criticize a world leader like Pandit Nehru) that he went to the extent of assaulting me:

I haven't met him since then — not that I don't want to, but because I don't want to embarrass him. Pandit Nehru's "internationalism" has not helped the Kashmiri Pandits. In fact it gave rise to a situation which culminated in their present plight, and the suffering they are going through in refugee camps.

When we talk of Kashmir, we may remind ourselves of the fact of partition of the country, namely that India was partitioned on the basis of religion, that is, Hindu majority to go to India and Muslim majority to Pakistan. So that the Nawab of Junagad had no business to accede to Pakistan, and the Nizam of Hyderabad had no right, according to the spirit of the partition plan, to declare Hyderabad an independent state. There is no point, we are told by our establishment intellectuals, in going into the legal niceties of the partition agreement. It is true, however, that many things have hapapened since 1947-48 — three wars between Pakistan and India, another partition (a new country, Bangladesh established), the assertion of different cultural identities in Kashmir, and so on.

India has no Kashmir policy except one, namely that our rulers want the Kashmir problem to be solved through armed might - militant's terrorism is to be combated by state terrorism. All political parties — leftists and rightists are agreed on this policy except that some parties make some feeble noise about human rights violation in Kashmir. This policy, I am afraid, has made the Kashmir issue almost intractable. A country which has no other policy except an armed solution cannot bring peace. Peace is established by thoughtful men and women, by statesmen. They are, one regrets to note, conspicuous by their absence in our country. In respect of Kashmir our "thoughtful" politicians including Pandit Nehru who thought thoughtlessly. The problem in Kashmir is political, and it must be solved politically; and for that we need fearless politicians who can challenge all irrational approaches even if they are preached and practised by all the political parties.

I may be pardoned to quote from my own writings under the title, "Hopeful Signs" — an editorial in the *PUCL Bulletin*, August 1990:

> One is tempted to feel, going by newspaper reports, that there are people, in our country now who are determined to challenge chauvinism, who are not prepared to be bullied by ultra nationalists and by people who are swayed by misguided patriotism. There was a time when men like M.N. Roy (in the late 1940s and early 50s) and Jayprakash Narayan (much later) used to be called traitors for their views on the Kashmir question. Today, thanks to selfless activities of human rights groups a good number of people have come to question government policy and also the conduct of our security forces in Kashmir and Punjab. Even some politicians particularly in the ruling front, seem to have realized that all that is being done in Kashmir by our security forces is not proper, and that excesses committed by our forces cause not only miseries and sufferings to ordinary Kashmiris but are also counter-productive in the pursuit of our objectives.

> There are some public men who were either swayed by thoughtless fervour or were ambivalent in the late 1940s and early 50s, are now criticizing the government not only with regard to actions of the security forces, but have also raised fundamental issues relating to Kashmir. The number of such people is not, however, large but the fact that these are being discussed in public is a hopeful sign.
>
> Another hopeful sign—again, going by newspaper reports—is that excesses committed by security forces in Kashmir seem to have declined. If this is true, one can hazard the guess that improvement in this direction is the result of objective reporting by some media persons, and human rights organizations.
>
> In this context we may refer to the question of the Amnesty International desiring to send its team to visit Punjab and Kashmir. Those who oppose the entry of a team are indeed short-sighted. After all a democratic government should have nothing to hide. We welcome the decision of the government in permitting the Amnesty International team to visit India. Let the team visit any part of the country it wants. Successive governments at the Centre have declined to permit Amnesty International or Human Rights Watch to visit Kashmir.

I need hardly add that I was not quite correct in my assessment — chauvinism and nationalism have not declined; on the country they have been on the rise.

The thoughtlessness and military approach have led to serious human rights violations, and they have alienated the Kashmiris from India. It is in this context that I give below a few instances of violations based on investigations by the People's Union for Civil Liberties. The middle class intelligentsia and most 'patriotic' intellectuals, and not merely politicians, have brushed aside these reports.

A few excerpts from an investigative report (1990) prepared by PUCL and a few other groups (the report was published in the June 1990 issue of the *PUCL Bulletin*):

> There were no overt threats held out to the minorities

from local Muslims. The militants killed people irrespective of community—in fact, more Muslims have been killed than Hindus. One thing about which the local people are particularly sore is the permission granted to non-Muslim employees to leave duty and draw their minimum salary even when they are not on duty. The exodus of non-Muslims is widely regretted by the common man in Kashmir ... Kashmiri Muslims wanted the Pandit families to return to their homes. The Kashmiri Muslims' contention is that their brethren Pandits are being evacuated under a conspiracy to communalize the situation in the Valley... All claims made by the Governer during his visits to Delhi and broadcast by the media that he is handling the difficult situation with utmost "love and compassion" are far from the truth. ... A large number of excesses were committed by the security forces. On March 23, 1990 at about 8.30 a.m., when curfew was not in force, security forces fired without any provocation upon a three-wheeler and a Matador van. This led to several deaths including that of a pregnant woman and her eight-year-old son. {The report gives an account of many such killings and excesses.} There are instances of molestations and raping of women in Chhanpura. ... For more than three and a half months, except for a break for a few days, Srinagar city and other major towns have been under curfew ...Without meaning any disrespect to Mr. Jagmohan [Governor of J&K in 1990] it is a fact which he too must realize — that today he is the most despised person in the Valley.... He is reported to have asserted in a Press Conference at New Delhi on April 2, 1990 that the story of alienation of the people of the valley is "not correct" and that the people are "terrified" presumably by the militants. This indicates that he is either out of touch with the Kashmir Valley, which is hardly possible, or that he does not want the Indian people to know the truth. The fact is that the entire Muslim population of the Valley is wholly alienated from India and due to the highly repressive policy pursued by the administration in recent months, especially since the

> advent of Mr. Jagmohan in January 1990, their alienation has now turned into bitterness and anger . . . . Cruelty and violence on the part of the militants in the Valley must be condemned. The militants by their violent activities are not only depriving innocent persons of their civil liberties but also having the cause of freedom and democracy in the valley. However, any policy of combating private terrorism by recourse to State terrorism must be condemned... It is necessary to replace the present repressive policy by a policy of reconciliation with the people of the Valley. At present there is hardly any contact between the people of the Valley on the one hand, and the government of Mr. Jagmohan and the heads of the paramilitary forces on the other.

When this report was released it came under fire. "Patriotic" elements including some national English language dailies criticized the report severely. I wrote a brief editorial note (see *PUCL Bulletin*, June 1990) under the heading, Kashmir and Human Rights.

"Of late there has been criticism, in fact, condemnation of the report on Kashmir presented by some Human Rights Organizations, including the PUCL. That some party politicians would always be hostile to such reports which plead for restoration of civil rights and respect for individual liberty and would even go to the extent of calling people belonging to Human Rights Organizations unpatriotic and anti-national, is understandable. What is depressing to note, however, is that even some intellectuals have been rather chauvinistic in their approach.

"We are not concerned here with the specific report with regard to presentation, etc., it is for our readers to make appropriate comments, particularly those readers who respect individual liberty and civil rights. We do feel concerned however about one aspect the Report has generated, namely the rise of misplaced and misconceived patriotism and also of chauvinism which could not care less about the denial of civil rights to our citizens living in J&K. It is indeed unfortunate that even some well meaning people have gone to the extent of calling stalwarts of civil liberties organizations unpatriotic and anti-national. Such men who have always raised their voice against authoritarianism and unreason. How thinking men could be so unthinking!

"It is, we believe, the duty of all sections of the people to raise their voice against authoritarianism which wants to curb democratic rights and deprive individuals of their civil rights. Let us not forget that the welfare of the people and the integrity and freedom of the country is secure in the hands of only those rulers who respect individual liberty and are tolerant enough to go beyond narrow nationalism and misplaced patriotism. We submit that curbing individual liberty and democratic rights is not only unproductive but also anti-national."

November 1991; One person was killed by paramilitary forces at Lal Chowk, Srinagar, Srinagar-PUCL inquired: I give below a summary account of the findings:

"On November 9, 1991 a grenade was hurled at a patrolling CRPF group. The grenade did not explode. The force fired a few rounds in the air. People ran away in panic. Commuters in buses disembarked. Mohammad Latif, a conductor of a Matador bus was unable to run away because of infirmity caused by polio. The CRPF personnel shot at him. They did not allow Latif to be taken to a hospital and he died. CRPF officers made no attempt to discipline their men. Latif was the only son of his widowed mother. The idea behind such killing was to spread terror or to teach a lesson'. But actually such killings have alienated the people, accusing the paramilitary forces to be occupation forces.

"Maulana Abbas Ansari, Convenor, Muslim United Front was arrested on April 19, 1990 under the Public Safety Act. According to a Srinagar-PUCL report, he was taken to the Jammu Interrogation Centre, then to Jodhpur, and later to Delhi Tihar Jail where he was kept for one year. After that he was taken to a BSF camp at Mehrauli, New Delhi. He was beaten at Jammu Airport by security forces. In spite of High Court orders the Maulana was not medically examined. He was denied medical treatment - his molar teeth was extracted by a non-technician at the camp."

The Government of India (ruling parties of all hues) have declined to permit Amnesty International to visit J&K.

A number of habeas corpus petitions were submitted to the J&K High Court. According to Srinagar-PUCL (May 1992), the authorities did not comply with the orders of the High Court. On May 3 a young woman and her baby were killed at Batmalloo in military cross firing. According to a Srinagar PUCL report, BSF personnel apprehended a boy from home when the local people testified that he had never been a militant, the boy was allowed to go. The Srinagar-PUCL report added that there was no reason why the BSF indulged in firing as there was no firing or assault on the part of militants. After three days of the incident the BSF personnel told the people that the boy had killed the woman and the baby.

According to a Srinagar-PUCL report, the J&K Pradesh Congress(I) chief, Mr. G.R. Kar expressed concern over alleged "excesses and custodial deaths" in Kashmir. Addressing conferences on September 16, 1992 at Srinagar he urged state authorities to restrain the security forces whom he accused of committing excesses.

I published the following report in the *PUCL Bulletin*, November 1992 originally published in *The Statesman*, October 1992.

> Kashmiri Pandits the first time in three years have joined their Muslim compatriots in protest against the forces in Kashmir Valley. They called for a bandh against 'continuing deaths of Kashmiris in custody' and alleged desecration of Jama Masjid Mosque in Srinagar early this month. Some of the Pandits, including women, protested against the custody deaths in the valley in recent weeks.

Killings at Wantipora, New Colony, Srinagar: I give below a summary account of the Srinagar PUCL report:

> On October 28, 1993 at 4.45 pm, 300 persons were waiting in a queue for kerosene oil at the local kerosene depot. Two flying squad gypsies approached Wantipora Road where people had assembled. The security personnel in the Gypsy fired on the fleeing persons killing a number of people. The dead bodies were taken to Nowshere Mill where the security forces were staying. The bodies were handed over to the relatives on the condition that they would be buried forthwith. Mr. Raja Bakshi, SSP Srinagar maintained that all the dead were millitants.

I give below excerpts from an article written by Balraj Puri on the Sopore Outrage (*PUCL Bulletin*, February 1993) The security forces burnt down 60 residential premises and killed about that many or more in Sopore;

> Is there still a sane person who is unmoved by the tragedy that is Sopore? Worst ever even according to the standards set in Kashmir ... If the security forces continue to become brutalized, would not they become a threat to the nation's cherished values instead of being their protectors? Would India be able to repair the damage to its moral and political claim over Kashmir? ... Sopore outrage coincided with tall official claims about an all-round improvement in the situation in Kashmir. In May 1990 the murder of Mirwaiz Maulavi Farooq had provoked a wave of anger against the militants suspected to be responsible for the murder. The unprovoked firing on the funeral procession successfully diverted the popular anger against India ... A theory acquiring wide currency [is that] a sort of vested interest [keeps] alive the Kashmir problem as some people are deriving rich dividends out of the flourishing anti-militancy business. Personally, I am inclined to attribute the excess to falling standards of discipline and commitment to duty, spread of communal knives, already prevalent in the society, to the security forces, physical fatigue and hostile environment.

Mr. V.M. Tarkunde wrote a letter dated February 6, 1993 to Mr. Chavan, Miniser of Home Affairs, Government of India. Given below are a few excerpts [*PUCL Bulletin*, March 1993];

> As you are probably aware, Mr. M.N. Wanchoo who was murdered by some unknown assailants in Srinagar on December 5, 1992 was a person of exceptional integrity and was an active supporter of human rights. Although like many of us he was totally opposed to the terrorist activities of Kashmir militants, he was of the view that they must be dealt with in accordance with law and that, in any case, innocent persons should not be either tortured or done to death by the security forces. A couple of weeks before his assassination he met me in Delhi on November 23, 1992, and, handed over to me several lists of innocent

> persons who were reportedly killed, while in custody or otherwise, by the security forces, during the months of July, August, September, October and part of November 1992. Every list given by Shri Wanchoo contains the name of the deceased and the places and dates on which they were reported to have been killed. [Killed by security forces; July list, 94 innocent persons killed; August, 79 persons; September, 116 persons; October, 136 persons; November, 60 persons]... The first essential requirement is that the same security forces must obey the rule of law while dealing with the militancy in the Valley. [The Home Minister or his office did not even acknowledge the receipt of Mr. Tarkunde's letter not to mention taking any action!]

National PUCL team visited Kashmir a number of times to investigate human rights violation. I give below a few excerpts from the May 22-27, 1993 report;

> The team concentrated on the following issues; (a) The January 1993 incident in Sopore, (b) The April 1993 incident in Lal Chowk, Srinagar, (c) Interrogation Centres, custodial deaths and jails; (d) the role and performance of the judicial system, (e) the role of the BSF. ... A number of interrogation forces have been established. People are picked up, interrogated and subjected to custodial torture. ... In a couple of cases [that the team followed up] the result was disconcerting. In one case, a Kashmiri Muslim student studying in Karnataka came home along with a classmate, the son of a Kashmiri Pandit. It being late, he spent the night with the Pandit family. Next morning the host family informed the father that in a night raid his son had been arrested and taken to an interrogation centre. In the second case an old man told the team that his son had been arrested over 20 months ago, and the family did not know anything as to his whereabouts or welfare.... Disappearances are a common phenomenon. Instead of such instances declining, their incidence was rising. ... The number of custodial deaths has not come down at all. If anything, it has gone up. ... One police constable, Riaz Ahmad was killed deliberately, according to policemen.

> According to the army, he was killed in cross firing. This led to widespread discontent and the police in Srinagar went on a strike. ... Policemen, too, are critical of the excesses committed by security personnel. ... According to people connected with the legal profession and a few retired officials, the judicial process is a part of the atrocity system. There was a circular dated December 14, 1992 specifically directing the SHOs that "FIRs should not be lodged without approval of higher authorities." ...The fact remains that the kind of system which obtains elsewhere in the country does not obtain in J&K. ... Two things that a large number of press persons mentioned need to be taken up; One, going by their experience, they had come to the conclusion that newspapers in Delhi and elsewhere did not always publish everything that they write; the news was suitably tailored to suit the policy of the paper or the passing national mood or any such consideration. Two, by now they had some idea of what was acceptable, and, by implications, unacceptable to the papers that they represented ... The condition of refugee camps in Jammu for Pandits was so appalling that it is difficult to believe that any civilized country could be party to such an arrangement for as long as three years... The whole set up is a disgrace...
>
> Violations of human rights and the large number of custodial deaths in particular lead to a feeling of bitterness and despair. What happens at the interrogation centres is too gruesome to be repealed. The general sentiment is undoubtedly in favour of *Azadi*. The state of alienation that exists between the people and the administration goes on widening and does not get bridged.

Human memory being providentially short, I have given a very brief account of human rights violations until 1993. This is an appropriate point at which to stop, for human rights violations have been on the increase and our people do not need to be reminded of the sad story of horrendous happenings in recent years and so far as our government of all hues is concerned it appears to believe — if human rights and violations are any indication — that the Kashmir problem has to be solved militarily. Our governments refuse to accept the fact that political problems are to be solved politically. And, politically problems are always solved, across the world, by statesmen, not by thoughtless, intoxicated politicians — the former conspicuous by their absence and the latter in abundance in our country. Let us not forget that human rights violations have often led to dangerous consequences in many countries. I have always maintained that in 1971 Pakistan was not defeated by India; Pakistan was defeated by its own army for its massive human rights violations in the then East Pakistan. We in India must draw a lesson.

Eight

Understanding the Kashmir Problem: The Beginning of the Present Phase

Balraj Puri

The Kashmir problem, in its present form, originated in November 1986 when the State entered into qualitatively a different phase of politics. One of the sources of confusion in understanding the present problem and hence seeking its solution is to ignore this qualitative change and treating it as continuation in the same form since the partition of the country.

In October 1947, the people of Kashmir Valley welcomed the Indian army to fight the tribal raid sponsored by Pakistan and till August 1953 they remained emotionally and politically a part of India. No doubt the issue of the future of the State was being debated in the Security Council and India was committed to decide it through a plebiscite. But there is ample evidence from Pakistan sources, to substantiate the statement of Alistair Lamb, a known protagonist of Pakistan's case on Kashmir, about its reluctance to hold a plebiscite. For according to him, "with horrors of tribal raid fresh in the mind of the people and Sheikh Abdullah's prestige intact, Pakistan could not gamble on a plebiscite and lose even that part of the state it had occupied."

Without going into the causes that led to the dismissal from power and arrest of Abdullah in August 1953, it must be conceded that the action of the Government of India against the architect of the State's accession to India was a rude shock to the people of Kashmir. However, despite his bitter differences with New Delhi, he and his followers did not cut their ideological umbilical cord with India. He remained committed to secularism and Gandhian principles and his best friends, who were his colleagues in the freedom movement were in India. Socialists and Gandhians, in particular, continued to protest against his detention and pleaded for his release and a dialogue with him.

In 1964, when he was released, he declared that he stood by whatever he said and did till August 9, 1953, when he was arrested, and that included accession of the State to India. He came to Delhi as Nehru's personal guest and went to Pakistan with his consent; though he was rebuffed there. On Nehru's death, he addressed a mammoth tearful gathering in Kashmir to mourn the death of the greatest Kashmiri of the century and a common bond between Kashmir and the rest of India.

In 1972, the Sheikh again declared that his differences with government of India were not on the issue of accession but on the degree of autonomy of the State within India. He received a hero's welcome when he returned to the Valley as Chief Minister of the State in 1975 after an accord with Prime Minister Indira Gandhi; which included his acceptance of the State as a part of India.

There was no serious challenge to him in Kashmir for signing the accord. The fact that he remained unchallenged and the most popular leader of Kashmir till his death in September 1982, and his decisions were endorsed by the people of Kashmir was eloquently demonstrated by the wailing funeral procession, the largest ever in the history of Kashmir that accompanied him on his last journey. The only challenge that was posed to his authority was by the Janata Party in the election to the State Assembly in 1977. The party, which was in power at the Centre, included all anti-Abdullah forces in Kashmir represented by till then pro-Pak leaders like G.M. Karra, Mirwaiz Maulvi Farooq, P.N. Bazaz and supported by Jamat-e-Islami and later day secessionists like Abdul Ghani Lone, apart from stalwarts like Maulana Massoodi.

This showed that these leaders had become secessionists for want of any pro-India anti-Abdullah or anti-government forum. The National Conference-Janata Party confrontation provided an outlet to discontent against the governments at the Centre and the State. The fair election of 1977 also demonstrated the integrating potentiality of Indian federalism and democracy. For defeat of the ruling party at the Centre proved that opposition to the

Government of India need not make a Kashmiri anti-India. That the central ruling party was routed in the Kashmir region, winning only two of 46 seats in the assembly, was indeed a great triumph of Indian democracy.

Farooq Abdullah inherited a unique heritage. He followed the policy of his father, after the death of the latter in 1982. He won a convincing victory against the Congress, which had meanwhile come to power at the Centre and was the main opposition in the state, in the election to the State Assembly in 1983. It again confirmed the faith of the people of Kashmir in Indian democracy. Farooq joined a series of opposition conclaves and hosted one in Srinagar which brought the State closer to the rest of India at the people to people level.

Apparently provoked by the defiance of Farooq, Indira Gandhi, the then Prime Minister of India, got Farooq dismissed. If he had fought back as N.T. Rama Rao did, who, too, was dismissed from the Chief Ministership of Andhra Pradesh at the same time, he would not only have won back the power in the next election and emerged as a legitimate political heir of his charismatic father but would have done a patrotic duty by demonstrating that as a loyal citizen of India, a Kashmiri had a right to oppose the Government of India.

But when the Congress party swept the parliamentary elections in India in 1984, after the assassination of Indira Gandhi, Farooq developed cold feet. He entered into protracted and humiliating negotiations with the Indian Prime Minister Rajiv Gandhi. In November 1986, on returning to power, after signing an accord with him and agreeing to share power with the Congress, Farooq realized that "any one who wants to form a government in Kashmir cannot do so without sharing power with New Delhi. For the people did not matter much. "This doctrine on Kashmir's relations with the Centre provoked and disillusioned the people of Kashmir. Farooq has been justifying his stand with the argument that his backward state needs special financial consideration of the Centre which a Central government of a friendly party can ensure. Secondly, closer understanding between the parties in power at the Centre and the State would enable them to face the challenge of the militancy better.

His logic is fallacious. In order to get legitimate financial share from the Centre, ruling party of a state need not be loyal to that at the Centre; unless the motive is to seek illegitimate share or the Centre's connivance over illegitimate ways of spending the aid. In any case no people are willing to barter their freedom for more money. Nor can any central government afford to refuse to help the state government in fighting militancy if it is ruled by a party opposed to it politically. It would simply not be tolerated by the nation.

The National Conference-Congress coalition government created a sudden vacuum in opposition politics. Both anti-state government and anti-Centre sentiments thus were deprived of a secular outlet. The rigged elections blocked democratic outlet of discontent also. The Rajiv -Farooq Accord towards the end of 1986 thus marked the beginning of the present phase of unrest in Kashmir which soon took a violent form in the absence of non-violent outlets. In fact the casual relationship between the two was so obvious to me that I had then warned about the consequences of the accord in a newspaper article which concluded with the remark that its "net effect would be that Kashmir would go the Punjab way (which was under the grip of militancy at that time) and Farooq would go Barnala (the then Chief Minister of Punjab) way."

It is now well known that the "defeated" candidates of 1987 elections formed the nucleus of the militant movement when the ballot lost its effectiveness as a means of protest. The parties that formed the government in New Delhi later did not insist on sharing power with the party in power in the State. For they did not have much of a presence there. Farooq re-framed his doctrine on Kashmir's relation with the Centre by declaring his loyalty to any party that came to power in New Delhi; thus reaffirming his basic thesis that people of his state did not matter in forming a government at the State or at the Centre.

From the Congress to the UF and to the BJP led NDA, he shifted his loyalty with extreme ease. In 1999, in an intelligent anticipation of the results of the Lok Sabha election, he joined the press conference of the NDA uninvited, as his party had not yet joined it formally, where its election manifesto was to be released, even though none of his party members had read it.

Farooq's logic has been so uncritically accepted by the rest of the country that their contribution to the alienation of the people have never been considered. Thus, no party ever raised any objection over the shifting loyalty of the J&K Chief Minister. The Congress leaders who, during the parliamentary election campaign of 1999, attacked all allies of the BJP for aligning with a "communal party" and did not visit the Valley to campaign against the National Conference, which, too, was an ally of the BJP; nor did they utter a word of criticism against this alliance.

The ease with which Farooq makes, unmakes and remakes his party alliances would be evident from the fact that a day after the fall of the Vajpayee government on a no-trust motion in 1998, he was on the breakfast table of Sonia Gandhi. Indeed leaders of almost all national parties were present to greet him on the occasion of his swearing in ceremony as Chief Minister of the state in 1996; as if to declare that he was India's representative to rule over the state. They had not campaigned against his party in the Valley as they would argue that Farooq is "our" best bet in Kashmir. Could he not run the state without almost no opposition in the Valley and less than two-third majority in the legislature (the opposition could get some seats mainly from Jammu region)?

Changing loyalties have eroded whatever popular support and credibility Farooq and his party had in the state; particularly after his alliance with the BJP. Without discussing the merit and demerits of the BJP, it is obvious that neither it nor any of its allies has been able to win over the loyalty of Muslims anywhere in the country, so much so that the NDA could not get a single suitable Muslim to be included in the central cabinet. Why should Kashmiri Muslims be expected to have an exceptionally flexible ideological commitment?

If the Farooq doctrine is applied to any other state, it is doubtful if it would remain loyal to India. For it denies to the people, the fundamental right of citizenship to change, choose and oppose the Government of India and the party in power. By denying this fundamental right to the people of his state, he merely reminds them that they are less than full citizens of the country. Moreover, the people in no other state or in the country will give to any regional leader monopoly to loyalty to India. For that is the surest way to divert the popular discontent against monopolistic power in Kashmir to a secessionist channel and to communal channel in Jammu.

Before attempting any lasting solution of the Kashmir problem, the people of the State should first be allowed to exercise those minimum rights which people elsewhere in India take for granted.

Nine

The Regional Dimension of the Political Crisis

G.M. Shah

Introduction

The history of studying the political behaviour of people in relation to their geographical environment dates back to the early Greek period. Aristotle recorded his observations in his politics, "the inhabitants of colder countries of Europe are wanting in political organization and unable to rule their neighbours...." Strabo in his geographical writings has explained how shape, climate and space relations of Italy affected the rise and strength of Rome. In modern geography Alexander Von Humboldt in his book *Cosmos*, describes the effect of configuration of the Mediterranean on the evolution of early civilization'.[1] H.J. Makkinder presented his `heartland theory' to suggest that one who rules inner Asia would rule the Euro-Asian supercontinent and one who rules the Euro Asian landmass would finally rule the world. Ellen Semple, a leader of deterministic thought in geography in her classical work, *Influences of Geographic Environment*, noted:

> "Man is a product of earth's surface: the earth has mothered him, fed him, set him tasks, directed his thoughts, confronted him with difficulties..... Whispered hints for their solution."[2]

The geographers belonging to the deterministic school of thought believe that the study of political behaviour of people in a regional framework can hardly be over emphasized. The geographical factors of a region influence the political life of the people both directly as well as indirectly in more than one way.

Firstly the topographic, climatic, pedological, vegetational and the resultant socio-cultural attributes of the inhabitants of an area give it a distinct physical personality as a region. The regional identity of a place promotes regionalism among its inhabitants. The river and glacial valleys in the mountainous areas having well-defined external limits develop a strong sense of 'territoriality' among the people. The limited land available for construction of buildings, agricultural farms and grazing land for the domestic animals, promotes competition among the people. The outsiders who invade the territory and privacy of the people in mountainous areas, normally face tough resistance from the indigenous people. The people in the mountainous areas are extremely conscious of their cultural identity and develop strong 'stranger anxiety' about the people who dilute their culture, and compete with them in the social, economic and political spheres of life. Such a mindset is referred to as 'hill-psychology' in behavioural geography. Consequently, the study of political aspirations of the people precludes the study of the physical features of a region in which the concerned people live.

Secondly, the inter-regional physical barriers, long distances between the two regions, inaccessibility, climatic variations and sharp socio-cultural differences between two regions hinder the process of inter-regional interaction and emotional integration among the people of such regions. Contrary to this, the geographical continuity, geographical vicinity, climatic homogeneity, accessibility and socio-cultural uniformity between the two areas help in promoting spatial interaction and emotional integration among the people.

Thirdly, the spatial distribution of human attributes such as ethnicity, language, religion, culture, caste, ideology, etc. in a regional pattern over an area gives its inhabitants a sense of distinct identity. The regional identity of an area based on physical uniformities or a single or multiple factor socio-cultural similarities of the people gives birth to regional political movements for the realization of socio-cultural and politico-economic objectives. More often than not, these political and socio-cultural movements transcend regional and national boundaries, depending upon the social composition of the people living across the borders as well as the basis of mass mobilization by the leadership. The shared socio-cultural traits, politico-economic interests of the people and spatial interaction on the geographical space promotes solidarity among the people, whereas the inter-regional and inter-national diversities promote the sense of alienation, mutual suspicion and isolation among the people.

In order to apply the above mentioned generalizations to the empirical situations of Jammu and Kashmir, the study of the political crisis of Jammu and Kashmir in a regional context becomes of utmost importance. A careful examination of the regional peculiarities of the State is necessary for arriving at a rational solution of the long-standing political crisis in the State.

Relevance of Regional Approach in the Empirical Situation of Jammu and Kashmir State

The political scientists and contemporary political historians dealing with the Kashmir crisis have studied the problem in its historical context only. There is also an equally important dimension of the problem, i.e. the regional aspect.[3] Any solution to the Kashmir issue that does not address the regional aspirations of people of the State cannot be said to be a democratic, one because of six main reasons. Firstly, the State of Jammu and Kashmir was a militarily organized political territory by the Dogra rulers between 1820 and 1890 rather than a democratically formed political entity. Secondly, the constituent regions of this erstwhile princely state have much stronger spatial and cultural bonds with their respective neighbouring countries than among themselves within the state. Thirdly, the State has sharp inter-regional physiographic, climatic, lingual, religious and cultural diversities. Fourthly, the landlockedness of different regions of the State in general and Kashmir Valley, in particular has deepened the sense of 'regional consciousness' among its inhabitants. Fourthly, the demographic dominance of various ethno-religious groups in different regions of the State have provided a conducive social environment for mass-support to the political movements based on ethnicity and religion. Fifthly, the claim over entire Jammu and Kashmir by both India and Pakistan have heightened the communal feelings among the people who can have a minority status in the probable future dispensations; and sixthly, located in the Western Himalayas, the inhabitants of various regions of the state possessing the 'hill-psychology' have their own perceptions, fears and preferences in deciding their association with or isolation from other regions of the state. The generalized solutions for the State as a whole, devised by the people not conscious of the regional sensitivities are bound to fail when applied to the empirical situations within a regionally diverse State like Jammu and Kashmir.

Keeping in view the above mentioned specialities of the State of Jammu and Kashmir, the role of a geographer becomes of paramount importance to understand the regional dimension of the Kashmir crisis. The regionalization scheme based on spatial variation in physiography, accessibility, distance from the nearest national capital, climate, language, religion, culture and political aspirations can help to delimit the political regions that have both geographical homogeneity as well as social cohesiveness. The present study is an effort in this direction to understand the regional dimension of the political crisis in the State. The study can go a long way in guiding the policy makers of the subcontinent to fulfil the political aspirations of the people living in different regions of the State of Jammu and Kashmir. The study has been divided into five sections, each one dealing with a particular sub-theme. A brief account of conceptual framework, political regionalization of the State and the main conclusion of the study have been discussed as under:

Conceptual Framework

The identity of an area as a 'region' in the field of geography is an old concept of space-explanation. According to available literature, Strabo (B.C. 64-64 A.D.) seems to be the first postulator of the concept of 'region'. In modern geography the idea of a 'region' was first stated by H.J. Mackinder and A.J. Herbertson. Initially the concept of region was well expounded by formulating natural regions and afterwards it developed further through the contribution of quantitative techniques into different kinds of regions.

'Region' can be defined as an area of specific location characterized by homogeneity of specific phenomenon, arising out of accordant relationships of different phenomenon and is distinct from the other adjacent or distant areas. The personality of a region or regions may not be of a static form. Unlike political or administrative regions, the delineation of the geographic regions is not an easy task. In order to solve the problem of such a complexity of phenomenon, the delimitation of a region is always based on certain criteria. The size of the region varies with the purpose in view. There may be as many types of regions as the criteria taken into account. Thus, it is a fact that regions do not exist in reality but are made by a person according to the adopted criteria.

The methodological framework in the process of identifying regional units and analyzing their spatial structure systematically is called 'regionalization'. It is a method of arriving at an operational scheme of purposeful regions purpose being either for analysis of spatial structure and or for formulating directional strategies with a view to achieve defined objectives at a regional level. Regionalization is a process aiming at how best a region can be conceptualized in a set of physical and socio-cultural variables through objective and subjective points of view.

Regionalization in its broader thematic explanation can be defined as a means of arranging an immense number of points on the earth's surface; discovering uniformities, regularities in it and establishing definite theories, systems, aggregations and structures. There are two main procedures of identifying regions. One is grouping and the other is splitting. Splitting means division of a larger area into smaller components using a set of criteria. Grouping means putting smaller units with common attributes, together to constitute a particular region. Regionalization is supposed to be a set of techniques for measuring spatial processes which can be dealt with two approaches of (i) 'Static elements of space based on the principle of internal homogeneity and (ii) dynamic aspects of spatial process related to intra-regional diversity, available resources and their levels of utilization and the changing settlement structure. In the first method, area is given for which regional character is to be identified, while as in the second, the context is given and the volume is to be determined.

Political Regionalization of Jammu and Kashmir State

Keeping in view the impact of regional, lingual and religious consciousness on the political life of the people in Jammu and Kashmir, both natural and socio-cultural variables have been taken into consideration for political regionalization of the State. These variables include physiography, climate, soil-cover, natural vegetation, geographical neighbourhood, accessibility, religion, language and political aspirations of the people of the State. The directly or indirectly expressed political aspirations of the people have been ascertained through the political manifestes of various political leaders, the voting behaviour of the people, non-participation in elections, participation of the local people in strikes, demonstrations and armed struggle against the security forces, and the political wishes expressed by the indigenous people through electronic and print media. A brief account of various political regions delimited on the basis of above mentioned criteria is given as under.

Pro-India Jammu Region

The pro-India Jammu region is spread approximately over an area of 10,000 square kilometres. It comprises the districts of Kathua and Jammu and Hindu majority *tehsils* of Udhampur and Doda districts geographically contiguous with Kathua and Jammu districts. The region is surrounded by the Lesser Himalayas in the north and Punjab plain in the south. It consists of two physiographic regions, namely Jammu plains and Siwalik hills or Sub-Himalayas. The Jammu plains are situated at an altitude of 300 to 600 metres above sea level and the Siwalik hills lying towards the north of these plains have an attitude of 600 to 1800 metres. The Jammu plain experiences the sub-tropical climate where the summer temperature rises even above 45°C with extremely humid and unbearable scorching heat. The Siwalik hills experience relatively a mild climate and the temperature seldom rises above 40°C in summer. During the winter season, the weather conditions remain pleasant with temperatures ranging between 25°C in the plain area to 15°C in the hills.

The summer rainfall in the Jammu plain ranges between 80 to 120 centimetres, whereas the winter rainfall is just 5 to 10 centimetres. The Jammu plain is covered by tropical thorny forest cover. The Siwaliks have a tropical dry deciduous forest cover. The Jammu plain has a sandy-loamy soil cover. The main crops grown are wheat, paddy and maize. The Siwaliks have mountain soil, where the lower slopes of the hills are devoted to dry farming. The important crops of the region include maize and wheat. The pro-India Jammu region is well connected with Delhi, the national capital through metalled road, railways and airways. Physically, climatically, and communication-wise most of the region is an extension of the Indian Plain rather than the Himalayan region.

The pro-India Jammu region has a population of 25 lakh people, out of which nearly three-fourths are Hindus. The religious minorities include Muslims, Sikhs, Christians and Buddhists. Nearly 75 per cent people speak Dogri. Punjabi is being spoken by 6 per cent, Gogri by 5 per cent and Kashmiri by 4 per cent population. The remaining 10 per cent people speak Hindi, Urdu and other dialects of the region. Though Urdu is the official language of the State the Dogras prefer to learn Hindi as a second language and write the same in Devnagri script. The dress pattern, food pattern, architecture, customs, traditions and the belief system of the majority community, i.e. the Hindus of this region resemble the north Indian states.[3]

From 1820 to 1947, the pro-India Jammu region was the homeland of the ruling dynasty, as the autocratic rulers of the State belonged to the Dogra community. In 1857 as well as the second World War the Dogra rulers supported the British to crush the revolt against imperalism in India and abroad. The last autocratic Dogra ruler of the State, Maharaja Hari Singh was throughout averse to the plans of the Indian National Congress and Jammu and Kashmir National Conference to forge constitutional ties of Jammu and Kashmir with the Indian Union to safeguard the sovereignty of the State as well as his dynasty's rule over Jammu and Kashmir. But when on October 21, 1947 the tribals from across the border raided the State and the Government of India declined to give him military assistance he was obliged to surrender defence, foreign affairs and communication to the Indian republic. Once the power at the state level was transformed from Maharaja Hari Singh to the National Conference led by a progressive Kashmiri Muslim, namely Sheikh Mohammad Abdullah, the Dogras of Jammu began to shift their loyalties towards the hardcore Hindu nationalists of India.

The Praja Parishad enjoying the support of Hindu nationalists of Jammu boycotted the State Constituent Assembly elections in 1951. The 'Praja Parishad' also opposed the special status to Jammu and Kashmir enshrined in the Article 370 of the Indian Constitution. When in 1952 the Delhi agreement between Jawaharlal Nehru, the then Indian Prime Minister and Sheikh Mohammad Abdullah, the Jammu and Kashmir Prime Minister was being finalized by the two leaders, the Praja Parishad used the slogan: 'One president, one constitution and one flag'[4]. The Bharatiya Janta Party demanding the abrogation of Article 370 of the Indian Constitution is the most popular political party of the region. The people of this region have been demanding a separate statehood for Jammu region within the Indian control, free from any constitutional link with the Kashmiri dominated Srinagar government. When in 2000 the National Conference introduced the Autonomy bill in the State Assembly, the BJP leaders tore the report into pieces. In May 2001 when K.C. Pant the Chief Negotiator of the Government of India, appointed to negotiate with the political parties of the state visited the Jammu, the Hindus of the region reiterated their demand for a separate statehood for Jammu province. On July 14, 2001 when the Pakistani President General Pervez Musharraf visited India to discuss the 'Kashmiri Issue' at 'Agra Summit' the radical Hindus of the Jammu gave a call for the 'Jammu Bandh' to launch their protest against solving the problem as per the wishes of the people of Kashmir. The above mentioned facts make it clear that the majority of the people in the Jammu region see their political future safe in the Indian republic. The region is thus geographically, climatically, culturally and politically very much a part of the Indian Union.

Pro-India Ladakh Region

The Pro-India Ladakh region is spread over an area of 92,000 square kilometres, out of which an uninhabited area of 37,555 square kilometres is under Chinese control since the 1962 India-China war. The region includes Leh district and the Zanskar *tehsil* of Kargil district. It is surrounded by the Karakoram mountains in the north, the greater Himalayas in the south, Baltistan in the west and Tibet in the east. The region comprises Shyok valley, Indus valley, Zanskar valley and the Ladakh plateau. The region has an average altitude of 4,000 metres above sea level. The region has a cold arid climate. The summer temperature at Leh rises up to 30°C, whereas the mercury falls upto - 55°C at the Siachen glacier in winter. The region receives a scanty rainfall of below 50 centimetres annually. The region is practically devoid of any forest cover, however, along the river and stream courses small patches of social forestry can be found closer to agricultural fields and human settlements. The region has a thin coarse textured sandy soil cover, with little humus content in it. A special kind of hard husked barley locally called as *grim* is the dominant crop of the region. The Changthang division of Ladakh region is famous for rearing the *pashmina* goats. The region is connected through the Srinagar-Leh National Highway with the Kashmir region. Another route originating from Leh joins it with Shimla while passing through Upshi-Keylong Kulu and Manali. The Srinagar-Leh route remains closed for five months a year. The Leh-Manali road remains open for only a few months in summer. While travelling upstream from Leh along the river Indus one can reach Damchok located along the Indo-Tibetan border. Similarly, while travelling down stream from Leh along the river Indus one can reach Skardu, the nodal centre of Baltistan. Geographically Ladakh region is a part of western Tibet. It also shares physical and climatic characteristics with Baltistan.

The total population of Pro-India Ladakh region is about 1.2 lakh persons. The region is predominantly a Buddhist majority area where 90 per cent people belong to the red and yellow sects of Buddhism. The remaining 10 per cent people are Sunni and Shia Muslims. In Nubra valley there are a few thousand people who belong to the Noor Bakshi sect of Muslims. The people speak Ladakhi as their mother tongue. Urdu is being spoken as the second language in the region. The people of the region have their historical, racial, lingual, cultural, religious and commercial ties with the surrounding regions of Tibet and northern Himachal Pradesh. The belief system, customs, traditions, food pattern, dress pattern, architecture, indigenous system of medicine, fine arts and literature of the region has its origin in Tibet and its neighbouring territories.

The Pro-India Ladakh region was a Buddhist Kingdom conquered by the Dogra general Zorawar Singh in 1834, and since then it continues to be a part of Jammu and Kashmir state much like the Hindu of Jammu region. The Buddhists of Ladakh have always remained against the Kashmiri dominated state government. In 1949 the Ladakh Buddhist Association sent a memorandum to the Prime Minister of India, suggesting that Ladakh be integrated with Jammu in some way either to become an Indian state in its own right or as a part of east Punjab, totally separate from Kashmir administration. Before China's annexation of Tibet, the head Lama of Ladakh had suggested secession and union with Tibet, 'their spiritual allegiance was to the Dalai Lama in Lhasa, so too might be their political future'. But after the communists took over Tibet in 1950, they lost the contact dating back seven centuries, which had influenced both their spiritual and cultural lives. In 1952 Kushak Bakula, the Abbot of Spituk Monastry declared that once power had been transferred from the Maharaja to the National Conference, the constitutional link with the state was shattered and we were morally and juridically free to choose our own course, independent of rest of the state[5]. The Ladakh Buddhists are mostly the supporters of the Indian National Congress. In 1989 the Buddhists of this region launched their struggle for the Autonomous Hill Development Council on a large scale. The Kashmiri Muslims serving in the public and private sectors of the economy had to face the strong resistance of local Buddhists. The Buddhist-Muslim divide widened to such an extent that there was a communal boycott by the Buddhists to buy goods from the Muslim shopkeepers. In the early 1990s the Ladakh district was granted Hill Area Development Council. During the previous state assembly and parliamentary elections the demand for Union Territory status for Ladakh within the Indian Union was the main political slogan of the Buddhists in the region. When in 2000 the Jammu and Kashmir State Assembly passed a resolution for the grant of pre-1953 status to Jammu and Kashmir the Ladakhi Buddhists observed the 'Ladakh Bandh' on that day. When in May 2001 Mr. K.C. Pant visited Leh, the Ladakh Buddhist Association reiterated its demand for Union Territory status for Ladakh region. The local Muslims who constitute less than 15 per cent population of Leh district opposed any such move, like the Balti speaking Shia Muslims of Kargil *tehsil* who prefer to remain as a part of Kashmir administration in the present circumstances. The Zanskar *tehsil,* predominantly a Buddhist majority area, is connected at present with Kargil town through Kargil-Padam road, In order to integrate the region politically with Leh District the Padam-Leh road needs to be constructed along the Zanskar river bank.

Pro-Pakistan Jammu Region

The Pro-Pakistan Jammu region includes the districts of Mirpur, Kotli, Rawalkot, Bagh, Poonch and Rajouri. The region is surrounded on its north by Pir Panjal range, on south and west by Pakistan Punjab and towards the east by the Lesser Himalayas dividing district Doda from the district Udhampur. The region is spread over three physiographic divisions, namely Jammu plain, Siwalik hills and Lesser Himalayas. Its altitude varies from 300 metres in Jammu plains to 4,800 metres along the Pir Panjal range. The region experiences sub-tropical climate in the south and temperate climate in the north. The region is covered by tropical thorny forests and subtropical decidious and temperate coniferous forests from south to north. The annual rainfall received by the region ranges between 100 to 150 centimetres. The southern plain has a fertile alluvial soil cover and the northern hilly tract has thin mountain soil profile. The south-western plains are devoted to the cultivation of paddy and wheat, whereas the northern part is under maize cultivation. The region is connected with Jammu and Rawalpindi through a motorable road. Both river Chenab and river Jhelum passing through the region enter into Pakistani Punjab to pour their waters into river Indus. The region is connected with Kashmir Valley through Srinagar-Rawalpindi road and the Bhimbar-Shopian route also known as Mughal Road. However, both these routes have been closed because of strategic reasons for the last 54 years.

The Pro-Pakistan Jammu region has a total population of 20 lakh people. In the Pakistani part of the region the people are entirely Sunni Muslims, whereas in the Indian part of the region there is a sizeable number of Hindus. The languages spoken in the region include, Mirpuri, Pahari Gojri, Hindi and Urdu. These Non-Kashmiri languages resembling the Punjabi language are collectively referred to as the Parmi group of languages. Though the region has its religious and cultivational ties with Kashmiri Muslims, ethnically they are closer to the non-Muslim Dogras of Jammu and Muslim Punjabis living towards their south. The Muslims of the region write their languages in the Persian script and share a common food pattern, dress pattern, customs, traditions, architecture and fine arts with the Muslims of Punjab province.

The Pro-Pakistan Jammu region, a fief of Maharaja Hari Singh had retained some degree of autonomy but in 1936 the region was brought under the full control of Jammu and Kashmir government. In spring 1947, the native ex-soldiers of the Second World War numbering above 60,000 launched their armed struggle against the autocratic Dogra rule. In October, the tribals from the North Western Frontier Province of Pakistan came to support their Muslim brethren to liberate the region from the control of the Jammu and Kashmir government. Politically, they have remained the supporting ground for the Jammu and Kashmir Muslim Conference led by non-Kashmiri Muslim leaders of the region. The people of the region have struggled from 1931 to 1946 for the restoration of democratic government in the State with the Maharaja as its constitutional head. But in 1947 fearing that after snowfall on the Pakistan-Kashmir border the Maharaja may accede to Hindu Majority India, the Muslims of the region accelerated their armed struggle against the autocratic ruler. The secular and Kashmiri character of the National Conference became the negative factors for the party to win many sympathizers from this region. Though politically the people of the region are labelled as Kashmiri but ethnically they are Rajputs speaking the Parmi group of languages. Parmi Muslim consciousness, geographical contiguity with Pakistan and ethnic dissimilarity with Kashmiris are the main factors responsible for pro-Pakistani sentiments among the people of this region. The autonomous status within Pakistan is a major political attraction for the people of this region to remain loyal to that country. The independent status or merger with Pakistan of the Indian part of the State would help the divided ethnic communities in this region to re-unify and thereby increase their numerical and geographical size. However any such development in future is bound to diminish their political authority over the state in the changed circumstances. The fear of the loss of authority is perhaps the most crucial factor that stops these people from launching a strong campaign for plebiscite in the Jammu and Kashmir State. However the political parties like Jammu and Kashmir Liberation Front, Jammu and Kashmir National Liberation Front, Plebiscite Front, etc., fight for freedom of the whole state.

The Pro-Pakistan Gilgit and Baltistan Region

The Pro-Pakistan Gilgit and Baltistan are spread over an area of 72,000 square kilometres in addition to Kargil *tehsil* with an area of approximately 10,000 square kilometres. The Pakistani part of the region includes the districts of Askardu, Ganche, Gilgit, Diamir and Ghizar. The region is located at a strategic position where India, Pakistan, China, Afghanistan and Central Asia meet together. The region is surrounded by the Karakoram mountains in the north and the North Kashmir range in the south. Towards the west it shares a common border with the North Western Frontier Province of Pakistan whereas the Ladakh region borders it in the east. The region has a mountainous topography with an average altitude of about 4,000 metres. The region experiences an arid type of climate. The region is practically devoid of any forest cover. The summer temperature at Gilgit touches 31°C, whereas during winter -40°C temperature is recorded near Dras, in Kargil district. The region receives an annual rainfall of about 75 centimetres. The region is connected with both China and Pakistan through the Karakoram Highway popularly known as the ancient Silk Route. The region is also accessible to Ladakh and Kashmir along the course of river Indus if one moves upstream from Skardu to Kargil. The region can be approached from Kashmir via Guris valley as well. Geographically the region is closer to northern Afghanistan and Sinkiang than Ladakh or Kashmir.

The Gilgit and Baltistan inhabit a total population of over 10 lakh people. The people of the region are predominantly Shia Muslims, though there is also a sizeable number of Sunni and Noorbakshi Muslims. The languages spoken in the region are

Balti, Dardi, Kohistani, Shina, Chilasi, Chitrali, Kafir, Badakshi and Yarkandi[6]. The people of Kargil and tehsils Skardu are known as Baltis whereas the other groups are known as Dards. Ethnically the Guris *tehsil* of Kashmir province is also a part of Dardistan. Since the people live in segregated river valleys, inter-ethnic interaction and integration among different communities of the region is very limited. There are profound Central Asian influences over the food and dress pattern, architecture and fine arts of the people of the region.

Baltistan was conquered by the Dogras in 1840, whereas they established their control over Dardistan from 1850 to 1890. In 1935 a part of the region lying towards the north of Indus was leased-out by the Dogra ruler Maharaja Hari Singh to the British India government to establish the Gilgit Agency. But following the announcement of the partition plan, the Gilgit Agency was returned to continue under the Maharaja's control. The Dardi principalities which included Hunza, Nagar, Chilas, Punjal, Yasin and Gilgit have always remained under a loose control of Jammu and Kashmir government. Keeping in view the strategic location of the region and involvement of the local people in defence of their territories against any aggression, the British established Corps of Gilgit Scouts in 1913. After the independence on August 15, 1947, the Gilgit Scouts were still under the command of a British officer Major William Brown. After Brown heard that the Maharaja had acceded to India, he met with the Dogra governor Gansara Singh and urged him to ascertain the wishes of the Muslim Mirs and Rajas, regarding the accession to India. The governor appears not to have taken Brown's advice whereupon Brown warned that he might have to take his own measures to avoid the bloodshed. On the night of October 31, Brown put in to operation a plan code-named 'Datta Khel'. A platoon of Scouts proceeded to the governor's house to take him into protective custody. Other platoons of Scouts and Muslim State Forces went to take over the key locations, In the early hours of November 1, Governor Gansara Singh surrendered. As Brown was to discover, amongst the rebels, whilst openly supporting Pakistan, there was a secret plan to set up an Independent republic of Gilgit-Astor, which claimed the backing of 75 per cent of the scouts. As the only non-Muslim, Brown was in no position to dissuade them, and went along with their plans to set up a provisional government. On November 2 after outmanouvering the pro-Independence group and securing the approval of Mirs and Rajas for accession to Pakistan, the Pakistani flag was hoisted in the region. The political future of the region, however, remains unresolved because Gilgit and its neighbouring states, which include the former kingdoms of Hunza and Nagar who signed the instruments of Accession to Pakistan on November 18, 1947, have never been formally accepted as part of Pakistan pending a resolution of the future of the entire state. As part of the Northern Territories, together with Baltistan they remain under Pakistan's administration without the same rights and privileges as the other provinces enjoy under the Constitution of Pakistan. In 1975 Zulfikar Ali Bhutto abolished the old landholdings and kingdoms of Hunza and Nagar and reorganized the whole area into five administrative districts.

The Northern Areas Motahida Mahaz (Joint Platform) is a popular political party of the region formed to press for the political representation in the Pakistani National Assembly and Senate. The Jammu and Kashmir Liberation Front in particular has made attempts to establish their representatives in Gilgit and Baltistan in order to foster the independence movement, but the people have little political affiliation with the Valley and are generally believed to favour full integration with Pakistan. The first choice of the people in this region would be integration with Pakistan and a provincal arrangement, secondly, a set up similar to Azad Kashmir and thirdly integration with Azad Jammu and Kashmir. In March 1993, the High Court of Azad Jammu and Kashmir declared that the Northern Areas were part of Azad Kashmir and ordered their administration to be returned to the government of Azad Kashmir. But the Shia population, who predominate in the Northern Areas were reluctant to amalgamate with Sunni-dominated Azad Kashmir. The decision of the High Court was quashed on appeal in the Supreme Court.[7]

Pro-Independence Kashmir Region

The Pro-Independence Kashmir region is spread over an area of about 16,000 square kilometres. It is surrounded by the Kashmir range towards the north and north west, the Greater

Himalayas towards the east and north east and the Pir Panjal towards the south and south west. It is a longitudinal depression in the west Himalayan ranges which was carved out tectonically. The region covers six districts of Anantnag, Pulwama, Srinagar, Badgam,Baramulla and Kupwara. The average height of the region varies from 1,350 metres to 4,000 metres above sea level. The most characteristic tablelands the *karewas* (morains) in the valley are the main hub of fruit cultivation. The valley experiences a temperate climate with a maximum temperature going upto 37°C in the month of July. The temperature in the region comes down even upto 10°C during the month of January. In the Kashmir region there is heavy snowfall in winter as a result of cyclonic disturbances from the Mediterranean Sea. During the summer season the monsoon rains occur from mid-July to September. The annual precipitation recorded in the region is between 75 to 125 centimetres. The region has an alluvial soil cover, whereas the Kandi areas have black sub-mountain topsoil rich in humus content. The temperate evergreen coniferous forests and alpine meadows are the characteristic features of the Kashmir region. The deciduous forest species of the region included poplar, willow, chinar and keekar. The irrigated tracts along the river Jhelum and its tributaries are devoted to paddy cultivation, the Karewas and Kandi areas are put to horticulture and maize cultivation respectively. The region is connected through the National Highway with both Jammu and Leh but the natural passage of the Valley to the outside world is along the course of river Jhelum via Uri towards the west of Srinagar city. Before the tribal raid in October 1947, the Srinagar-Rawalpindi road, as it is called, was the most important communication link between the Kashmir Valley and the Punjab plains. There is a seasonal pattern of mass-movement between Kashmir and the Indian plains. During the summer it is the tourists and the Amarnath pilgrims who come to visit Kashmir. During the winter the Pashmina shawl traders, wholesale fruit sellers and government employees of the civil secretariat, come out of Kashmir to Jammu, Delhi, Poona, Calcutta and Bombay and other places to conduct their economic activities.

The Pro-Independence Kashmir region has a total population of 50 lakh people. More than 94 per cent people speak Kashmiri.

The other languages spoken in the region include Gojiri (3.5 per cent), Punjabi (1.5 per cent), Shina, Pahari and Pashtu. Almost 95 per cent people of the region are Muslims and the remaining 5 per cent are Hindus, Sikhs, Christians and Buddhists[8]. Before the fourteenth century Kashmir was civilizationally a part of the Indian subcontinent, but after the arrival of Persian and Central Asian Sayyids since the early 14th century, Kashmir was civilizationally transformed to the Sufi-Muslim way of life. Sanskrit was replaced by Persian as the official language of the region. Similarly the Sharda script of the region was replaced by the Persian script. The Buddhist and Hindu architecture, dress pattern, food pattern, morality and ethics, religious and political institutions, and fine arts were all transformed under the Persian and Central Asian influences. It was during the early 20th century that Persian was replaced by Urdu as the official language of the state, Hindustani music and cinema gained some popularity in the region and some affluent families of the state begain to send their children to receive higher education at Lahore University and the Aligarh Muslim University. The construction of Srinagar-Jammu National Highway via Banihall pass also became an important factor in promoting interaction and some emotional integration of Kashmiris with northern India. The continued presence of Indian military and paramilitary forces in Kashmir has not been welcomed by the Kashmiris, especially following the dismissal of Sheikh Abdullah from Prime Ministership on August 8, 1953.

The pioneers of political awakening in Kashmir were the highly educated members of the Muslim Conference who formally launched their campaign in 1931 for improving the educational and socio-economic conditions of the Muslims of the State in general, and Kashmiris in particular. The movement launched by the Muslim Conference shifted its thrust towards the political rights of the people and in 1938 the Muslim Conference was converted into the National Conference to launch a broad based struggle for what came to be known as 'New Kashmir'. The basic principles of the National Conference were secularism, socialism and democracy. The party enjoyed very little support outside the Kashmir Valley among the non-Kashmiri Muslims, Hindus, Buddhists and Shia Muslims.

The Kashmiri political struggle has undergone evolutionary change in the 20th century. In 1931, the Kashmiri Muslims formally started their struggle to improve their socio-economic conditions, especially to improve their educational status, enhance their participation in government services. In 1938 they began pressing their demand for responsible government in the State, whereas in 1946 they started the 'Quit Kashmir movement' to force the autocratic ruler to leave Kashmir. Following the announcement of the partition plan, the Kashmiri leaders were manouvering for getting an autonomous status within India or Pakistan, which they finally achieved within the Indian republic, but the developments between January 1948 to August 8, 1953 shook the balance of trust between the Kashmiris and the Government of India. From 1953 to 1975 the Kashmiris were struggling for a 'Third Option', i.e. the freedom of Kashmir from both India and Pakistan, but following the Indira-Abdullah Accord of 1975 there was some political calm in Kashmir. But after Abdullah's death the anti-India political forces re-emerged on the scene. After their defeat following the rigging at some polling booths in 1987 elections, the armed struggle for the liberation of Kashmir from India was the ultimate resolve of the Jammu and Kashmir Liberation Front, Hizbul Mujahideen and other militant organizations of the Valley.[9] In 1994, the All Party Hurriyat Conference was established by 23 political parties of the Valley to launch a political struggle for liberating Kashmir from India. The pro-independence political organizations enjoy mass support in the Kashmir Valley.

The Pro-Autonomy Doda Region

The Pro-Autonomy Doda region is spread over an area of about 11,700 square kilometres. The region is surrounded by the Pirpanjal range on its north, Himachal Pradesh on its south, Greater Himalayas on its east and the Lesser Himalayas on its west. The region can be divided into five physical divisions, namely the Greater Himalayas, the Chenab-Maru valley, the Pirpanjal West, the Pirpanjal East and the Doda Lesser Himalayas. The region comprises five *tehsils*, namely Kishtwar, Baderwah, Doda, Ramban and Banihal. The average altitude of the region ranges from 1,800 metres to 4,800 metres above sea level. The region has a mountainous topography and through the Banihal pass and Patnitop it is accessible to Kashmir and Jammu respectively. The region experiences a temperate type of climate. The summer temperature rises upto 35°C in the month of July at Ramban. The winter temperature falls upto -15°C in the month of January at Patnitop. The region receives an annual rainfall of about 100 centimetres. The mountain ranges of the region remain under snow cover for about five months a year. The region has a sandy-loamy mountain soil cover. The mountain tops of the region are covered by alpine vegetation, below which there is a coniferous evergreen forest cover and the sub-mountain slopes are covered by deciduous forests. The Ramban town is equi-distant from both Srinagar and Jammu cities. Through Chenab valley the region is accessible to Rajouri and Poonch towns as well. The Baderwah is closer to the Chamba district of Himachal Pradesh. The *tehsil* of Banihal and Kishtwar are closer to the Kashmir Valley.

The Pro-Autonomy Doda region has a total population of about 6.5 lakh persons. Four-fifths of the population of the region is Muslim and one-fifth is Hindu. Nearly 50 per cent people speak the Kashmiri. The other languages spoken in the region are Pahari, Hindu, Gojiri, Dogri, Baderwahi and Pogli. About 9 per cent population of the region belongs to the Scheduled Caste category. The people have their ethno-religious ties with all the three regions, i.e. Pro-Independence Kashmir region, Pro-India, Jammu region and the Pro-Pakistan Jammu region. But because of the geographical nearness to the Kashmir Valley, Muslim majority demographic composition and a large proportion of Kashmiri speakers in the region, the region is culturally closer to the Kashmiri people. Some of the famous poets and singers of the Kashmiri language belong to this region.

Though apparently the Pro-Autonomy Doda region is politically a neutral region, the people of the region are very sympathetic, especially in Banihal and Kishtwar towards the ongoing freedom movement launched by people like Shabir Ahmed Shah, Mirwaiz Umar Farooq and Amanullah Khan. the Pro-India political parties like the National Conference, Indian National Congress, and Bharatiya Janta Party have also some following in the region. The people of the region have been demanding for more than a decade an Autonomous Regional Council for the Doda district. They are mostly interested in their socio-economic upliftment and political empowerment at the regional level rather than the issues of national and state concern.

The Pro-Unification Muzaffarabad Region

The Pro-Unification Muzaffarabad region comprises Muzaffarabad district and Uri and Karnah tehsils of the Kashmir Province. The total geographical area of Muzaffarabad district under the Pakistani control is 1,648 square miles. Before the tribal raid in October 1947 the Muzaffarabad district comprised three *tehsils*, namely Muzaffarabad, Uri and Karnan but following the implementation of ceasefire between India and Pakistan on January 1, 1949 the Muzaffarabad *tehsil* was put on the Pakistani side of the ceasefire line. The whole Muzaffarabad region has a mountainous topography. It is surrounded by north Kashmir range on its north, Pir Panjal range on its south, Pakistan on its west and the Kashmir Valley on its east. The region has an average altitude of 1,500 to 4,500 metres above sea level. The region has a temperate type of climate. A maximum temperature of 40°C is recorded near Kohala Bridge in July. The winter temperature goes down upto 5°C at Muzaffarabad in January. The region has black mountain soil cover. The lower ridges are covered by the deciduous forests and the higher reaches are forested by coniferous evergreen trees. The river valley floor is put to the paddy cultivation and the submontane slopes and Kandi areas are devoted to maize cultivation. The region is connected through the Srinagar-Rawalpindi road with Srinagar, Lahore and Islamabad.

According to the 1941 Census, the Muzaffarabad region had a population of 2,64,671 persons, out of which 2,45,858 persons were Muslims and 18,813 persons were non-Muslims. The total population of Muzaffarabad *tehsil* was 1,25,585, persons followed by Uri and Karnah with a population of 80,223 persons and 58,963 persons respectively[10]. The present population of the entire Pro-Unification Muzaffarabad region is nearly 8 lakh persons out of which about 3 lakh people live in the Indian part of the region.

Punjabi is the mother tongue of the majority of the population. Kashmiri is spoken in certain parts of the region bordering the Kashmir Valley.

The Muzaffarabad town is the capital of the Pakistani part of Kashmir. Since the region is divided into two parts and the people of the region have their relatives living on both sides of the Line of Control, the demand for the re-unification of the region is being heard in both parts. The people of the region prefer to have an independent status for the entire state or a semi-independent status within Pakistan. The people of the region have at no point of time expressed their willingness to be an integral part of India. The popular political parties of the region are the Jammu and Kashmir Liberation Front, Jammu and Kashmir Muslim Conference and the Jammu and Kashmir Plebiscite Front.

Conclusion

The regional analysis of the popular political aspirations of the people of Jammu and Kashmir State based on a 'cause and effect relationship' discussed in the above sections makes it clear that there is no consensus among the people living in different regions of the State with respect to their political future. They stand divided along the regional, religious and ethnic lines. On the basis of the political aspirations of the people, the State of Jammu and Kashmir can be divided into three main regions, namely: (i) Pro-India Jammu and Ladakh region; (ii) Pro-Pakistan Jammu, Gilgit and Baltistan region, and (iii) Pro-Independence Kashmir, Doda, and Muzaffarabad region. Considering the physical and social diversity of the State and its spatial and cultural ties with its neighbouring countries, any effort to make Jammu and Kashmir State either an independent country or a part of Pakistan or a part of India will not be acceptable to the people of the State in its entirety.

In order to find a permanent solution to the Kashmir crisis, the people of all the regions need to be consulted by both the countries, to ascertain their regional aspirations. More importantly the people of the State need to be allowed to have an inter-ethnic, inter-religious and inter-regional dialogue to develop a consensus either to unify the whole State or to bifucrate it, or to trifurcate it to fulfil the mutually antagonistic political aspirations of the people living in different regions of the State. Democratically speaking, the people whose political future is involved, need to be taken into confidence irrespective of their religion, language and political ideology to find a mutually acceptable solution of the Kashmir crisis. No single party of the State can exclusively claim to represent the wishes of the people of Jammu and Kashmir State. Therefore, what is required is to initiate a dialogue and discussion with the popular political parties of all the constituent regions of Jammu and Kashmir State to diffuse the present political crisis.

References

1. Humboldt Von, Alexander (1859) *Cosmos*;Vol. 1 p. 484.
2. Semple, E.C. (1911) *Influences of Geographic Environment*, pp. 1-2.
3. Census of India (1988) *Regional Divisions of India*, Jammu & Kashmir State.
4. Puri, Balraj (1966) *Jammu: A Clue to the Kashmir Tangle*, p. 93.
5. Verma, P.S. (1994) *Jammu and Kashmir at the Political Crossroads*, New Delhi, p. 42.
6. Saraf, Mohammad Yusuf (1977); *Kashmiris Fight for Freedom*, Feroz Sons Ltd., Lahore, Vol. 1, pp. 1-42.
7. Schofield Victoria (1997), *Kashmir in the Crossfire*, Viva Books Private Ltd., New Delhi, p. 275.
8. *Report of the Jammu and Kashmir Commission of Inquiry* (1968) Government of Jammu and Kashmir, Jammu Government, p. 17.
9. Qureshi, Z.M. (1979), *Elections and State Politics India*, Sunder Prakashan, Delhi, p. 60.
10. Saraf, M.Y. (1977), *op. cit.*, pp. 37-42.

Ten

Ethnic Identities and Political Deadlock

Hari Om

A number of leading social scientists, political analysts and jurists like Bhikhu Parekh, Bhabani Sengupta, Prem Shankar Jha, Kuldip Nayar, A. M. Khusro, B. G. Verghese, Praful Bidwai, Ajit Bhattacharjee and A. G. Noorani, have suggested solutions which, according to them, alone can end the ongoing turmoil in the Kashmir Valley, resolve the 53-year-old Kashmir imbroglio to the satisfaction of all and ensure peace and stability in South Asia.

Solutions

Parekh maintains that the solution to the problem lies in the recognition by the Union Government of "Kashmir's different history, needs and circumstances" and grant of "a differential status" to the people of Jammu and Kashmir [*The Times of India*, March 3, 1994]. Sengupta and Prem Jha assert that if New Delhi sincerely wishes to break the political deadlock in Kashmir, it has no other alternative but to accept and implement what is being termed as an "Autonomy- plus, independent-minus" formula [*The Hindustan Times*, February 2, 1993; December 24, 1993; and February 10, 1994] or to grant "autonomy [to the State] to the point where it is almost indistinguishable from independence" [*The Hindu*, January 22, 1992]. Verghese and Bidwai vouch for a solution that seeks joint control of India and Pakistan over the State, as also what Bidwai calls "special autonomy" for the people of Jammu and Kashmir [*Indian Express*, May 5, 1992; *The Hindustan Times*, December 12 and 13, 1993 and March 25, 1993; *The Frontline*, June 2, 1995; *The Times of*

India, August 6, 1992, November 19, 1993 and August 25, 1994]. Bidwai also describes it as a "Trieste solution". [Trieste, it may be pointed out, was disputed region between the Slovenian Republic of the former Yugoslavia and Italy till 1954. Bhattacharjea wants the Central Government to grant "independence [to the State] in stages on the model of Bhutan" [*Indian Express*, March 3, 1991]. The suggestions of Kuldip Nayar and Khusro are no different [*The Hindustan Times*, July 15, 1991; *Indian Express*, February 5, 1994]. And, Noorani strongly urges the Central Government to start parleys with the gun toting militants forthwith in order to strike a truce over Kashmir [*The Statesman*, March 7-8, 8-9 and 9-10, 1994]. He says that "those with no blood on their hands are irrelevant." The upshot of his whole formulation is that the only way to "forge a lasting peace in Kashmir" is negotiations with those "who are firing on our soldiers."

Indifferent Response

It needs to be noted that these persons have been saying so for quite some time, but without evoking any favourable response from the people of the troubled State minus a few individuals here and there. The reasons for such an indifferent attitude to these proposals are not far to seek. One of the most potent reasons is that all these solutions are based on the misguided notion that the nearly 2,000 square kilometres of the Kashmir Valley represents the entire State of Jammu, Kashmir and Ladakh; that the political aspirations of all the people in the State are identical or nearly identical and that the contradictions among them, if any, can be easily reconciled. This has turned out to be the prime cause of our failure to break the deadlock in the State. None of these formulations enjoy any universal support in Jammu, Kashmir and Ladakh. The two prime factors are :

- the State of Jammu and Kashmir houses a number of religious and ethnic groups; and
- the political aspirations and needs of the people of Jammu and Ladakh, who constitute more than half of the State's population and inhabit about 90 per cent of the State's land area, and Kashmiri Pandits and Muslims are conflicting.

Prudent

It would be only prudent if we examine both these factors and that too dispassionately. Such an exercise would surely help us to evolve some definite Kashmir policy and restore peace in the State. Jammu and Kashmir, it must be remembered, is a multi-lingual, multi-religious and multi-ethnic State [for details see Census of India, J&K Part, 1981]. The principal languages spoken here are : Dogri, Kashmiri, Pothwari, Balti, Ladakhi, Gojri, Dardi. Punjabi and Urdu. The main religious groups, as per the 1981 Census, are : 38,31,292 Muslims [64.3 per cent], 19,08,288 Hindus [32.1 per cent], 1,29,393 Sikhs [2.17 per cent] 69,796 Buddhists [1.17 per cent] and 6,916 Christians [0.12 per cent].

The largest region of the State is Ladakh. It has a land area of 96,701 square kilometres and is predominantly Buddhist [52 per cent]. The Jammu region is next in size. It has an area of 26,293 square kilometres and is predominantly Hindu (66.3 per cent) with 29.7 per cent Muslims and 3.58 per cent Sikhs. The Kashmir province, having a land area of 15,853 square kilometres, is predominantly Muslim [94.85 per cent] with 3.89 per cent Hindus and 1.04 per cent Sikhs.

The State of Jammu and Kashmir is, in fact, a blend of several ethnic groups. Some of the major social and ethnic groups in the State are: Kashmiris, Dogras, Gujjars and Bakerwals, Darads, Baltis, Gaddis, Ladakhis and Pothwari-speaking Muslims and non-Muslims and Chibalis. Kashmiris are mainly concentrated in the Kashmir Valley. Dogras are spread all over the Jammu region. Gujjars and Bakerwals inhabit the mountainous and Kandi area of the State. They are mostly herdsmen. They are said to have migrated from Rajasthan and embraced Islam. They trek along with their sheep, goats and cattle from the plains to the higher regions in search of green pastures in summers, the Darad and Balti Muslims have their abodes in Gurez, Tilel and parts of Dras. Gaddis inhabit the South-East of the middle mountain region of the Jammu province. Pothwari-speaking Muslims and non-Muslims and Chibalis live between Chenab and Jhelum and Ladakhis inhabit the trans-Himalayan Ladakh. They are all Mongolites.

The Muslim population of the State can be broadly divided into Kashmiri Muslims inhabiting the Southern portion of the

Kashmir region, Gujjars and Bakerwals and Darad and Balti Muslims. In Kashmir there are more than six lakh Gujjars and Bakerwals and one lakh Darad and Balti Muslims. Nearly eight lakh Kashmiri Muslims are Shias. Added together, they form about half of Kashmir's population, the other half being Sunni Muslims. Nearly one lakh Shias live in different parts of the Jammu region and one lakh in Kargil district of Ladakh. The distribution of most Gujjars and Bakerwals in the State—over 12 lakhs—is as follows: Poonch—one lakh fifty thousand, Rajouri—two lakh, Udhampur—one lakh, Jammu—eighty thousand, Kathua—thirty thousand, Doda—one lakh, Baramulla—one lakh fifty thousand, Pulwama—one lakh, Kupwara—one lakh fifty thousand, Srinagar—fifty thousand, Badgam—thirty thousand. The population of Pothwari-speaking Muslims and non-Muslims is nearly four lakh. About one lakh of them inhabit Poonch, eighty thousand, Kupwara, fifty thousand, Baramulla, thirty thousand, Srinagar and about one lakh Rajouri.

Militancy in the State of Jammu and Kashmir is basically confined to the Kashmiri-speaking Sunnis. These were the people who dominated the State's political and economic institutions between October 1947 and January 19, 1990. And, these are the people who have been controlling the State's polity and economy since October 1996. [Between January 1990 and October 9, 1996, the State was under Governor/President rule.] More than half of Kashmir's population, which includes eight lakh Shias, one lakh Darad and Balti Muslims and six lakh Gujjars and Bakerwals, are totally indifferent to the separatist movement that has been going on in the Valley since December 1989, when the protagonists of the State's separation from India abducted the then Union Home Minister Mufti Mohammad Sayeed's daughter, Dr. Rubiya Sayeed, to secure the release of eleven top-ranking activists of the so-called secular Jammu and Kashmir Liberation Front (JKLF).

Important Factor

The composition of population is indeed an important factor in the State's political situation and just cannot be overlooked by policy planners while evolving a solution to the vexed Kashmir problem. Even more important, perhaps, is the attitude of different people inhabiting different parts of the State towards India, as also to the State's existing politico administrative structure. For instance, Shias and Gujjars and Bakerwals in the State, in general and in the Kashmir region, in particular, vehemently oppose the concepts of "*azadi*", merger of the State with the theocratic, feudalistic and medievalist Pakistan and "pre-153 constitutional position" on the ground that under the dispensation the militants and other Kashmiri leaders have been striving to achieve since 1990, their fate would be no better than that of the Mohajirs, Shias, Ahmediyas, Sikhs, Hindus and Christians in Pakistan. They, in addition, advocate a radical change in the State's politico-administrative and economic structure so that they obtain what they call their legitimate due in the State's political and economic processes. How else can one explain the statements made repeatedly by some influential leaders of the Shia and Gujjar and Bakerwal communities, including Sadiq ali, Mian Bashir, Taj Mhi-Ud-Dind, Chaudhary Jalal-Ud-Din, Anwar Chaudhary and Chaudhary Shah Mohammad.

Sheikh Abdullah's close associate, National Conference M.L.A. and a prominent leader of Shias, Sadiq Ali, has declared in unequivocal terms that, "The one million Shias in Jammu and Kashmir are in danger as they face discrimination from the Pakistan-supported militants and 1.8 million Sunnis [of Kashmir]...Now they will brook no further exploitation. I know the crimes being committed under the garb of secularism. Secularism never means selectism. If we are 20 per cent of the population, why shouldn't we get 20 per cent of what the State offers? Give each section its due and there will be secularism" [*The Sunday Mail*, July 17-23, 1994].

Similarly, the former Senior Vice President of the Jammu and Kashmir Pradesh Congress (I) and a highly revered leader of the Gujjar and Bakerwal communities, Mian Bashir, has strongly urged the Prime Minister to "use force to crush the Jamait-e-Islami which wants to have a stranglehold" on the minorities by "terrorizing them." He has also justified the Kashmiri Pandits' "demand for a separate homeland" [*The Sunday Mail*, July 31 – August 6, 1994; *Indian Express*, August 11, 1994]. Identical was the stand of the Gujjar and Bakerwal-dominated Militancy Mukhalif Morcha [Anti-militancy Front] top-ranking leaders, Taj Mhi-Ud-Din and Chaudhari Jalal-Ud-Din. They have been consistently helping the Government of India in its endeavours to crush militancy and integrate the State fully with India. Besides, they have sought the Centre's support in favour of a change in the state's politico-administrative set-up that ensures the representation of Gujjars and Bakerwals in all spheres in proportion to their population [*The Times of India*, February 24, 1994. *The Tribune*, May 28, 1995, *The Hindu*, January 28, 1995]. The Gujjars United Front leaders, including Anwar Chaudhary and KK Chaudhary Shah Mohammad, have gone a step further and repeatedly declared that the solution to the problems being faced by their communities lie in the segregation of all the six districts of Jammu region from Kashmir and their conversion into a full-fledged "Gujjar and Duggar Jammu State within India and under the Union Constitution." Their refrain is that Kashmiri rulers will under no situation enable them to enjoy the fruits of Indian democracy or exercise those rights to which they are entitled as a Scheduled Tribe community [*Daily Excelsior* and *The Tribune* January 16, 2001].

Such an attitude on the part of the Shia and Gujjar and Bakerwal communities, barring a couple of Shia leaders like Maulvi Abbas Ansari of the 23 – Party Hurriyat Conference, simply cannot be dismissed as something ludicrous and preposterous. They have a point when they, or for that matter all other religious and ethnic minorities in the State, articulate their grievances against the Valley leaders and demand proportional representation which, they believe, alone can protect them against exclusion by the Valley Sunnis [*The Tribune*, February 23, 1994 and April 4, 1995; and *The Times of India*, October 4, 1993]. For example, Gujjars and Bakerwals, Shias, Darads, Baltis, Pandits and Sikhs have at no point of time during all these, 53 years of independence been allotted more than four seats in the Legislative Assembly out of over 40 seats meant for the Kashmir region. This despite the fact that they constitute nearly 55 per cent of Kashmir's population and dominate a number of assembly constituencies, including Kangan, Bandipur, Pahalgam, Tangmarg, Noorabad, Kokarnag, Ganderwal, Verinag, Beerah, Badgam, Zadibal, Nagin, Pattan, Sonawari and Habbakadal.

On the contrary, the Valley Sunnis, who form about 45 per cent of Kashmir's and just 22 per cent of the State's population, have all along returned no less than 40 legislators to the Assembly. But this unfair and preponderant share of representation of the Valley Sunnis in the legislature and State Cabinet, which decide questions of supreme importance to the happiness and well-being of the population, constitute just one example. They enjoy a similar position in the State Secretariat, Government services, professional and technical institutions and recruitment agencies like the Public Service Commission and recruitment boards. The reason: they control all the political organizations, including the Congress, the National Conference, the CPI, the CPI-M, the Janata Dal, the People's Democratic Party, the People's League, the People's Conference, the JKLF, the Hurriyat Conference and the Jamait-e-Islami.

It is indeed ironical that those who have been ruling since October 1947 are feeling alienated from India and challenging the nation's unity, integrity, and secular and democratic ethos. It is again a paradox that those who suffered, and continue to suffer, gross discrimination and political neglect at the hands of the Kashmiri Sunni-dominated successive State Governments as well as New Delhi are bitterly opposing the separatists and doing everything under the sun to defeat the Pakistan design on Jammu and Kashmir and enter the arena of mainstream politics.

The attitude of the people of Jammu and Ladakh and the displaced Pandits towards India is no different. The political demands of the people of Jammu include "statehood within India", "regional autonomy" and "a statutory development board" with or without Article 370. On the other hand, the demands of the distant Ladakhis range from "Union Territory status" to "an autonomous Hill Council", invested with "full political, administrative and economic powers and without Article 370" under which the State enjoys a "special status" to a "security zone within Kashmir" to "reservation for the Pandit minority in all spheres and at all levels and application of the Indian Constitution to the State in full."

Cleavage of Opinion

More importantly, even the Kashmiri Sunnis are not a homogeneous lot. In fact, they are vertically divided into four groups demanding independence from both India and Pakistan, merger of the State with Pakistan, pre-1953 constitutional status [limited accession of the State to India] and close integration of the state with India.

That there exists a profound cleavage of opinion among the leaders of the Sunni community with regard to the State's political future can be seen from the former JKPCC[I] President, Ghulam Rassol Kar's outright repudiation of his close friend and Chief Minister, Dr. Farooq Abdullah's clamour for the pre-1953 position on the ground that the ongoing process of the State's integration with India just cannot be allowed to be reversed. This is also clear from the statement of a former Hurriyat leader, Shabir Shah. And, it reads like this: "The Hurriyat Conference cannot claim to represent the entire State as it only has members from six of the 14 districts and there is no representation from Jammu and Ladakh." Former Jammu and Kashmir Chief Minister and son-in-law of Sheikh Abdullah, G. M. Shah, and Dr. Farooq Abdullah also say the same thing and feel that if we are really interested in solving the Kashmir problem, we have no other option but to involve the people of Jammu and Ladakh in the proposed dialogue with the Hurriyat Conference. They add that the solution has to be such as is acceptable to all the people inhabiting different regions of the State. And, that even the Hurriyat Conference is a divided house is too well known. But these are just a few of the several such statements which serve to demonstrate how much the Kashmiri leaders are divided in their political perceptions.

It is thus fairly obvious that the people of Jammu, Kashmir and Ladakh are not Palestinians, who are one against Israel as far as their struggle for a homeland is concerned. The people of Jammu, Kashmir and Ladakh are a divided house, with, of course, an overwhelming majority of them vehemently opposing the clamours for Pakistan, independence and demanding a political system which not only promises to unite Jammu, Kashmir and Ladakh and the rest of the country together in closer bonds, but also ensures their effective and real participation in the State's political and economic processes.

Way Out

What then is the way out? Should we continue to devise solutions based on the outmoded and archaic assumption that the Valley Sunni leaders represent the general will, and that accepting and implementing the political demands of a section of the Kashmiri leaders would be the same as meeting the political needs of the people of Jammu, Kashmir and Ladakh? Or, should we go in for the reorganization of the State in order to first accommodate the political aspirations of the people of Jammu and Ladakh and then start parleys with Kashmiri leaders of all shades of opinion, including those representing the displaced Pandits, to determine what could satisfy them and their constituencies?

These are the only two options available and we have to choose one. The first option we simply cannot exercise because it has the potential of creating more problems than resolving the existing ones. Clearly, we have to opt for the second alternative.

Time is running out and there are potent reasons to believe that unless the State is trifurcated, the best opportunity for any action would be lost forever. This action is imperative. Even otherwise there is no logic in maintaining the State as a single political unit. The people of Jammu and Ladakh are conspicuous by their absence in Kashmir. Most of those who had some immovable property anywhere in Kashmir have already sold it and settled down permanently in Jammu or Ladakh. A few employees from Jammu and Ladakh, who used to hold certain positions in the Government and semi-Government departments in Kashmir before the eruption of militancy there, have either got themselves transferred to Jammu or Ladakh or have gone on long leave. If there are some officials from Jammu and Ladakh still in the Valley, their number is not even 1,000 out of nearly 2.4 lakh Government employees.

Not only this, no person from Jammu and Ladakh could ever become Chief Minister of the State. For, the Valley leaders hold the view that since Kashmir has 42 seats (now 46) in the 76-member assembly (now 87-member assembly), the office of the Chief Minister is their sole preserve.

These and several such things have only created an extreme form of inter-regional rancour and animosity. In fact, while the people of Jammu and Ladakh consistently complain that "they are being treated as second class citizens by the Kashmiri leaders," the Valley leaders always accuse the legislators of Jammu and Ladakh of hobnobbing with the Centre to bring down what they call their "legitimate governments" and foist "Delhi agents on the State." In this context they refer to the role of the legislators of Jammu and Ladakh which actually led to the fall of Sheikh Abdullah's Government in August 1953 and 1977, Farooq Abdullah's ministry in 1984 and the ouster of Gul Shah in 1986.

The trifurcation of the State, it must be borne in mind, would remove all negative trends, and promote in each region politics based on purely democratic and economic issues. In such a situation the Kashmiri Sunnis may become less vulnerable to the "syncretic pulls of fundamentalism from Pakistan". R. Venkataraman, former President of India, it may be recalled, had realized it as early as 1983. As a matter of fact, that year, he had urged the then Prime Minister, Indira Gandhi, to make Ladakh a "Union Territory as demanded by the local people", confer the status of "statehood" on Jammu and deal with the Valley as a "separate entity" (R. Venkataraman, *My Presidential Years*, 1994).

The Vajpayee Government would do well to take all these things into consideration, respect the sentiments of the people of Jammu and Ladakh as well as religious and ethnic minorities and heed the advice of the former President. Not to do so and cultivate the otherwise unpopular Hurriyat Conference alone would be to play with dangerous tools or provoke political explosions not only in Jammu and Ladakh, but also Kashmir.

Eleven

Problems of Power Sector Development

Dost Mohammad
A.S. Bhat

Abstract

Power shortage has hampered the growth of agriculture, industry and commerce in the State. The planning for power development has been faulty, concentrating exclusively on the imports rather than the creation of additional capacity. No new power project was commissioned during the past twenty years. The power projects commissioned by the Central government in the State have given little relief to the power starved Valley. The cavalier attitude of the state government towards the power sector has widened the gap between demand and supply which is estimated at 2,000 MW by the year 2000 AD. Lack of transmission lines to carry bulk power to Kashmir has further aggravated the situation. The state has also suffered on account of the Indus Water Treaty, which has inflicted huge losses on the generation front. The State has also failed to claim its due share from the centrally sponsored projects and power generated from the three rivers included in the Treaty. The state government has recently decided to take up four new power projects in collaboration with the international consortia. However, this requires huge finances for which sources are yet to be identified. The power scenario is likely to remain grim in the years to come.

Introduction

Inadequate power supply has been acknowledged as the most important infrastructural bottleneck to the economic development of the State of Jammu & Kashmir. Despite huge hydro power potential, no new power project was installed during the past 20 years. The generating capacity of the power projects has stagnated at 180 MW which is unparalleled compared with other states and the country as a whole. The State has exclusively relied on the import of power rather than the creation of additional generating capacity. The centrally sponsored projects with an installed capacity of 690 MW provide only 12 per cent as royalty to the State. The State is not given any compensation for the losses inflicted on it by the Indus Water Treaty signed between India and Pakistan. Due to faulty planning and the denial of its legitimate rights over the power generated from Ravi, Sutlej and Beas, the State is facing a crippling shortage of electricity restricting the growth of agriculture, industry and commerce.

Since 1997 new initiatives have been taken to solve the grim power situation in the State. The government has signed MOUs with multinationals for commissioning of four power projects—Kishenganga (330 MW), Baglihar (450 MW), Sewa-II (120 MW) and Uri-II (280 MW)—which requires a total investment of Rs. 8,000 crores. In addition various power projects have been identified for participation by the private sector. The State is also building transmission lines to improve the supply position, particularly in the Kashmir Valley which faces acute shortage of power throughout the year. Since hydro power projects have long gestation periods and sources of finance are yet to be identified, the power scenario is unlikely to improve in the near future. Power shortage will continue as a serious social and economic problem. The present paper attempts to identify the main problems involved in the development of electric power in Jammu & Kashmir. The main issues discussed are: Indus Water Treaty (Section II), hydro potential (Section III), installed capacity (Section IV), demand-supply gap (Section V), cost of power imports (Section VI), transmission losses (Section VII), and rural electrification (Section VIII).

II. Indus Water Treaty

The Indus Water Treaty signed between India and Pakistan in 1960, has far-reaching implications for the power position in Jammu & Kashmir. It is, therefore, imperative that a brief description of this Treaty and its impact on power planning in the State is given at the outset.

According to this treaty, India has the exclusive right on the waters of Ravi, Beas and Sutlej, while Pakistan possesses the right to use the waters of the Indus, Jhelum, and Chenab—the main rivers traversing through the State of Jammu & Kashmir. As a result of the restrictions on water storage in these rivers, all power projects in the state are to be "run-of-the-river-type". This adversely affects the cost effectiveness not only on construction of the projects but also on the generation of electricity from these projects.[1] The generating capacity of all run-of-the-river projects falls by about 60-75 per cent during winter because the water level in different rivers gets depleted substantially. For example, the water requirement for rated generation of lower Jhelum Hydel Project is about 7,500 cusecs. In the winter average discharge remains 1,600-2,000 cusecs. This discharge corresponds to 22-28 MW. The generation from other power houses falls correspondingly (See Table 1).

Table 1
Hydel Power Generating Capacity at Peak Hours in Jammu & Kashmir: 1996.

S. No.	*Name of the Project*	*Installed Capacity (MW)*	*Effective Capacity at Peak Load Hours*	
			Summer	*Winter*
1	Lower Jhelum Power Project	105	105	40
2	Upper Sind Hydel Project (Stage I)	22.5	18	16
3	Mohra Power House	9*	6	0
4	Ganderbal Power House	15	10	7
5	Chenani Power House	25	20	10
6	Stakna Power House	4	4	4
7	Iqbal Power House	3.75	3.75	3.75
	Total	184.25	166.75	80.75

*not functional due to economic and technical reasons.

Source: Chief Engineer, Power Generation Wing, Srinagar, July 1997.

This state has not been compensated for the forced perusal of uneconomic projects and only 15 MW of power are provided to it from Bhakra and Beas which have the total installed capacity of 2,704 MW (Kaul, 1989, p. 23). In consonance with the principle of natural justice the State should have been given a partner status with Punjab and Haryana in the distribution of power from Bhakra and Beas. According to the Gadgil Formula which provides the home state 10-12 per cent power, the legitimate share of Jammu & Kashmir would be around 325 MW. In addition, the power is sold to the State at exorbitant rates compared to the partner states which in accordance with the Gadgil Formula are entitled to "free of cost" power from these projects. Thus, the State suffers on account of restricted access to the power generated from Bhakra and Beas and also from a market-based rates charged on electricity supplied. Since 1997, there is a growing concern both in official and private circles about the implications of the treaty to the State. For the first time, the state government has put forth the demand for 200 to 300 MW share from the Bhakra-Beas Project.

III. Hydro Potential

Being a mountainous region with four major rivers—Chenab, Jhelum, Indus and Ravi—traversing through it, Jammu & Kashmir has immense hydro power potential[2] which remains mostly unidentified as no scientific survey has been conducted during the past quarter century or so.[3] The Centre for Monitoring Indian Economy (CMIE) has reported the state's hydel power potential at 7,487 MW which constitutes about 9 per cent of the total hydel potential of the country. (CMIE, 1996), p. 29). Undoubtedly, these estimates understate the actual potential because Chenab alone provides the possibility of generating 550 MW of power. The CMIE estimates are based on the mean flow of rivers flowing through the State. Since the flow of water is severely reduced in winter, the mean flow of any river in the State is a misleading guide to the hydro power potential. The restrictions on the construction of dams on the State's waters, is another factor responsible for gross under-estimation of power potential in the State. The official estimates of the state government put this potential at 15,000 MW. However, it is accepted by the official circles that no scientific survey has been conducted to identify the hydro power potential of the State. There is thus a pressing need for a comprehensive survey to determine the actual hydro power potential of the State and also the feasibility of various power projects. The State has also an immense possibility of pump set storage generation to meet the power shortage at peak hours. These sources are yet to be fully identified and their technical and economic feasibility to be worked out in the State.

IV. Installed Capacity

During 1977-97, no new power project was commissioned in the State except the Gas Turbine Station (GTS) which functions only during winter. This period has witnessed phenomenal growth of power generation capacity in other states and the country as a whole. It is, therefore, evident that huge allocations made periodically were spent on imports of power rather than creation of additional generating capacity in the State.

The installed power generating capacity of the State is 366 MW of which 182 MW are thermal and 184 MW are hydel (See Table 2).

The generating capacity of hydro electric projects declines by about 60-75 per cent in winter due to lower discharge in the rivers feeding various power projects. The effective capacity of hydro power stations thus falls only about 80 MW in winter (see Table 1). In order to ease out the grim power situation, the GTS with an installed capacity of 175 MW remains the major source of power in the Valley. The effective capacity of the station is only 140 MW and power is generated at an exorbitant cost of Rs. 6.25 per unit including depreciation. The cost of diesel is Rs. 3.50 per unit of power generated. The other sources of thermal power, namely Kalakote Thermal Station (22.5 MW) and Bemina Diesel Station (6.76 MW) are non-functional owing to economic and technical reasons. There are no solar and tidal power stations because solar power is impracticable and wind generated electricity offers little opportunities for practical applications.

The current utilization of less than 1.5 per cent of hydro-electric power potential of the State indicates the total neglect of this sector over the years. As a result, the State of Jammu &

Kashmir remains at the bottom in terms of hydro power generation in the country in general and the northern region in particular. The State accounts for 0.9 per cent of the hydro power generated in the country which is lowest among the northern states, as shown in Table 3.

Table 2
Statistical Power Profile of Jammu & Kashmir: 1995-96

	Unit	*1990-91*	*1991-92*	*1992-93*	*1993-94*	*1994-95*	*1995-96*
Installed capacity (utilities)	MW	262	262	262	337	362	366
Hydro	MW	180	180	180	180	180	184
Thermal	MW	82	82	82	157	182	182
Power Generation (Utilities)	Million KWH	3265	3074	2905	2745	2837	2881
Transmission and distribution lines	000 Ckt.km	42	42	42	42		
T&D Losses	Percent	42.3	49.2	48.3	47.7		
Power Requirement	Million KWH	3132	3345	3640	4045	4385	
Power availability	Million KWH	2795	2984	2932	3296	3309	
Power deficit (–)	Million KWH	–337	–361	–729	-749	-1076	
Power deficit (–)	Percent	–10.8	–10.8	–19.5	–18.5	–24.5	
Overall power consumption (utilities)	Million KWH	1477	1480	1505	1595	2007	
Domestic	Million KWH	386	386	405	353	520	
Agriculture	Million KWH	150	150	155	269	215	
Industry	Million KWH	370	370	370	282	489	
Commerce	Million KWH	239	240	241	217	307	
Per Capita power consumption (utilities)	KWH	189	188	195			
Village electrified	Number	6153	6170	6175	6175	6188	6252
Village electrified	Percent	95	95	95	95	95	95
Pumpset energized	Thousand	2	3	3	3	3	5

Source: Centre for Monitoring Indian Economy, India's Energy Sector, September, 1996, p. 80.

Table 3
Power Generating Capacity in Northern India, 1996

	Hydel		*Thermal*		*Solar*		*Total*	
India	20976	(100.00)	60087	(100.00)	2225	(100.00)	83288	(100.00)
North	7158	(34.1)	15890	(26.4)	895	(40.2)	23942	(28.7)
Haryana	884	(34.1)	896	(1.5)	—	—	1780	(2.1)
Himachal Pradesh	289	(1.4)	0	(0.00)	—	—	289	(0.3)
Jammu & Kashmir	184	(0.9)	182	(0.3)	—	—	366	(0.4)
Punjab	1799	(8.6)	1710	(2.8)	—	—	3509	(4.2)
Rajasthan	896	(4.7)	1014	(1.7)	—	—	1981	(2.4)
U.P	1505	(7.2)	4570	(7.6)	—	—	6075	(7.3)

Source: Centre for Monitoring Indian Economy, India's Energy Sector, September,1996, Tables 28-29

Demand-Supply Gap

The State is facing a crippling shortage of electricity for domestic as well as industrial uses. Demand has continuously increased due to increased population, rural electrification and better standards of living while as domestic generation of electricity has stagnated as no new power stations was commissioned during the last 20 years. This has resulted in a huge gap between demand and supply which is partly filled through imports and generation by GTS. The import of power from neighbouring states and supply from Salal Hydro Project (NHPC) cater to the requirements of Jammu region (this project is located in Jammu region). Kashmir Valley remains under darkness throughout the year, except the summer months when local power stations generate electricity to their full capacity. The Valley faces acute shortage of power in winter due to cold weather conditions and scarcity of fuel like firewood, etc. Electricity is being mostly used for heating purposes during the winter when temperature falls to subzero level. The power shortage as evidenced by frequent and unprecedented load shedding (four days curtailment in a week in Srinagar) are producing negative effects on the people's psyche besides adversely affecting the industrial and agricultural development in the Valley.

With the commissioning of the Uri Hydel Power Project (480 MW) in 1996-97, the power situation has improved somewhat in the Valley as the project supplies 240 MW of power to the Valley.

However, the immediate increase in the availability of power through this project cannot exceed 150 MW owing to the limiting capacity of the local grid station. The capacity of 220 KW Pampore Grid Station is 240 MW. Due to some technical reasons, the grid is actually loaded to 200 KW. The limiting capacity of the grid has become the bottleneck for feeding the power from the Uri Project or other parts of the state/country in the power network of the Valley. The commissioning of Zainakote Grid Station and that of 400 KV double circuit Uri Wangoora Pampore transmission line has improved the absorption capacity of the State from 720 MW to 960 MW.

The Uri Hydel Project roughly requires 10 cusecs of water for generating 1 MW power. Since in winter the discharge of river Jhelum is only 2,000 cusecs, the maximum generation can only be 200 MW. Previously, the water was stored in the barrage of the Lower Jhelum Hydel Project during night and day hours to allow a maximum generation from the project during morning and evening peak hours but now such storage is not possible as this will affect the generation from the Uri Hydel Project. Finally, the supply from this project involves an element of uncertainty as it has yet not been transferred to Kashmir despite the public commitment made by the Prime Minister of India in 1996.

The gap between the demand for and supply of electricity has been increasing over the period (see Table 2). The estimated gap between demand and supply widened from 337 MKWH (10.8 per cent) in 1991 to 1,076 MKWH in 1995-96 (24.5 per cent).[4] However, the estimates regarding the availability of electricity are highly exaggerated as these are based on unrealistic assumptions about the timely commissioning of ongoing projects in the State and the Central sector. Most of the power projects under construction are likely to take much longer gestation periods because of the prevailing conditions in the State. Hence the actual gap is likely to be much wider in the years to come. In order to overcome the actual shortage of electricity, attempts should be made to reduce the demand and increase the supply from local as well as central power projects. In view of the environmental considerations and the availability of a vast hydro electric potential, the State should go in for only hydroelectric power projects because

(1) hydro power projects use natural resources which are renewable and indigenously available; (2) have a relatively large life and low depreciation; (3) unforeseen breakdowns in hydro projects are less frequent and maintenance required plant shut downs are of very short duration; (4) operation and maintenance costs are low and plants can be designed for automatic and supervisory control from remote locations; (5) hydro projects are cleaner and basically non-polluting (Guha, 1990). In addition, hydro projects are favoured for good peaking capability and greater efficiency. The planning for economically feasible and technically viable hydel projects should be undertaken earnestly because the gestation period in a hydel power house is not less than 9 years.

The other means of increasing power availability in the State are as follows: First, construction of 400 KV line from Jammu to Srinagar to transmit power from major power houses to be constructed in the Jammu region. Second, the construction of 220 KV transmission line from Jammu and Srinagar. In this regard work has been started by the Power Grid Corporation on a single circuit 400 KV line from Dul Hasti (Doda) to Kishenpur (Udhampur). It has also decided to take up the construction of 400 KV double circuit transmission like from Kishenpur to Wagoora (Baramulla).[5] Until now, the power system of the Valley was linked to the rest of the country through a double circuit 132 KV line, having a restriction of power flow of about 100 MW. With the new transmission lines, about 250 MW of power can be transmitted from Salal, Dul Hasti (under construction) and Sarna (Punjab) to meet the demands of the Valley to a great extent. Third, power availability can also be improved by taking up mini and micro level hydro power projects for which there is immense scope in the State.[6] A number of mini hydel projects catering to the local requirements have already been commissioned in many parts of the State including Leh and Kargil in the Ladakh region. Many others are envisaged to provide electricity to far-flung areas which have been denied modern amenities of life including electricity for long. Fourth, the State has also submitted a number of small and medium hydel projects to the Central Electricity Authority for approval.[7] The Central sector has also identified and also taken up for construction some of the hydro power projects in the State.

These include Dul Hasti in Doda (390 MW) and Salal in Udhampur (345 MW) and Ratli in Doda (170 MW).

These projects are huge in size and need colossal investments for which the State and Central Governments have to make special efforts for implementation.[8] The financial resources for these projects can be arranged either through financial institutions of the country or borrowed from international institutions like the Asian Development Bank, and the World Bank. In view of the economic liberalization, private sector participation can also be envisaged. The state government has already, identified 17 projects with an installed capacity of 5415 MW for private sector participation.[9] Multinational firms (like Enron, etc.) can be involved in the construction as well as financing of the projects.[10]

On the demand side, energy conservation can reduce power requirements significantly. The means for conservation of energy include: (1) education of people about conservation and value of energy; (2) florescent tubes fitted with a condenser and an electronic choke (to make these operative at low voltage) should replace lamps to bring down the power consumption; (3) the conservative use of electricity in Government establishments including public utilities can also help in an improvement of the power situation; (4) the use of high efficiency, good quality and ISI marked electric appliances can also reduce power consumption in the State. In addition, special feeders for industrial and irrigation load may be taken up to make them independent of domestic load. This will help in the distribution of electricity and implementation of load shedding programmes in an effective way.

V. Cost of Power Imports

In order to fulfil the power requirements, the State has to import electricity at market rates from outside. The cost of importing electricity is much higher than the cost of generating it in the indigenous power stations in the State. For example, the total expenditure on import of power during 1996-97 was Rs. 400 crores which could install a generating capacity of over 150 MW in one of the identified hydro power projects in the State. This suggests that the accumulated expenditure on import of power could have created enough generating capacity to meet the entire requirements of the State. The present position with regard to power is highly uneconomical and calls for a shift of emphasis from purchase to generation in the feasible power projects. The State Electricity Board (SEB) which is managing the generation, transmission and distribution of electricity in the State is running huge losses due to high import costs and lower tariffs per unit and non-realization of tariffs from customers. At present the tariff rates levied per unit are 28 paisa for domestic, 50 paisa, for commercial, 10 paisa for agricultural use, and 40 paisa for industries. The corresponding figures for the country as a whole are: 88 paisa, 190 paisa, 22 paisa and 202 paisa respectively.

VI. Transmission Losses

The transmission and distribution (T&D) losses in the State are the highest among the states and the country as a whole. Table 4 provides information on T&D losses in the country and the states of the northern region.

Table 4

Transmission and Distribution Losses as per cent of Electricity Generation in Northern India.

	1980 -81	*1985 -86*	*1987 -88*	*1988 -90*	*1989 -90*	*1990 -91*	*1991 -92*	*1992 -93*	*1993 -94*	*1994 -95*
Haryana	22.6	19.8	25.4	26.6	29.2	27.5	26.8	26.8	24.5	25.2
H.P.	19.3	20.2	21.6	22.1	18.7	21.5	20.4	19.5	17.3	20.3
J&K	48.1	35.9	41.8	41.5	49.5	42.3	49.2	48.3	47.7	43.3
Punjab	19.6	18.8	18.4	18.3	18.1	19.0	21.5	19.2	—	18.8
Rajasthan	26.6	26.5	21.0	25.3	24.4	25.9	23.1	22.7	25.2	24.2
U.P.	15.6	20.5	26.8	27.4	26.1	26.9	26.1	24.4	23.2	24.6
India	20.6	21.7	22.1	22.3	22.9	22.9	22.8	21.8	21.5	22.2

Source: CMIE, India's Energy Sector, September 1996, p. 38.

The main reasons for huge T and D losses is due to the pilferage of electricity. The check on pilferage of electricity at distributional level appears an uphill task. Instead of putting an all out effort to stop the excessive misuse of electricity, the SEB officials concerned with the distribution of electricity connive with consumers to tamper with the power meters to steal electricity.

The meters are unsealed, reading is reversed and finally the seal is reset. Some consumers even make these meters 'dead' so that electricity is stolen without any limit. In view of these, the reduction of T&D losses amount to around 22.2 per cent (the national average) in the near future seems highly unlikely. In addition, technical reasons also account for around 12 per cent of the total T & D losses. These losses can be minimized by designing a foolproof transmission and distribution system.

VII. Rural Electrification

Rural Electrification programme was initiated in early 1950 but a major breakthrough was achieved only during the mid 1970s when the Rural Electrification Corporation (REC) undertook finance of the programme in the State. Till 1996, about 6,000 villages (96.5 per cent of all villages) had been electrified in the State. However, these figures are illusory keeping in view the acute shortage of electricity particularly in the Valley. The power supply to most of the villages is unreliable and inadequate. The problem can be overcome by developing mini power stations at low cost in short periods of time. These plants are especially suitable for Kashmir as they use renewable resources and cause no air and water pollution. The energization of rural pump sets as a component of the rural electrification programme has not made headway in the State, indicating limited opportunities for productive application of power for agricultural sector of the State.

Conclusions

Adequate power supply is essential for economic development and consequent improvements in the quality of life. Without an efficient and sufficient power supply the government cannot initiate programmes for development of industry, agriculture and commerce in the State. Being a mountainious region, Jammu and Kashmir has immense hydropower potential over its four major rivers. The actual hydroelectric potential is, however, yet to be assessed for which a comprehensive survey needs to be taken up in the State.

During the past two decades no new power project was commissioned in J&K, resulting in a yawning gap between the availability and the requirements of electricity. The shortage in supply is partly met through imports and generation by GTS in winter but the overall situation remains grim. The huge allocations made to the power sector have been spent on imports rather than the creation of new sources of generation. The three medium power stations—Mohra Power House, Ganderbal Power House, and Chenani Power House—are virtually defunct beacause of obsolete and worn out machinery. As a result, the power position in the State is highly critical. The State Government must view the efficient exploitation of a vast hydro power potential as an important priority for economic and social development. The emphasis should be on the creation of additional generating capacity in the identified hydro power projects. The funds spent on imports of power would have created enough generating capacity to fulfil the growing needs of the people, army and the establishment.

The State has not been given its due share from Central power projects including those located in the State. The Indus Water Treaty is highly unfavourable to the people of Jammu and Kashmir and nothing has been done to compensate it for the losses incurred over the years. The state government must fight for the legitimate rights of the people over electricity generated on Ravi, Beas and Sutlej over which India gained exclusive rights by sacrificing the rights on rivers—Indus, Jhelum and Chenab—traversing through Ladakh, Kashmir and Jammu respectively.

The decision of the State Government to allow the National Hydroelectric Power Corporation to construct Kishenganga (330 MW), Baglihar (450 MW), Sewa-11 (120 MW) and Uri-II (280 MW) is most appropriate and timely. However, it will put a huge financial burden for which domestic and international sources need to be identified. New transmission lines for bulk power supply to Kashmir and designing of fool proof distributional system need to be given priority. These measures are likely to end the acute problems of power shortage in the State.

Footnotes

1. CEA (1994) Public Electricity Supply. All India Statistics – General Review, Central Electricity Authority, Government of India, New Delhi.

2. CMIE (1996): India's Energy Sector, September, Centre for Monitoring the Indian Economy, Mumbai.
3. ET(Various issues): *The Economic Times.*
4. Kaul. K. L. (1989): *Power Scenario in Jammu and Kashmir*, Srinagar.
5. McDonald. A. and Kay D. (1988): *Water as Power Resource in Water Resource-Issues and Strategies*, Longman, London.
6. Ministry of Power, Annual Reports, various years, Government of India, New Delhi.
7. Government of India, Ministry of Non-Conventional Sources of Energy: Non Conventional Sources of Energy- A Decade of Achievement, Special Supplement, Indian Express, October 28, 1992.
8. ———, Harnessing Hydel Power without Dams or Deforestation, Special Supplement, Indian Express, October 29, 1992.
9. Government of Jammu and Kashmir, Power Development Department: Feasibility Cum Project Report for Gas Turbine Power Project.
10. Parikh, Kirti (1995). Enron Episode: Lessons for Power Policy, *EPW*, October 14-21, pp. 2543-46.
11. Roy, S. N. (1995): T and D losses: The Hidden Factors, *The Economic Times*, September 22, p. 7.
12. Morris, Sebastian (1966): Political Economy of Electric Power in India, *EPW*, May 25.

References

1. It has been estimated that the cost of the "run-of-the-river" projects which use small head fall is about 75 per cent higher than hydro projects with high head fall for a given plant capacity of say, 250 MW (McDonald and Kay, 1988).
2. Even this meagre quantity has been withdrawn. The State is vigorously pleading for its restoration.
3. In theory, the hydro power potential is determined from the quantity of available water multiplied by its fall and so can be estimated from the mean land elevation and the mean annual run-off.
4. The demand projections are carried in the fifteenth Annual Power Survey of the Central Electrical Authority. There is a need for an overall assessment of energy needs and uses to project the demand scenario of electricity in the State.
5. This 200 km long transmission line will take 4 to 5 years
6. Small and mini hydro power plants have many advantages: (1) readily accessible resources of renewable energy suitable for hilly regions isolated from main grids but endowed with hydraulic resources; (2) can be exploited wherever sufficient water flows

exist — along small streams, medium to small rivers, irrigation dams, canal drops, over descent heads as low as 2m and above; (iii) use reliable, mature and proven technology. These plants can be made even more attractive through standardization and better planning and management to reduce initial cost and commissioning schedules; (iv) does not involve setting up of large dams or problems of deforestation, submergence or rehabilitation; (v) least polluting, entail no waste, no production of toxic gases and no adverse effects on environment and (vi) initial investment, maintenance costs and gestation periods are low compared to thermal, diesel and gas based stations (Government of India, 1992).

7. These include: Lower Kalnai, Doda (50 MW), Mawar, Hindwara (6 MW), Lower Ans, Udhampur (37 MW), Parnai, Rajouri (37 MW) Lidder, Anantnag (30 MW), Wangat, Srinagar (30 MW), Sonamarg, Srinagar (83 MW), New Ganderbal Srinagar (30 MW) Panikhar Parkhachak, Kargil (30 MW) and Chutak, Kargil (7 MW).
8. In 1996, Government of India exempted all power projects with investments upto Rs. 1000 crores, approximating 250 MW capacity from the mandatory techno economic clearance for investment. The State can go ahead with these projects depending upon the availability of funds, etc.
9. These include projects at Parnai, Bursar, Pakal Dul, Sawalkote, Chatuk, Parkachak, etc.
10. The new policy of the Centre has opened up power generation and distribution to private entrepreneurs including multinational firms. Maharashtra is the first state which has opened up power sector to the private entrepreneurs. The State of Jammu and Kashmir presents immense scope for private participation in the generation of power from small and medum hydro-electric projects. These projects can also be integrated into area plans for development of tourist sites and places.

Twelve

Democratic Decentralization: Past, Present and Future

M.S. Bhat

Perspective

The configurations of the inter-governmental divisions of powers/functions and transfer of resources are primarily determined by the objectives of fiscal federalism. Transfers of resources from the Centre to the states and from the states to the districts/local-self governments are broadly justified to :

i. Offset differences in the revenue raising capacity;
ii. Account for the variations in the unit cost of public/merit goods and services due to the external diseconomies;
iii. Ensure optimal output or minimum levels of public services; and
iv. Harmonize the tax structure

To achieve these objectives conceptualization and measurements of parameters (Such as taxable capacity, unit cost of public/merit goods, public services; negative spillovers; capital-output ratios; terms of trade; expenditure needs; state/district/block specific price indices, etc.) are needed.

Transfers designed to ensure optimal levels of output in the wake of negative spillovers or to provide minimum levels of public services have to be necessarily for specific purposes (with or without matching requirements). These could be used to impose donors' preferences on the recipients. Transfers meant to neutralize fiscal disadvantages have to be unconditional.

Debates on fiscal federalism or fiscal relations of a particular state with the Union are seldom analyzed against this background. "Centralization" versus "decentralization" has been viewed either as inimical to the national integration (via disintegration) or as the only solution to clear the rot created by the crude statism at different levels of governance. The myth of a strong centre resting on the weak states is untenable. The opposite myth of strong states propping up a weak district/local self-government is also untenable. There is a need for a paradigm shift in our approach to the debate on democratic decentralization. The experiences of each state has to be put in perspective.

Development via democratic decentralization was regarded as a strategic factor in the development process of the state since the inception of "planned" economic development in 1951. Programmes of restructuring economy were initiated through a series of structural and institutional reforms. Consequent upon these changes the State made considerable headway in economic development and social transformation. However, the extreme initial backwardness of the State coupled with the absence of a sustainable and vibrant mechanism of democratic decentralization has constrained the harnessing of the potential gains to a considerable extent. Poverty, unemployment and backwardness across the regions/districts and within the districts persist. Performance, on the front of democratic decentralization has been far from satisfactory despite periodic reiteration of intentions and setting up of formal structures like Panchayati Raj Institutions (PRIs) on the statutory basis. There is credible evidence to suggest that lack of effective decentralized democracy and planning have obstructed the process of tapping potentialities in men and material. Despite introducing Single Line Administration (a unique form of governance at the district level), inter-district imbalances have not only persisted but increased over the years.

It will, therefore, be rewarding to know why democratic decentralization failed to work. Without understanding: the forces operating against it, operational limitations and technical requirements constitutional mandates are bound to result in repetitions. Interface between planning and democracy, on the one hand, and democracy and socio-economic structures, on the other, is the basic parameter within which this exercise needs to be carried out. It will be too naïve to think that democratic decentralization does not involve any opportunity cost or it is the panacea for all the problems of development. A policy with regard to institutional building is a function of complex interaction between ideological pre-disposition and pragmatic considerations. Given this perspective an attempt has been to recast the experiences and prospects of democratic decentralization in the State.

The study has been divided into six sections. Section-I presents a resume of the major developments during the pre-1947 period. The main focus of this section is to trace the historical roots of the Panchayati Raj Institutions (PRIs) in the State. Attempts at democratic decentralization during 1947 to '1975 have been covered in Section – II. Democratic decentralization from 1935 to 1975 is synonymous of development of Panchayati Raj institutions in the State. Therefore, Sections I and II deal mainly with the Panchayati Raj Institutions in the State. District governance, called Single Line Administration, has been described in Section III. Attempts to revive PRIs in the State against the backdrop of district governance have been discussed in Section IV. Section V deals with the problem arcas and outlines the possible remedial measures.

Concluding remarks have been presented in the last section.

Section-1: Pre-1947 Scenario

The history of Panchayati Raj, in its present form, can be traced back to promulgation of Jammu and Kashmir Village Panchayat Regulation No. 1 by Maharaja Hari Singh in 1935 (1935 Act). The preamble of this act states, "whereas it is expedient to establish in Jammu and Kashmir State village Panchayats to assist in the administration of civil and criminal justice and also to manage the situation and other common concerns of the village." The act provided for election of Panchas numbering five to seven out of which one would be appointed by Panchayat Officer called Wazir-re-wazarat. This officer was empowered to frame rules and procedures for conducting elections. Panchas were to be elected with simple show of hands. A cluster of several villages constituted a Panchayat. Sarpanch of Panchayat or voting in a Panchayat election a person had to fulfil the following requirements:

(a) He should be I) hereditary state subject, ii) living in the rural area, iii) not insane, iv) 21 years age, and v) possessing any kind of property worth Rs. 1,000/-;
(b) His tax should be at least five rupees;
(c) His annual income should be at least Rs. 700/;
(d) Should at least be a matriculate or possess an equivalent academic qualification.

As per the 1935 Act Panchayats had to :

(a) Assist civil administration in the administration of criminal and civil justice;
(b) Carry out public utility works as village sanitation, supply of drinking water, maintenance of village tanks etc;
(c) Maintain government and public property and supervise the work of village officials and labourers and construction of public buildings.

The main functions of the Panchayats were "judicial". For example, out of 58 provisions of the Act, 47 dealt with the judicial functions. The act was amended in 1941 with a view to widen the list of functions. Litigation to settle petty disputes took a lot of time to get settled through courts. These were costly too and had become an important cause of mounting rural indebtedness. The Government thought that Panchayats could probably settle most of these cases with a greater degree of equity and speed than the ordinary courts. Since these cases do not involve intricate legal matters, therefore, their disposal could be quicker and cost effective. According to the available official data, it appears that the government's assessment about the efficacy of the Panchayats had some rationale behind it. The number of cases brought before the Panchayat courts in 1939 was 8,830 and by 1941 this number exceeded 25,000. The amount of money reported to have been saved was Rs. 1,00,000.

The responsibilities of enforcing the 1935 act (original/ amended) was assigned to the revenue department. A department of Panchayat and Rural Development, affiliated to revenue department, was established in 1936. In 1937 this department was further reorganized and was placed under the supervision of a director. The director had to formulate the general policy for development and provide necessary funds to the Panchayats for the development of their respective areas and supervise their functioning.

In addition to judicial functions, the Panchayats were also held responsible for: Improving civic amenities (like supply of pure drinking water, village sanitation, comunication, roads, etc.), and consolidation of agricultural holdings. For carrying out developmental activities at the village level (such as improvements of culverts, drains, approach lanes, bathing places, bunds etc.) an amount of Rs. 2.5 lakhs was kept at the disposal of Panchayats. One of the significant works done by the Rural Development and Panchayati Department was a survey of 1,300 villages listing their economic, social and cultural conditions. The data generated through this survey was utilized to assess the comparative merits of the requests for financial assistance. The results of the survey revealed that in over 50 per cent of the cases surveyed, family consumption expenditure (food + non-food) exceeded income which in turn was considered the main cause of indebtedness in the rural areas. Yet another interesting feature of the Panchayat Raj during this period was initiation of the first ever Adult Education drive in collaboration with the state education department. Number of village libraries were opened and community radio sets installed in 24 villages. In addition to the resources mobilized by levying taxes and tolls government provided an assistance of Rs. 40,000 in 1937-38 and Rs. 3,85,000 for the period 1945-49 to the Panchayats.

Despite all the above initiatives, policy statements and even some initial successes, the Panchayat Raj institutions could not become effective and viable instruments of grassroots development. These could not even administer quick cost-effective justice. The primary reason being that these operated under feudal socio-economic structures which could be conducive to anything but not to development via democratic decentralization.

Section II—1947—1975 Developments

After the achievement of independence the state government launched an ambitious programme of rural reconstruction. Political commitment to democratic decentralization, social justice and the reconstruction of the economy were outlined in the policy document of "Naya Kashmir" of 1944. While launching "Naya Kashmir" in 1944, Sheikh Abdullah said, "All Jammu and Kashmir National Conference considers the 'New Kashmir' programme as a blue print for the future political and economic set-up in the State. We have formulated this programme with this objective in view. From the political angle it aimed at achieving a responsible government based on democratic principles. All institutions of democracy from Panchayats to national assembly shall be constituted through the due process of elections. Indpendent judicial system shall be an important component of the system and executive shall be made accountable to the people" (Shafi, 1990).

In line with these directive principles a series of agrarian reform measures were initiated and implemented as early as 1948. These reforms proved "the most important single factor which engineered basic changes in the economic structure of the State". (Jha Committee, 1975). Besides agrarian reforms and establishment of cooperatives, the Panchayat Raj Institutions were considered necessary. Accordingly, the 1935 Panchayat Act, (amended) was replaced by the Act V of Samvat 2008 in 1951. The act provided for the establishment of Panchayat of village/villages. Five to seven villages were covered by one Panchayat and Panchayat units were generally co-existence with the revenue Halqas. A majority of the Panchayat members were to be elected. Elections were to be held on the basis of adult franchise. The act also empowered the Panchayat officer to nominate the members. Members were to be elected by a show of hands. However, rules also provided for vote by ballot. Members of the Panchayats and not the electorate were entitled to elect the president of the Panchayat called Sarpanch. No executive officer could function under the Panchayat.

Panchayats, subject to rules as would be prescribed, had to perform administrative/developmental, municipal and judicial duties. Compared to the 1935 Act, these functions covered all important aspects of village life and Panchayats were given a lot of freedom to formulate the modus operandi of implementation according to local conditions. For each *tehsil* the Act provided for a Panchayat Board with the following functions and powers:

(a) To establish a judicial committee for deciding the cases mentioned in Section 118;

(b) To draw plans for the improvement of communication and irrigation facilities, granting of stud bulls for the improvement of breeds of cattle, distribution of improved seeds, etc.

A special feature of the 1951 Panchayat Raj Act was the provision for a joint committee of Panchayats. These committees mostly were empowered to perform inter-Panchayat developmental works. The main sources of revenue were (I) Fee levied in judicial cases; (ii) Fines imposed under the act; (iii) Voluntary contribution from the people; (iv) Taxation; (v) Contribution from village cess fund and (vi) Contribution from the government.

Administrative Set up

Along with the rest of the country two important programmes of rural development — Community Development Programme and National Extension Services—were launched in the State between 1952 to 1958. Community Development Programme was launched in 1952 with a view to achieve rural development via people's participation. The National Extension Services were conceived as a necessary adjunct to the Community Development Programme. The Service was constituted at the block level with a network of village level workers. Public participation was sought to be incorporated through the nominated members. Training of Panchayat workers was accorded top priority.

Panchayats undertook the works of highest utility and material benefits under Hallashri system of labour wherein villagers participated in the work free of cost or on payment of nominal wages. The Department of Panchayats and Rural Development was reorganized and made responsible for enforcing the provisions of the 1951 Panchayat Raj Act. The Department possessed the power of superseding a Panchayat. The Department had its staff at state, provincial, district, *tehsil*, and sub-*tehsil* levels. There was one director, two provincial Panchayat officers, seven assistant rural development officers, sixteen inspectors and sixty sub-inspectors. The director functioned at the state level as the controlling and coordinating head of the different provincial administrative units of the Panchayat department. Below the director there were two provincial officers. The provincial unit was further sub-divided for the purpose of administration into divisional units. Each unit was under the charge of a gazetted officer designed as assistant-rural development officer. At some places the jurisdiction of assistant rural development officer extended over to an administrative district and at other places it was extended to over two districts or even more. Below the assistant rural development officer there was a Panchayat Inspector whose jurisdiction extended over to fifteen Panchayats depending upon the density of population, area and topographical conditions. The sub-inspectors were responsible for supervising and guiding the works of village Panchayats.

Up to March 1951 forty Panchayats were established in the state. By March 1954 this figure went up to 751 covering 4,774 villages (excluding villages in Pakistan occupied Kashmir). Panchayats performed a prominent role in rural reconstruction works. On many occasions these aided peasants particularly when some natural calamity befell the countryside. Out of the 685 villages Panchayats as on April 30, 1950 re-elections were held in case of 126 panchayats and new establishments were put in order. These were increasingly involved in: nation building programmes; irrigation improvements, grow more food programmes; plantation, raising of bunds/flood control measures and provision of safe drinking water. In 1948-49, 63,599 seedlings and saplings were planted. In the eight plantation blocks of Kashmir Valley 147094 stems/seedlings of various species of willows, poplars and fruit plantation) were planted in 1949-50. Seeds to the extent of 13,423 Khirwars (107.4 metric tones) were distributed in 379 villages among the cultivators of flood affected areas of Anantnag district at concessional rates. The villages that were affected by the floods of 1948-49 were given rations for four months. During the autumn and winter months 4,456 manure pits were dug in over 72 villages. Preliminary economic surveys to determine the socio-economic conditions of the rural people were conducted in the three *tehsils* of Anantnag district. Panchayat staff, in cooperation with the agricultural department, collected the produce of the China Paddy for further propagation. The total quantity of seeds collected the produce of the China Paddy for further propagation. The total quantity of seeds collected and stored at eleven centres in the six Tehsils was 5020 Kirwars (402 metric tons). Works undertaken by the Panchayats varied from region to region. For example in the Kashmir province, improvement works included:

1. Improving irrigation facilities.
2. Construction of flumes, and
3. Construction of dams (to ensure equitable distribution of water) and retaining walls to strengthen the banks of Khuls (Traditional Zamindari Canals) and blasting of boulders (which prevented free and smooth flow of water).

In the Jammu Province the works mainly comprised: improvements of ponds, construction of tanks and water supply works in Kandhi areas. Works of general nature such as construction of roads and laterines were undertaken at places where Panchayats had funds.

Response to the Balwantrai Mehta Committee Report

Various evaluation reports compiled by the Planning Commission (GOI) showed that the initial thrust on creating viable Panchayat Raj Institutions, as necessary adjunct to community development and National Extension Service, had lost its momentum. A feeling also developed that public involvement was not representative enough and as such was not effective. Following these reports, the Balwantrai Mehta Committee was appointed in January 1957 to study and report on community development and national extension with a view to assess the extent to which the movement had succeeded in utilizing local initiatives. The committee recommended that (i) there should be administrative decentralization, and (ii) decentralized administrative programmes should be under the direct control of elected bodies.

Based on these directional thrusts the Jammu and Kashmir Village Panchayat Act, 1958 replaced the 1951 Panchayat Raj Act and envisaged a two-tier Panchayati Raj System—Gram Panchayat at the village level and Block Panchayat Board at block level. The

Act empowered the state government to establish by notification a Panchayat in every village or group of villages and to define territorial jurisdiction thereof.

The Act did not differ much from the 1951 Act as far as the major functions and sources of revenue were concerned. The government had the powers to: suspend, supersede or dissolve a Panchayat on the grounds of default in the performance of duties or abuse of power; and make alternative arrangements for carrying out the work of the Panchayat for a period not exceeding six months. However, the Act also had certain distinctive features. For instance, the Act provided for the establishment of Panchayat Adalats to decentralize the administration of justice. The main features of these Adalats were:

1. Every Panchayat shall at its first meeting elect, out of its members, in the manner prescribed, five persons for the purpose of constituting a Panchayat Adalat;
2. The five persons so elected shall constitute a Panchayat Adalat;
3. The term of office of the member of the Panchayat Adalat shall be co-extensive with the term of their office as the member by Panchayats;
4. Every Panchayat shall have a chairman. The Chairman shall be elected by the Panchayat Adalat from amongst the members of the Panchayat Adalats. The term of the Chairman of such Panchayat Adalat shall be co-extensive with the term of the Panchayat Adalat.
5. The government, if it thinks fit, may remove any member elected on Panchayat Adalat after giving him an opportunity of being heard and after such inquiry as the government deems fit; and
6. No Panchayat Adalat shall entertain or hear a suit or a case in which any member of Panchayati Adalat is party to the suit.

Block Panchayat Boards

Creation of Block Panchayat Boards his was novel feature of the Act. It provided that :

1. There shall be constituted a Panchayat Board of such members of the Panchayat as the government may determine;

2. Every Block Panchayat Board shall consist of one representative from each Panchayat area in the block. The Board may co-opt one woman member interest in the work of women and children's welfare;
3. The term of office of every member of the Block Panchayat Board shall be coextensive with the term of Panchayat it represents;
4. The non-official members of the Block Panchayat Board shall annually elect from among themselves a person who is able to read and write to act as chairman of the Board;
5. Provided that during the first three years the government may appoint any person as chairman of a Block Panchayat Board.

The Panchayat Board had to advise in the development of the block in respect of: (a) Communication; (b) irrigation facility; (c) Government Dispensaries; (d) Veterinary dispensaries; (e) Schools; (f) Local Industries (g) Medical relief (h) Drinking water.

By 1962 the entire rural population and inhabited villages numbering 6956 were covered by the Panchayats and average population per Panchayat worked out to be 3,098. The number of Gram Panchayat increased from 936 in 1962 to 1483 in 1977-78 covering all the inhabited villages. Average population per Gram Panchayat decreased from 3,098 in 1961-62 to 2,543 in 1977-78 but in 1990 this figure again increased to 3,218 compared to 2,386 at the all India level. The number of villages per Gram Panchayat works out to 4.7 in 1990 compared to 2.8 at the all India level.

Setback to 1958 Act

Between 1952 and 1969 (beginning of the Fourth Five Year Plan) two developments of far-reaching consequences took place. First: at the national level the focus on the Community Development Programme was overshadowed by the grow more food campaign originating out of the report by the Ford Foundation Expert Group on "India's food crises and steps to meet it (1959)". To overcome the problem of food shortages several programmes were introduced in the subsequent years. Agriculture development received top priority and the concern for "grow more food" became the main driving force behind the new seed-water-fertilizer technology. The results of this new package were encouraging and instant. It helped to reduce the pressure on the food front to a large extent. But the gains were not only region-specific but were disproportionately garnered by the rural elite. The pattern of benefits aggravated the regional and interpersonal inequalities of income and assets. Though nobody could find fault with the policy of growing more food. But agricultural development becoming synonymous with rural development (though as a consequence and not as a cause) was a development fraught with serious consequences.

Second: The dismissal of Sheikh Abdullah Ministry and his subsequent arrest marked the beginning of a prolonged period of political instability. Democratic institutions were subverted and democratic aspirations of people were viewed as inimical to national integration. Governments were often imposed from above. This eroded the people's faith in democratic institutions. Democracy at the grass roots became grassless. The formal structures created with great expectation and speed remained in a state of suspended animation for a long time. The development activities were mostly carried out by the line departments in the name of community Development and National extension services.

One of the instant fallout of these developments was that the process of democratic decentralization receded to the background in the State. It was only in the Fourth Five Year Plan that the question of poverty, unemployment and need for social services and decentralized planning were brought back at centre stage of planning. But these efforts could not help in retrieving the lost ground. Even the official documents concede this. For instance, for the development programme under Panchayats Rs. 109.00 lakhs were earmarked in the State's Third Five Year Plan. Against this provision utilization was only Rs. 46.00 lakhs. The shortfall was attributed to non-implementation of the Panchayati Raj Programmes in respect of tiers above the village level, and non-conduct of Panchayat elections. The system of paying grant-in-aid to Panchayats was abolished in 1967-68 and instead it was decided to give loans for creation of remunerative assets. The Fourth Plan outlay of Rs. 35 lakhs proposed for Panchayat was to be utilized for the creation of:

i. Purchase of land for Panchayat Plantation;
ii. Nurseries and orchards;
iii. Raising of nurseries/orchards and plantation in community/lands;
iv. Development of fish ponds;
v. Development of Panchayat mulberry and silkworm rearing centres;
vi. Setting up of Panchayat rice hullers floor mills;
vii. Development of bee keeping poultry dairy;
viii. Construction of residential shops/residential quarters; and
ix. Installation of tubewells and pumping sets.

Retrospect

If we compare the pre-1947 Panchayati Raj Acts with 1951 and 1958 Acts the difference between the guiding principles and actual orientation becomes obvious. Though all these acts professed to create and strengthen the Panchayati Raj institutions as instruments of local self-government yet political economy in the ultimate analysis proved the decisive factor in determining the actual working of these institutions. For instance, before 1947 Panchayati Raj Institutions (PRIs) had become subservient to a feudal power structure. These were anything but instruments of local self-government. Pre-1947 Kashmir like any pre-democratic society had feudal and autocratic value premises which in turn determined its concepts of freedom, equality, development, local self-government and people's participation. Under these conditions any legal or institutional arrangement was bound to be designed to supplement the functioning of feudal institutions at the village level. By the very definitions, of some of the main provisions of these acts only privileged few had to dominate the institutions of the local self-government and appropriate the benefits of developmental activities. Panchayats could never become people's institutions as arbitrariness was the hallmark of these acts. A predominant majority of the villagers could neither vote or seek election for Panchas due to the explicit disqualification clauses. These institutions were structured to strengthen feudalism. Similarly in the name of democracy, Panchayati Raj Institutions created under the provision of the 1951 Act became tools of arbitrariness in the hands of undemocratic regimes.

All these Acts provided overriding powers to the ruling parties to dissolve, supersede and suspend the Panchayats and nominate members. At the end of the day this proved an alibi for stifling the growth of those very institutions which these acts sought to create. Uniformity in the core developmental functions assigned to the Panchayats in each act, in a way, highlights the failures of the successive governments to solve these problems on the priority basis. Another hallmark of these acts was a deliberate gender-bias. The provisions of these acts stipulated everything in terms of he and not in terms of he/she.

The Panchayati Raj Institutions, were never allowed to grow as a tier of governance in their own right. Formal constitutional/ Administrative structures were never created to work out: their resource endowments; expenditure needs/resource needs; extent of external diseconomies; resolutions of inter-Panchayat disputes and creation of a sound database. Panchayats which existed were treated as appendage to the centralized administration.

Though the number of Blocks and Panchayats per Block has remained by and large the same from 1977-78 (when six new districts were created) yet plan provisions and expenditure under Community Development and N.E.S. have registered a sharp decline over each plan period. From a peak of 64.22 per cent of total plan expenditure during the Second Five Year Plan the relative share of expenditure has gone down to 2.59 per cent during the annual plan 1991-92. Plan provisions have also decreased to 0.3 per cent from the high of 39.80 per cent during the Third Five Year Plan.

Section III: Single Line Administration

The Indira-Abdullah Accord of 1975 marked the beginning of an era of political stability and revival of democratic traditions. By this time the Planning Commission had also recast the guidelines for the district planning. The planning was decentralized with the constitution of district planning boards with adequate public representation and making district as a planning unit. The board was given powers to formulate long and short-term plans and oversee their implementation. The district development commissioner and the district superintending engineer were given the powers of the major head of the department. The meeting of the district developments boards, in which the entire State Cabinet and major heads of the departments at state level participate, are held in the district to take on the spot policy decisions and approve the district budget. This whole process has been termed as Single Line Administration. Its purpose was to decentralize the administration and build up a participatory base at the district level. The State was amongst the first few states in the country to introduce decentralized planning at the district and block levels. In the early 1960s some steps were taken by the State Government in this direction when district level planning was introduced in Ladakh with single line system of administration. Consequent upon this experiment the State Government in 1976 took the decision to introduce the decentralized planning in all districts of the State with the twin objectives of:

i. Making planning more reflective of the hopes and aspiration of the common man;
ii. Ensuring speedy implementation of development programmes.

Institutional Framework

In order to achieve these objectives district development boards for each district of the state (composed of people like members of parliament, members of state legislature, elected representative of development blocks, chairman local bodies and some nominated members from backward classes and women) were constituted. The Deputy Commissioner of the district was appointed as ex-officio District Development Commissioner (DDC) with delegation of wide financial and administrative powers. The DDC is also the chairman of the district development board. All the departments in the district are placed under the administrative and operational control of the DDC concerned.

Role of District Boards

The main functions of the district development boards are as under:

a) To consider and guide the formulation of development programmes for the district and indicate priorities for various schemes and consider issues relating to the speedy development and economic upliftment of the people of the district.

b) To review periodically the progress and achievements of development plans and schemes in operation and make such recommendations as it considers appropriate; and

c) To function as a working group for formulation of periodic and annual plan for the district.

Each district has a superintending engineer who functions as Vice-Chairman of the District Development Board and is in-charge of the public works programmes and staff of the district in different branches. The Superintending Engineer, however, works under the overall control and direction of the concerned DDC.

The district development commissioner and superintending engineers of each district issue the bulk of administrative approvals and technical/financial sanctions that are involved in respect of district plan, at the district level itself. All heads of the departments function as ex-officio technical advisors on behalf of the state government. On an average 40 per cent to 50 per cent of the total state plan outlays are earmarked for district sector schemes every year. Multiple criteria are applied for determining outlays for various districts which among other things include:

i) Population of the district;
ii) Relative backwardness of the district;
iii) Number and size of the identified bad pockets within the districts; and
iv) Development potential and needs of the district.

Cabinet Review

A novel feature of the decentralized planning in the State is the annual review of the cabinet with the district development boards. The cabinet, along with senior officers of the government including heads of departments, participate in the district development board meetings of each district at various places in the districts to review the performance and assess the position of development works. The main objective of these reviews is to reduce the delays in decision making and implementation of programmes.

Block Level Planning

Decentralization of planning from the district downwards was deemed necessary to match the sectoral financial allocations with location-specific needs and to regulate the distribution of benefits of development. The state government, therefore, decided to decentralize the planning process further and adopted block as a primary unit of planning. Consequently, the district development plan was supplemented by a separate plan for each block of the district with earmarked outlays to be determined by the district administration in consultation with the district development board. The state plan is subdivided into the following sub-heads:

1. State level plan;
2. District level plan; and
3. Block level plan.

The composition of the 'block plan' district plan and state plan is determined broadly with reference to the following criteria:

(a) All programmes, which can be planned and executed at the block level without sacrificing planning efficiency, are included in the block plan. Schemes like research/ training and higher education, etc. form a part of the state level plan;

(b) Schemes and programmes handled by corporations and companies and government departments working as commercial undertakings are presented in the state level plan;

(c) State component of programmes figuring in the district or block plans form a part of the state level plan. For example, elementary and secondary education figure in the block plan and district plan respectively but expenditure on the office of director education is charged on the state plan. Likewise, district component of block plans forms a part of the district level plan;

(d) Projects physically spread over more than one block necessarily figure in the district level plan irrespective of the location of such projects. Likewise projects physically spread over more than one district are presented in the state level plan.

(e) Projects physically located in one block or district but the benefits from which flow to other blocks or districts in the normal course included in the district level or state level plan as the case may be irrespective of their physical location.

Size of population and relative backwardness of a district/ block are the guiding principles for determining the plan outlays. A planning cell has been provided at the district level to assist the district development board in the formulation and implementation of the plan. An officer designated as Chief Planning Officer heads the cell.

Section IV — Revival of PRIs

As a sequel to the efforts to revive the democratic traditions, the state government repealed the Jammu and Kashmir Village Panchayat Act 1958 and replaced it by Jammu and Kashmir Panchayati Raj, 1989. The act has been described as a "radical" step as it aims to, "promote and develop the Panchayati Raj system in the State as an instrument of vigorous local self-government to secure participation of the people in the implementation of development planning." The full involvement of the people is proposed to be secured by the process of direct election of the Panchas, Sarpanch and Chairman of the Block Development Council. For the effective participation of the rural population in the development programmes and self-governance the Act has conceived a three-tier Panchayati Raj system. These tiers are:

(i) Halqa Panchayat;
(ii) Block Development Council; and
(iii) District Planning and Development Board.

The distinctive features and flaws of the Act have been widely debated (See "Panchayati Raj in Jammu and Kashmir", published by the Concept Publishing Company on behalf of the Institute of Social Sciences, New Delhi, 1990). We shall, therefore, concentrate on only a few features of the Act in order to find out in what way it is a step forward in the evolution of Panchayati Raj Institutions in the State. Some of these features are the functions assigned to the three tiers of the system.

The Act has conceived the Halqa as the crucial tier for the entire process of democratic decentralization by giving it wide-ranging functions. Every Halqa Panchayat shall consist of such number of Panchas (not less then seven and not more than eleven, including the Sarpanch) as the prescribed authority may, from time to time, fix in this behalf. Provided that if the prescribed authority is satisfied that women or Scheduled Castes or any other class are not represented in the Halqa Panchayat, it may nominate not more than two persons to be members thereof. With minor exceptions, the disqualification for a person to be the member of the Halqa Panchayat are the same as prescribed in the 1958 Act. If in the opinion of the government a Halqa Panchayat is incompetent to perform or persistently makes default in the performance of duties imposed on it by or under this Act, the Government may, by notification, supersede such Halqa Panchayat is called upon to show cause why such an order shall not be passed. The period of suppression shall not exceed six months during which the elections shall be held.

Functions

According to the provisions of this Act, Halqa Panchayat has to perform the following functions subject to availability of funds:

(i) prepare development plans;

(ii) undertake measures for the implementation of the developmental plans;

(iii) deal with soil conservation, water management, social forestry, rural industrialization, agriculture, sheep and animal husbandry, sanitation, health and other welfare programmes;

(iv) regulation of buildings, shops and entertainment houses and checking of offensive or dangerous trades;

(v) construction and maintenance of slaughter houses, regulation of sale and preservation of meat and processing of skins and hides.

(vi) Regulation of sale and preservation of fish, vegetables and other perishable articles and food;

(vii) Regulation of fairs and festivals;

(viii) Preparation and implementation of special development plans for alleviating poverty and employment generation through programmes like Integrated Rural

Development Programme, National Rural Employment Programme, Rural Landless Employment Guarantee Programme and Housing for Scheduled Castes and Backward Classes;

(ix) Implementation of schemes of universalization of elementary education and other educational programmes; and

(x) Administration of all matters involving regulation, supervision, maintenance and support, incidental to, or necessary for the more efficient discharge of the above functions and those which may be entrusted to Halqa Panchayat under the provisions of the Act.

Halqa Panchayat Fund

Every Halqa Panchayat shall have a fund to be called "Halqa Panchayat Fund" which shall comprise the following:

(i) Taxes and fees levied by Panchayat;

(ii) Proceeds from the property and enterprises run by the Halqa Panchayat;

(iii) Court fees, fines and compensation paid to the Halqa Panchayat;

(iv) Donations and contributions paid by public for works undertaken by the Halqa Panchayat;

(v) Proceeds of the sanitation cess collected by the government on the revenue being loaned within the Halqa Panchayat area;

(vi) Grants from the government for general purposes on per capita basis and also for specific functions;

(vii) Loans from government of other agencies approved by government or other financial institutions; and

(viii) All other income of Halqa Panchayat and such grants as may be assigned to the Halqa Panchayat by the government, keeping in view the topography and backwardness of the area.

Block Development Council

For every block in the State, government shall, by notification, constitute a Block Development Council bearing the name of the Block. The Block Development Council shall consist of:

(i) a Chairman; (ii) all Sarpanchs of Halqa Panchayat falling within the Blocks; and iii) Chairman of Marketing Society within the jurisdiction of the Block. Provided that if the prescribed authority may (if it is of opinion that women or Scheduled Castes or any other class are not represented in the Block Development Council), nominate not more than two persons to be the members thereof. Every Block Development Council shall have a Chairman who shall be a person qualified to be elected as a Panch and shall be elected in accordance with the provisions contained in Section 41. Every Block Development Council shall have a Vice-Chairman who shall be elected by the members of the Block Development Council from amongst themselves. The Block Development Officer shall be the Secretary of the Block Development Council. The term of office of the Chairman of the Block Development Council shall be five years from the date he is declared as such by Election Authority. The Block Development Council shall perform the following functions :

(i) Constructions, maintenance and supervision of Inter-Halqa Panchayat Communication System;
(ii) Administrative and technical guidance to Halqa Panchayats and review of their work.
(iii) Supervise plans relating to agriculture, rural development, animal husbandry/sheep husbandry, social forestry, education and public health;
(iv) Supervise and monitor the implementation of poverty alleviation programmes;
(v) Undertake measures for effective supervision and monitoring of various developmental programmes; and
(vi) Carry out such other functions as may be entrusted to it by the government or by the District Planning and Development Board.

Elections

The election to the Panchayat Halqa and Chairman of Block Development Council shall be held under the direction and control of the Chief Electoral Officer. There shall be no bar on holding of election on party lines. The Electorate of the Halqa Panchayat shall elect the Sarpanch of the Halqa Panchayat. The Chairman of the Block Development Council shall be elected by the electoral college comprising elected Panchs and Sarpanchs of Halqa Panchayat falling within the Block. The election to the Halqa Panchayat shall be held one month before the expiry of term or within six months from the date of suspension, as the case may be. No civil court shall have jurisdiction to question the legality of any action taken or any decision given by an officer or authority appointed under the Act in connection with the conduct of election thereunder.

District Planning and Development Boards:

Each district shall have a District Planning and Development Board to be constituted by the government by notification in the government gazette. The Board shall comprise the following:

(i) Chairman of the Block Development Council of the District;
(ii) Member of Parliament representing the area;
(iii) Members of the State Legislature representing the areas within the District;
(iv) Chairman of the Town Area Committees at the district; and
(v) President of the Municipal Council, if any.

The Chairman of the board shall be nominated by the Government from amongst the members of the District Planning and Development Board. The members of the District Planning and Development Board from amongst themselves shall elect the Vice-Chairman. No government servant shall be elected as Vice-Chairman of the Board. The District Development Commissioner shall be the chief executive of the Board and he shall be assisted by the district level heads. The main functions of the board shall be to:

(i) function as a working group for formulation of periodic and annual plans for the district;
(ii) formulate and finalize the plan and non-plan budget for the district;
(iii) lay down the policy guidelines for Block Development Councils and Halqa Panchayat;
(iv) approve the budget of the Block Development Councils and supervise and coordinate their work;

(v) undertake special measures for alleviating poverty and employment generation and extending assistance to Halqa Panchayat in this behalf;

(vi) promote and assist cooperative institutions; and

(vii) perform such other functions and duties as may be assigned to it by the government from time to time.

Finances

All the funds provided by the government or any other agency, meant for the development of the district will flow through the District Planning and Development Board as per the District Plans.

Section V — Problems Areas

The above description of Democratic Decentralization in the State shows that the steps taken by the government do not go far enough. It is not possible to describe in detail the shortcomings/ failures of the Institutions of democratic decentralization in the State. However, some of the major concerns and problem areas have been outlined in the following paras.

It is worthwhile to recall that the Constitution of J&K contains a specific provision to encourage organization of village Panchayat in the Directive Principles of State Policy. Section 16 of the Constitution casts an obligation that the State shall take steps to organize village Panchayats and endow them with such powers and authority as may be necessary to enable them to function as units of self-government. While this has been done to some extent through the provisions of the PRA, the two higher tiers have been totally neglected.

It is time we accept the fact that the state government cannot look after all developmental work through its line departments and that there is a distinct advantage in entrusting these responsibilities to people's elected representative at lower levels for better supervision, monitoring, accountability and performance. In this sense, the enactment of some other states such as Maharashtra, Gujarat, Karnataka and others are more progressive. It will be worthwhile that the state government examines the provisions of these enactments (Godbole Committee, 1998).

The 73rd Amendment of the Indian Constitution envisages a much larger devolution of powers and functions to the institutions of local self-government in the rural areas. This amendment is not applicable to J&K. There are some important differences between the State enactment and provisions of the 73rd Amendment. It is seen that, under the 73rd Amendment, Panchayats are to be constituted at the village, intermediate and district levels. This three-tier structure does not exist in J&K. There is no provision in the State Act for setting up a state Finance Commission once in every five years to review the financial position of the Panchayats and recommend suitable devolution of resources to them. There is also no provision in the State Act for the appointment of a State Election Commissioner.

The State Finance Commission appointed by a number of other states have submitted their reports. Some of these commissions have delineated the basic minimum functions of the village Panchayats. The commissions have recommended that revenues pertaining to a number of tax and non-tax avenues be transferred to the villages Panchayat. In some other cases, the commissions have recommended the share of local bodies as a percentage of total tax revenues of a state.

The system of single line administration has been in vogue in the State for nearly 25 years. According to the official assessments, "The introduction of this system has yielded considerable benefits in terms of widening the impact of development programmes and reduction of regional disparities." However, the empirical basis of these studies is suspect. Impartial studies suggest that the system has not worked well (Misri and Bhatt, 1994).

The State has a large proportion of population living in the far-flung, inaccessible and backward regions. These areas remain cut off from the mainstream for the large part of the year. The inadequacy and uncertainty of road and other means of communications have many unfortunate consequences. Prices of essential products, which have to come to the main trading centres of the State, tend to be extremely high. Such products are often in short supply despite a network of public distribution system. At the same time, the prices realized from whatever people produce locally tend to be very low. Quality of the existing meagre social infrastructure like schools and health services are greatly affected by the non-availability of reliable roads, particularly in winter and monsoon. Leh and Kargil districts and some sub-regions in the Kashmir Valley have the most difficult terrain in the State. The area being hilly and climatic, conditions reaching arctic cold, large tracts are devoid of any vegetation and means of communication are quite inadequate. The land being unsuitable for cultivation of the cereals, people necessarily depend upon supplies from outside the region. The cost of these supplies becomes highly prohibitive in view of the exorbitant freight and incidental charges. The problem is further compounded in the far-flung villages owing to lack of transport and communication facilities. In the Jammu region, the hilly districts of Doda, Udhampur, Rajouri and Poonch face the same problems.

These areas have a preponderance of primitive primary activities. The people living in these regions are socially underprivileged. The quality of life is very poor, with high birth and death rates. Complete dependence on the natural conditions have forced the people to utilize the natural vegetations leading to deforestation, thereby increasing the quantum of soil erosion. This has damaged the only possible economic activities of tourism, horticulture and animal husbandry in these regions, which in turn has created serious ecological problems and water scarcity.

To deal with the backwardness and imbalances in the development, the government formulated the policy of multi-level planning, involving redefinition of the lowest development unit related to "terrain, geographical features, topography, compactness, accessibility, population density, duration of working season, distances separating habitation, remoteness to market, existing level of development and administrative structures and the resource endowment to ensure mobility of development machinery for the effective implementation and supervision of projects in execution."

The State had initiated the regional approach of planning as far back as in 1996 when efforts were made to identify the Border Community Development Blocks for special treatment in view of their peculiar problems and locational constraints.

The "balanced growth" of various sub-regions was also

debated by the multi-disciplinary team constituted by the state government in 1974. The team pointed out, inter alia, that, "within the State there are pockets of extreme backwardness which have only marginally been touched by the planning processes during the last two decades. This is partly due to the conscious policy of making investment only where it is most efficient, where the income-investment ratio is the highest and where economic gains are quickest. The backwardness is, however, the cumulative result of a number of factors like the lack of communications, harsh climatic conditions, difficult terrain, lack of irrigation facilities, etc."

The need for balanced regional development was emphasized in the Government Policy Statement in 1975. The Statement said that "balanced economic development of the State will obviously be one of the foremost concerns of the government. The government would like to emphasize maximum self-reliance consistent with the need to promote the requisite and desirable degree of inter-dependence with the other parts of the country. The objective will be to secure the most prudent and beneficial utilization of the natural resources and skills peculiar to the State, to achieve the maximum possible rate of economic growth, consistent with the need to secure a degree of balance between the rural areas and the urban areas, to maximize the State per capita income and to generate the maximum employment potential" [Government of J&K, Governnor's Address to the Joint Session of Legislature, March 6, 1975].

Similarly, in 1976 the State Government set up a committee under the chairmanship of the Chief Minister for intensive development of the identified backward regions. In 1991, the Central government declared the whole area of Ladakh with Scheduled Tribe population. In spite of these efforts, the area continues to suffer socially and economically.

The envisaged programmes of balanced regional development within the broader framework of development in the State have generated some controversy. The controversy was partly ideological and political in nature. However, a number of studies suggested that sectoral and sub-regional imbalances in the levels of living/development have not only persisted but increased over the years (For details see Sikri Commission Report, Zutshi, (1987) Service Centres and Their Impact on Surrounding Hinterlands—A Case Study of Kashmir Valley).

Geographical resource endowment and technological factors constitute the basic causes of the inter-district variations in the State. Secondary and tertiary economic activities are mainly concentrated in Srinagar and Jammu districts. Growth impulses are weak in other districts. The maximum labour force is dependent on primary activities in the State. Long winter months in the Kashmir region and some sub-regions in the Jammu Division not only hinder but also hamper early maturity of crops and cause large-scale seasonal unemployment. Capital formation suffers due to this. Growth centres, concentrated in Srinagar and Jammu districts, have not succeeded in disseminating information about prices and other magnitudes to the hinterlands. This has cumulatively caused migration and also witnessed that the towns adjacent to the rural areas, that enjoy better infrastructural facilities and the benefits of the growth of the services sector, attract the rural unemployed. The rural areas where orchards and related economic activities have gained momentum as they attract labour from the neighbouring rural areas. Spread-effects of the development process can be brought within the reach of the backward areas by special government efforts. The resource endowment position of these pockets/regions needs to be investigated along with projects formulated to generate income and employment. Local skills and entrepreneurship needs to be promoted. However, the removal of the key infrastructural bottlenecks—accessibility of electric energy and transport facilities have the potential of giving an immense boost to the development tempo in these regions/areas/pockets.

The development strategies of these areas will have to be formulated keeping in view, the resource endowment position, geo-physical setting, socio-cultural units and levels of social and economic infrastructure.

There is no ready-made approach for tackling the problems of inter-district and sub-regional backwardness. A package of policies with a definite area and spatial planning approach has to be thought of for this purpose. The development unit has to be the agroclimatic or resource unit. Since the main occupation of the majority of population dwelling in the identified backward regions is agriculture, the main development strategies should be oriented to get the maximum output from agriculture and allied activities.

Agricultural production may be increased by the optimum use of water and land resources, together with the election of crops most suited to the areas from the scientific point of view. Scientific cropping pattern and time and space sequence of crop affect the agricultural production as it ensures the greatest efficiency of land in fragile ecosystem.

In order to maintain the soil fertility and productivity, it is necessary to have good soil management practices including the supply of inorganic matter, the adaptation of proper rotation of crops and other recommended package of practices. The provision of modern seeds and spread of technological awareness could transform the present agricultural situation in the backward areas.

The Sher-i-Kashmir Agricultural University of the State has conducted surveys in the Kandi areas for the alternative-cropping pattern so as to increase the yield from these areas. These surveys should be continued on an extensive scale as these would help in evolving proper crop management in these areas.

The Sikri Commission in its Report submitted in 1980 had recommended that "in order to study and correct development imbalances, it is recommended that the government compile figures of per capita income at current prices by regions, district administrative units and undertake studies which will indicate per capita expenditure by fractile distribution of population in the State, region and distinct administrative units, using as appropriate, the surveys that the National Sample Survey and the Reserve Bank of India undertake." No action has been taken by the State Government on this recommendation so far.

The Sikri Commission's other recommendation was that, "Data in respect of the number of under-employed and unemployed persons and not only of the educated unemployed should be compiled periodically by regions and districts in order that the employment generation programme may be related to regional and district development activities." (Paragraph 5.3, 3.2). At present only unemployment figures are published district-wise. Other data are not compiled in the manner proposed by the

Sikri Commission. The committee believes that compilation of data as suggested by the Sikri Commission would be an important input in preparation of plans and programmes for the backward regions. This work may be taken up in hand without loss of any further time. Less developed and backward districts should be given a special weightage in allocation of Plan as also non-Plan development funds from such districts to schemes and programmes in other districts be permitted on any account. If grants for any particular department cannot be used during the year, re-appropriation may be allowed only in respect of departments within the same district. This will ensure that funds allocated to these backward districts get used within the same district (Godbole Committee, 1998).

While the decentralized planning process has been able to evoke public participation and reflect felt needs to some extent, it has also given rise to some problems with regard to plan implementation. Because of the growing demand for development programmes and the rising expectations of the people, the number of schemes taken up in the district plans has been mounting from year to year. This has resulted in a somewhat thinner spread of resources. In the engineering sector this has also led to considerable time and cost overruns. In the context of limited plan funds real benefits in sectors like water supply roads and minor irrigation are slow to accrue. With the passage of time, the number of continuing schemes have increased and tend to spill over into successive plans thus limiting the scope for initiating new programmes or shifting priorities. In one sense these problems are also encountered at the state and national level and perhaps inevitable within a democratic structure. At the same time, awareness is also growing of the need to plan and fix priorities in a situation of limited resources. With them this should bring about greater rationality in the district plans as has been the experience at the national and state levels.

A second difficulty being experienced is the diffusion of plan schemes. In the engineering sectors, which consume a substantial part of the total outlay of the district plan there is sometimes a conflict of authority and control between the district superintending engineer and the state level chief engineers who continue to be separate for the various disciplines, viz. road irrigation and flood control and public health engineering. This has adversely affected technical control over the schemes because the superintending engineer is heavily burdened with the planning and administrative functions and thus does not have enough time to devote to technical inspections of schemes. At the same time, the authority of the state level officer (viz. The head of the department) in this set up has also become somewhat tenuous. On the one hand, he continues to function as the liaison point with the State Government but on the other hand, his communication with his own field organization is only through either the superintending engineer or the district development commissioner.

While there are diverse sectoral plans being implemented in the specific area, there are at the same time many core programmes being implemented by local authorities under the umbrella of IRDP, NREP, RLEGP, DPAP, etc. Quite frequently one can discern an absence of coordination in the efforts and activities of different authorities in a specific area. There is a twofold problem of a lack of coordination among different departments operating in the same area and a lack of harmony between sectoral and core agencies. The need for decentralized planning and coordination arises specially to correct these lacunae. Unfortunately, this aspect of decentralized planning has been sidetracked.

Another important implication of decentralized planning is that the development personnel at the district/block/HP level should be in a position to generate feedback for themselves on the impact of development programmes and resultant charges. This would obviously need systematic periodical collection of disaggregated data about the incidence of poverty. Special profiles of the poor, schemes to be undertaken, resources inventory, poverty line norms, household incomes, etc. At present this is the most neglected area in the poverty alleviation programmes. The state revenue records are in a mess. Highly exaggerated information is collected by using obsolete methods of data collection. This type of data is absolutely irrelevant for micro-level planning. Thus, a high degree of decentralization in data collection and use of modern techniques is unavoidable. During the seventh Five Year Plan the planning process was taken down to the block level. Multiple criteria have been evolved for the distribution of outlays among the blocks giving due weightage to area, population and extent of backwardness.

Section VI — Summing Up

Legal/administrative structures of democratic decentralization, in different forms, are in place in the State for the last seventy-five years. Some of these structures are indeed in line with the true spirit of our federal polity. However, in practice even the official records and assessments suggest that these have failed to deliver. Looking retrospectively long spells of political uncertainty have severely impeded the growth of these structures. Democratic decentralization, particularly Panchayati Raj, is viewed by many as one of the viable means of ending the people's alienation and diluting the crisis. There is no harm in trying this option. However, institution building is an ongoing process. No law or administrative framework can offer "a once for all" solution to the problems of democratic decentralization. The issues of people's participation at the grassroots level cannot be seen in isolation. These are linked to the broader issues of political economy and survival of the State as a democratic polity.

References

1. Government of India, "Report of Study Team on Panchayat Raj Finance 1963" Part I and Part II, Ministry of Community Development and Cooperation.
2. Government of India, "Panchayat Raj at a Glance", Department of Rural Development, 1960-61, 1977-78 and 1990.
3. Government of India, "Report of the Committee on Panchayati Raj Institution", Ministry of Agriculture and Irrigation" Department of Rural Development, August, 1978, New Dehi.
4. Government of Jammu and Kashmir, "Report of the Development Review Committee" (Jha Committee), Part-I, 1976.
5. Government of Jammu and Kashmir, "Report of the Committee on Economic Reforms" (Godbole Committee), 1998.
6. Government of Jammu and Kashmir, "Report of Jammu and Kashmir Commission of Inquiry" 1980 (Sikri Commission).
7. Malaya, H. D., "Village Panchayats in India", Economic and Political Research Department, All Congress Committee, New Delhi, 1956.

8. Mathew George (ed.), *Panchayat Raj in Jammu and Kashmir*, Institute of Social Sciences and Concept Publishing Company, New Delhi, 1990.
9. Misri, M.L. and Bhatt, M. S. *Poverty, Planning and Economic Change in Jammu and Kashmir*, Vikas Publishing House Pvt. Ltd., New Delhi, 1994.
10. Rao, C.H.H., "Decentralized Planning: An Overview of Experiences and Prospects", *EPW*, Vol. Xxxiv, No. 8, February 25, 1989, pp. 411-416.
11. Shafi, M., "Revival of Democratic Tradition", In *Panchayati Raj in Jammu and Kashmir*, ed. George Mathew, ISS and Concept Publishing House, New Delhi, 1990.
12. Shivak, M. and Srivastava, "Factors Affecting Development of the Panchayati Raj System", NIRD, Rajendra Nagar, Hyderbad, 1990.
13. Sultan, M., "Poverty Alleviation Requires More Attention" in *Panchayat Raj in Jammu and Kashmir*, ed. George Mathew, ISS and Concept Publishing House, New Delhi, 1990.

Thirteen

Peace Through Autonomy and Reconciliation

Aijaz Ahmed

Any discussion of Kashmir must begin, first, with the scale of violence and atrocities; second, with the underlying structural problems and historical issues which underly the conflict; and, third, with a distinction between what is indigenous and what the role of foreigners, mainly Pakistan, really is, so that we can have some sense of the kind of settlement we shall require within Kashmir, which must always have the priority, and between India and Pakistan without which a durable peace in Kashmir cannot be secured.[1]

The first thing to be said about the scale of violence and atrocities is that it is only in relation to the size of the country as a whole, and thanks only to a kind of moral numbness that pervades our society generally, that this scale appears to be small and manageable. The figure of between 50 and 70 thousand casualties in a population of roughly 5 to 6 million which is commonly accepted, as against the figure of 20,000 which the government puts on, gives us a ratio of one casualty out of every one hundred, which would then mean that the killing fields of Kashmir are in no way less savage than the orgies of blood that the Serbian army and the ethnic militias perpetrated in various parts of the former Yugoslavia.

This, then, has to be considered in relation to the ratio between the population, the security personnel and the supposed number of militants at any given time. *India Today* of August 14 this year put the total number of armed militants at well below two thousands: 965 for the *Hizbul Mujahideen*, 250 for *Lashkar-e-Toiba*, 283 for *Jaish-e-Mohammadi*, and small contingents of a couple of other organizations. One wonders how the journal obtained such precise figures about top secret operations of the enemy, but we shall let that pass. The point, rather, is that the generally accepted figure for the total number of security forces engaged in counter-insurgency, including the former militants working now for the government forces, is roughly half a million. It rather boggles the mind that half a million trained security personnel cannot put out an insurgency that involves less than two thousand gunmen on the other side, most of them said to be foreigners with no roots in the terrain or the population. And if it is indeed true that the insurgency is really a matter of cross-border terror engineered by Pakistan, then it again boggles the mind that half a million security men, equipped with modern weapons and with all kinds of air cover, cannot seal a Line of Control merely 740 kilometres long. The main task of these forces is not fighting against infiltration but controlling the indigenous population itself, and the ratio of one security man to about a dozen civilians is said to be the worst in the world.

There is of course the indiscriminate, savage violence practised by the terrorists, but by any count, including notably the government count which our newspapers dutifully reproduce, the ratio of security men dying is relatively low. In the Death Count which *The Indian Express* has taken to publishing on a daily basis, very much on the model of the infamous "body count" released by the Americans during the Vietnam war, we could simply look at the statistics given on November 5 where it is said that out of the 2,351 who died in the first ten months of this year, there were 356 security men, as against a combined total of 1,995 militants and civilians. If security men account for roughly 15 per cent of the casualties even by the doctored statistics of the security forces themselves, the actual ratio is in fact likely to be lower. Second, if *India Today* is correct in saying that there are less than two thousand militants operating in J&K at any given time, and if *The Indian Express* is also correct in saying that 1,343 of them have been killed over the past ten months alone, then it becomes unclear how the insurgency continues unabated if it is simply a matter of cross-border terrorism' as the government claims. Third, any distinction between civilian and 'militant' in such accounts of popular insurgency must always be greeted with great scepticism; it is, after all, the security forces themselves, which largely determine whether a particular corpse is that of a 'civilian' or a 'militant'.

Let me now refer you back to *The Indian Express* of November 5 to illustrate the kind of casualness with which the dead get reported. In the box of the Death Count, on page 5, we are told that 6 civilians, 17 militants and 7 security men died the previous day—which comes to a total of 30. But the first column of the front page had carried on to page 7, we learned that the 44 had included 25 militants, 8 security men and, presumably, 11 civilians. How the number of the dead could be 30 on page 5 but 44 on the front page and on page 7 was left very much to the reader's imagination. This kind of casual irresponsibility in reporting the dead is a regular feature of our dominant media and it indicates not so much a lack of professionalism in this or that newspaper but a settled moral numbness in society as a whole, so that it does not really matter how many have died, through what means and as to who is actually responsible. The fact that this moral numbness pervades the polity as a whole is well reflected. The fact that neither the government, nor the security apparatus active in the field, nor the government's Human Rights Commission, nor any of the political parties either within the NDA or in the Opposition have ever undertaken a comprehensive, credible public inquiry into the abuses of power by the security agencies. Everyone seems to have settled down to the rhetoric of "cross-border terror" and "fundamentalism" on the one hand, and to cliches of "insaniyat," "alienation", etc., on the other.

I shall soon come to the substantive questions of politics and diplomacy, ceasefires and alternatives for a final settlement, and so on, which do and should preoccupy us all. But I think that all those other, very necessary discussions should not obscure the actual levels of cruelty and deception involved in the very picture we get from official sources and the dominant media. Unlike Pakistan, we are still, outside such regions as Jammu & Kashmir, a reasonably democratic polity; we can, and we must, hold our government accountable if this polity is to remain democratic and if we are to restore democratic norms where such have ceased to operate. Unlike the makers of Pakistan, who were obsessed with the Hindu-Muslim difference leaders of the national movement in India had made rather large moral claims about how we were going to build a religiously ecumenical and pluralist society, a secular polity, and a state bound strictly by law, constitution and ethical responsibility. In the early years of the Republic, when belief in those claims was still powerful, the people of J&K had opted to become a part of secular India rather than the Muslim Pakistan not simply by virtue of the Instrument of Accession, which is the legal basis for the association of the State with India, but also because of those promises of building a progressive, pluralist, secular India in which the people of J&K were to have a very special status and the maximum degree of autonomy within the Union. Those promises were contained in Article 370 of the Indian Constitution and in the Constitution of J&K itself. These are constitutional obligations without which the Instrument of Accession itself is rendered meaningless; to deny this fact, as the RSS and its affiliates punctiliously do, is to undermine the Union itself.

There were, in other words, two sides to the moral bond. There was the translation of it in the form of a constitutional obligation. But there was also a visionary idea which we then took to be a practicable horizon and which was best expressed by Mahatma Gandhi when he said that the kind of religious tolerance and plurality that he envisaged for the whole of India was most evident in Kashmir, and it was therefore not Kashmir that had to be re-made in the image of India, but India itself that had to be re-made in the image of Kashmir.

The Indian State has increasingly conspired with Pakistan to destroy that particular Kashmir, the one that the Mahatma had held up to India as an idea to be emulated. Actually, Pakistan has at least a perverse kind of honesty in its enterprise; their rulers practice a politics of religious hysteria and they are quite forthright about it. On February 5 this year, General Musharraf, in some other ways more decent, observed that his immediate predecessors, said jubilantly that the *jehad* that had been won in Afghanistan, had now been transferred to Kashmir. I shudder to think of people who can soberly think of making of the Valley something resembling what their friends, from Hekmetyar to the Taliban, have made of Afghanistan, In a newspaper column, Saeed Naqvi recently quoted extensively from the website of the *Lashkar-e-Taiba* and urged us all to visit that website, to have some sense of the kind of barbarian that has come into the Valley.

Such facts must never be used, however, to condone the kind and degree of counter-terror routinely practised by the Indian State itself. In actual practice the counter-terror against the terrorist frequently extends into terror in its own right, plain and simple, directed at the innocent population itself, targeting the Muslim segment of the population in particular. Indeed, if we, as a polite people, ever had the courage to institute something resembling the Commission for Truth and Reconciliation which the Mandela Government instituted in South Africa after the dissolution of Apartheid there, it may so turn out that routine terror against the population far exceeds the violence used against the terrorist.

What happens in Kashmir is, of course, a matter of life and death, first of all, for the Kashmiris themselves. But it was also, from the very beginning, a test case for the two nation-states that two-nation theory, as propounded by Mr. Jinnah, was that there could be peace between Hindus and Muslims only if both got their own separate states. The claim of the Indian national movement, by contrast, was that ours was historically and structurally a composite culture and we could build a secular, multi-denominational society encompassing peoples of all religions; religious difference was not a political liability, we said, but a cultural asset. Kashmir became a testing ground for both these claims. What actually happened is that neither of these new nation-states that arose out of decolonization in South Asia proved able to leave behind them the bitter legacy of the Partition, and it was in Kashmir that competing claims of territory and belief proved the most intractable.

For us to understand the scale of our mutual failures, we might recall how in the process of building modern democracies France and Germany were eventually able to leave behind them the memories not only of the wars over Alsace-Lorraine that had occupied them through so much of the 19th century but the experience even of the two World Wars, so that they could then emerge as the main pillars of European unity. In South Asia, by contrast, the Partition did not solve the problem of communalism but made it permanent, institutionalizing it in organs of the State itself, in the form of religious bigotry in Pakistan and, increasingly over the years and decades, as a ferocious majoritarianism and great-nation chauvinism in India. There has been almost a traumatic failure in both countries to bury the hatchet and to arrive in Kashmir at an imaginative solution that would bypass the maximalist positions held by the two adversarial nation-states and would pave the way for peace there through maximum autonomy for the region and an honourable reconciliation among all its peoples. We have never even considered the possibility that the task of the two nation-states is not to dictate a solution but to help the people of the state, on both sides of the LoC, find a solution that would be peaceful, progressive, secular, in conformity with their aspirations as well as with their historic ties with the region as a whole, including security ties. Nor have we considered the possibility that the solution may well lie in softer, more flexible ideas of sovereignty than the rigid ones that we have inherited from nation-states of the 19th century. This is the historic failure of our two countries, for which the people of Kashmir are paying with their blood and their honour.

The peace that Mr. Jinnah had promised as a result of the Partition never materialized. Not only did the Partition itself come with unimaginable levels of communal violence and the largest migration of refugees in human history, but that strife was immediately extended to Kashmir and made permanent. This is the one region in South Asia where the violence of the Partition has never ended. It is indicative of the ferocity of Pakistan's determination in this regard that it has never renounced its own territorial claim to the whole of Kashmir, has never allowed the emergence of a force that spoke autonomously for Kashmir, has always claimed that the issue of self-determination in Kashmir was an issue of integration with either India or Pakistan, and has always assumed, peremptorily and pre-emptively, that, given such a choice, Kashmiris would necessarily choose in favour of Pakistan.

Wars were initiated both in 1948 and in 1965 with the aim of obtaining through the force of arms what it could not achieve through political or diplomatic means, and its conduct during the more recent insurgency dating from 1988-89 has been dictated by these implacable objectives and presumptions. I shall return to the matter of Pakistan's policies in a moment, but it is worth remarking here that it has done all it can to prevent the emergence in Kashmir of a force that is secular in its own territorial claims; and it has actively financed and given training and weapons to outfits of the most rabid theocratic orientations. Meanwhile, it has allowed political formations in the so-called Azad Kashmir less freedom than has been available, for the most part, to their counterparts in J&K on the Indian side. Basically, it has never accepted that there could be—on its own borders, no less—a Muslim-majority state that was willingly a part of India; that seemed to negate the two-nation theory itself.

For India, meanwhile, there were two quite different questions in years immediately after Independence. India had of course declared itself not a Hindu Rashtra but a secular Republic. However, it had done so without at the same time fully facing the majoritarian communalism that was even then a major force in at least the northern regions of the country—not weakened but strengthened by the Partition—and a considerable presence within the Indian National Congress itself, as Prime Minister Nehru was the first to recognize and condemn. Could this formally secular India, arising out of a communal holocaust really live with a Muslim-majority state within the Union, and one, moreover, that was accorded a very special degree of autonomy, which majoritarian communalism was bound to represent as 'minority appeasement' that was compromising security and integrity of the nation? One can grasp the gravity of this question if one recalls that Shyama Prasad Mukherjee, whom the RSS has taken to eulogizing as the first martyr in the Indian struggle for Kashmir, was in fact a colleague of Nehru in those early years when Article 370 of the Constitution was crafted as embodying the terms of acceptance of the Instrument of Accession. Communalism was not entirely external to some pockets of the national movement itself. So, that was the first question; could the promised autonomy for the State of Jammu and Kashmir survive the creeping institutionalization of majoritarian communalism in large parts of Indian society and state after Independence?

But this too was connected with another equally basic question about the shape of the Republic, and the place of J&K in it: the question, one might ask, of the viceregal traditions of governance which Independent India had inherited from the Raj and towards which even the finest of our leaders, perhaps including Nehru, were very much inclined. It is sometimes said that Mountbatten was able to make arrangements that could prevent the Partition by arguing that the kind of constitutional arrangements that could prevent the Partition would make the Centre permanently weak in relation to its federating units, so that the processes of national integration shall be impeded in the political sphere and the Centre's ability to undertake major initiatives would be curbed in the economic sphere; better to let go of some regions than to weaken the Centre. Be that as it may. The structure of the Union that emerged out of Independence was formally federal but substantively unitary: a strong Centre with weak federation units. Could this system accommodate a unit of a very different kind—one that entered the Union with its own Constitution and its own flag? It is chastening to recall that what Namboodripad was to face some years later was a much milder version of what Sheikh Abdullah had to face in 1953; it was with Kashmir that the history was repeated there more often than in any other state, just as elections were rigged there more blatantly than elsewhere. It was in Kashmir, in other words, that Indian federalism and Indian democracy, India's commitment to its own constitutional provisions and its claims of a composite culture as a politically positive value, were tested the most strongly, and here it was that the Indian State was found the most wanting.

I hardly need remind this audience that the erosion of Article 370 began not under a communal dispensation but in the 1950s, the "golden decade " of Indian democracy and secularism, and that between 1953 and 1986 no less than 42 amendments were passed so as to restrict the powers of the state. Nor does one have to go into details as to how the so-called 'Hindu card' was played in Jammu in 1983 by the very custodians of Indian secularism, from which the BJP benefited only later; how the elections of 1987 were rigged; and how the Muslim United Front of 1986, the insurgency dating from 1988 and the emergence of the Kul Jama'at Hurriyat Conference (APHC) in 1993 were initially at least, responses to these events. It is indicative of larger trends, through, that even in its founding moment APHC affirmed the specifically "Islamic character" of the struggle; with the JKLF already sidelined, neither the Pakistan-based Muttahida Jehadi Council (MJC) which had already been established in 1991, nor the APHC which emerged two years later, even claimed to speak for the non-Muslim populations of the composite state. What is crucial to understand, in any case, is that Islamization of considerable sections of the insurgency and its affiliates in the Valley grew in tandem with the increasing communalization of Indian politics in general and of Jammu politics in particular—a turn of events in which the Congress itself proved entirely capable of practising a pragmatic kind of communalism which often paved the way, inadvertently perhaps, for the more programmatic communalism of the majoritarian Right. Moreover, these developments which were internal to Kashmir and, more generally, to India coincided with certain fundamental changes which were then in place within Pakistan, a matter to which I now turn briefly.

After the failure of its bid to capture the whole of Jammu and Kashmir, in 1948, Pakistan had initiated the 1965 war with the express purpose of capturing as much of the J&K as possible while also trying to capture some other Indian territory which it dreamed of exchanging for whatever part of Kashmir still remained in India's hands. In that project it had failed miserably and the next few years, until after the Bangladesh crisis, were years of great internal turbulence within Pakistan. The 1971 war was then fought on Indian initiative resulting in what we call the liberation of Bangladesh but what was perceived by the Pakistani leaders as an elaborate and successful Indian conspiracy for Pakistan's military humiliation and territorial breakup. That traumatic experience brought about three fundamental changes. Pakistan had until then claimed to be home for majority of South Asian Muslims but was now home to fewer Muslims than not only Bangladesh but also India. In this crisis of identity, then, the Islamicist vocation of the

State was found; no longer the home of the majority of Muslims, Pakistan was to be the home of the truly pious. Second, the markets it had lost in East Bengal were to be compensated for with markets elsewhere. The answer was the Muslim world, specifically the socially and religiously conservative monarchies of the Gulf region. This too contributed to the rise of orthodoxy there, but what it meant above all was that the Pakistani State began to think of itself not as a merely South Asian entity but as a strategically located middle-sized power straddling both South and West Asia.

The third fundamental shift was in security perceptions. Having been cut to half its size by a much bigger neighbour, it took a leaf out of Israeli textbooks and decided that in order to command strategic depth, the defence parameters of its own security should be drawn inside the territory of the two neighbours that Pakistan considered hostile: India principally, but also to a certain extent Afghanistan. Pakistan's relatively successful role in the insurgencies in Punjab and Kashmir came in the wake of this new strategic doctrine of forward defence because there was fertile ground in those states for Pakistan to exploit. These changes were already emerging in the Bhutto years, in the mid-1970s, but reached their final form only after Zia-ul-Haq's coup d'etat, especially after the Afghan revolution of 1978.

Zia was a man of much more orthodox, even theocratic persuasions, and he carried out a very conservative kind of systematic Islamization of Pakistani society, state and, especially the armed forced, though it could also be argued that this process of conservative Islamization of some of the armed forces there was an older process of which Zia himself was a product. This religious zealotry became particularly ferocious after Pakistan started fighting America's proxy war in Afghanistan. By the time a full-fledged insurgency began taking shape in Kashmir in response to the rigged elections of 1987, the PDPA government in Afghanistan was already beginning to tatter, the Pakistan Army had gained almost a decade of experience of that war and had at its disposal very considerable military resources as well as thousands of experienced irregular combatants and freelance seekers of martyrdom, so that it was now much better equipped to take advantage of the crisis that was by then brewing within J&K.

Meanwhile, the ISI had emerged as a virtually autonomous centre of decision-making, thanks to the CIA which had sought to largely bypass the Pakistan GHQ and manage the war itself, with direct channels to Pakistan's Intelligence Services.

ISI had tried to recruit the JKLF as early as 1984 but had been turned down by the Valley-based leaders, and it was only after Amanullah Khan's arrival in Pakistan in 1986 that the relationship seems to have been firmly established. However, 1989 was the crucial year. Not only did militancy gain ground very rapidly but, more importantly, the highly successful general strike and election boycott of that year, ordered by the militants, convinced Pakistan that Kashmir was witnessing a new kind of mass movement which it had to capture so as to ensure that it was led by groups loyal to itself. It was in this atmosphere that differences between JKLF and the ISI began to widen, and the Jama'at–e-Islami, never popular in Kashmir previously gained ascendancy only after the ISI threw its weight behind it as the force selected to eliminate JKLF and to Islamicize the insurgency, just as it was the ISI that had given the Jamaat a pre-eminent role in Afghanistan, until Benazir for her own reasons curtailed that role and gave much more support to the Deobandis groups. Since the Jama'at was connected with the Hizb-e-Islami of Hekmetyar in Afghanistan and with the Hizbul Mujahideen in Kashmir, and had a number of its own Pakistani cadres active in J&K, Syed Salahuddin's outfit was ideally positioned to take on the JKLF on the one hand and to try and occupy the pre-eminent position among the rest of the groups.

However, just as the ISI had learned from the CIA in Afghanistan never to rely only on one or two groupings, several groups were created for Kashmir as well, many of whom were then brought together in the Tehrik-e-Hurriyat-e-Kashmir (TEHK) and the Muttahida Jehad Council (MJC) which were created in April 1991 and from which JKLF was pointedly excluded. Pitched battles were fought against the JKLF, which was caught in a pincer between Indian security forces and the Pakistan-sponsored Mujahideen. This was combined, then, with systematic killings of non-fundamentalist and secular people belonging to the National Conference, the Left parties, Congress and Janata Dal. That the Hizbul Mujahideen is by no means the only fighting force of the insurgents in J&K, but also that it is the pre-eminent one, are facts that were determined initially in Islamabad and Muzaffarabad, even though the majority of its cadres are of Kashmiri origin. In context, then, it is very ironic that Mr. Advani would certify the Hizb as "our own dissidents" because they offered a short-lived ceasefire, while his colleague in the BJP, J.P. Mathur called Farooq Abdullah an "Islamic fundamentalist" and Mr. Advani's parent organization, the RSS, characterized the Autonomy Resolution passed by the State Assembly as only "a step short of actual cessation."

Much of this is well enough known and I mention it here to make several points. First, the problem in Kashmir is rooted in the failure, in different ways, of both India and Pakistan to overcome the trauma of the Partition. In Pakistan's perception that a Muslim-majority Indian state on its borders is an unacceptable refutation of the two-nation theory and the whole of Kashmir belongs to it by something of a divine right; and in India's failure to honour the commitments it made to the Kashmiri people, a failure that is itself rooted not only in the communal pressure to teach the Kashmiri Muslims a lesson but also its much more fundamental fear that the grant of any extensive autonomy there may serve to dismantle the viceregal tradition of centralized dispensation and administration. The least that India could do is to grant real autonomy to the state and then work out mechanisms of real political and administrative devolutions to the respective regions within the framework of that autonomy, but for that we lacked the will and the imagination.

Second , the politics of communalization is now a fact of life in Kashmir but it is something that has been smuggled into it by the dominant forces in India and Pakistan, and in the Indian case the RSS-BJP combine has been the main beneficiary but the Congress itself has been an accomplice in it. The price has, of course, been paid by all the religious communities there, Muslim and non-Muslim, and there are strong indications that sectarian strife is now on the rise among the Muslims themselves. This too was predictable. Religious zealotry has already polarized the Afghan and Pakistani populations on lines of Shia-Sunni sectarian divide, with powerful armed militias on both sides but especially ferocious among the Sunnis. Some of the same Sunnis, largely Deobandi militias are deeply intertwined with the so-called Mujahideen operating in Kashmir. I have long feared that this turn of events may destroy the rich diversity and happy plurality of sects ecumenical, largely Sufic ambience of Kashmiri Islam and instituting, instead, an orthodox, scripturalist, puritanical and punitive Islam.

Third, it is well to remember that it is always the internal crisis which gives to hostile neighbours the chance to intervene. Pakistan's crisis of 1971 was not of India's making; Bhutto and the Generals brought it upon themselves by refusing to abide by the democratic mandate, which then paved the way for Indian intervention. Similarly, it was an internal crisis within Kashmir—brought about by methodical dilutions of its autonomy, by communalization and corruption, electoral fraud by the political parties and repression by the security agencies—which paved the way for armed insurgency to gain ground and for Pakistan to take hold of much of that insurgency and turn it into something resembling low-intensity warfare. India can fight back but there is no military solution to it. The insurgency was in fact largely contained by the mid-1990s and the elections of 1996, which Farooq Abdullah agreed to fight on the plank of real autonomy after receiving extensive assurances from the highest source, was a very real chance which, like all such chances before and since then, was squandered. For some two years, it did seem that the plank of *azaadi* in its more extreme form had been overtaken by the alternate plank of "maximum autonomy" as the United Front Government of the time put it, extending the promise that Narasimha Rao had held out in 1995 with his statement that so far as autonomy was concerned "the sky was the limit". But our leaders are always seeking short-term tactical advantage, with little capacity for strategic thinking or the courage to make a historic breakaway from the rigidly held positions. By the time the BJP-RSS combine came to power in 1998, the lack of movement on the autonomy question had already eroded Farooq 's position. In 1999, then, he lost what little relevance he still had by joining the BJP-led government. In a significant poll that *Outlook* published in its October 16 issue only 2 per cent of the respondents in the Valley felt that the government needed to talk to Farooq but 54 per cent were in favour of talks with the Hurriyat and 36 per cent in favour of talks with all parties (surprisingly, only 8 per cent favoured talks with the Hizb). The internal crisis remains, however, and it is foolish to imagine that the Pakistan-sponsored groups can be contained without major breakthrough on the political front within the country.

Fourth, however, it is also a fact that Pakistan has always been a party to this dispute, whether or not it has always acted honourably. And, as numerous influential commentators, from J.N.Dixit to Malini Parthasarthy, have emphasized over the last few months, none of the members of the Security Council subscribe to the idea that J&K belongs unproblematically to India as such, no matter how much they may sympathize over the issue of LoC violations; that is why, all of those countries punctually call upon India and Pakistan, equally, to desist from fighting and negotiate a settlement. So, the internal settlement that has to be made between the Indian State and the people of J&K cannot yield a stable peace unless Pakistan too is a party to it. Maulvi Muhhamad Yusuf Shah, now more commonly known by his assumed name Syed Salahuddin, the chief of Hizbul Mujahideen, made rather interesting points in his recent interview which *India Today* published in its September 7 issue: "Before 1990," he said, "Kashmir never knew the gun culture. My name is Salahuddin. I have fought elections thrice in Kashmir. That was the time when we tried to get our right in a peaceful and democratic manner. But, we were crushed, tortured and dishonoured. *Tan aamad, ba-jang aamad* (when you are finally fed up , you take up arms). What we are asking for—a tripartite dialogue—is a ground reality, a historical fact that nobody can deny.......How can India forget the political future of 1.20 crore Kashmiris on 84,000 square miles of Kashmir in command and control of Pakistan?" One does not have to be an admirer of Mr. Salahuddin to concede that "the historical fact" is undeniable, although one is not quite sure of the population figures.

What little chance there was for negotitated peace faded with the emergence of the BJP-led government and then went up into a ball of fire, first at Pokhran and then at Chaghai. The subcontinent is yet to recover from the ill effects of these explosions, which strengthened the more belligerent elements in both societies who then concluded, on both sides of the border, that possession of nuclear weapons makes it safer to fight limited conventional wars. In India, certainly, the military budget has gone up dramatically.[2] The Lahore Declaration was essentially an eyewash, undertaken to placate the Americans with claims of peaceful intention after having demonstrated the worst of aggressive designs. And it had to be Mr. Vajpayee who travelled to Lahore because he was the man directly responsible for authorizing the nuclear explosions in the first place.

The real wages of Pokharan were actually earned in Kargil and then, after Pakistan was forced to vacate its positions there, in the shape of qualitatively new kinds of offensive by the militants: more attacks on police and army posts, more pitched battles with concentration of personnel and fire power, even suicide bombers and, now, perhaps the more crude kinds of SAM missiles.[3] On the other hand, communalization of politics in the State has meant that some version of a plan to separate Jammu and Kashmir, combined with various proposals for alterations of other sub-regional boundaries—bifurcation, trifurcation, re-division of the whole into eight newly-created provinces'—have come from a surprisingly large number of sources: U.S.-based think tanks, National Conference, MLAs from Muslim majority districts of Jammu, Karan Singh, BJP-associated academics and politicians in J&K, RSS-sponsored fronts, and of course the state-appointed Regional Autonomy Committee (RAC) whose own report resembles remarkably the blueprint prepared by the Kashmir Study Group in consultation with the U.S. Administration.

Meanwhile, Farooq Abdullah has accumulated a new record of non-governance and governmental corruption over the past four years and has signally failed to build bridges with the non-Muslim majorities of Jammu and Ladakh; he is thus trying to take the limelight away from the Hurriyat and the Hizb through the Autonomy Resolution but also trying to strike bargains with the other constituencies with the RAC report. The Hizb's offer for a ceasefire and negotiations is still as shrouded in mystery as is its quick withdrawal. Four gains they, and Pakistan behind them, seem to have made. First, it was the prospect of this offer which helped the BJP kill the Autonomy Resolution; the attention was soon going to be focussed elsewhere. Second , they were able to show to the Americans that they were open to negotiations. Third, India was seen as rejecting the very idea of involving Pakistan at any stage, contrary to the demands from all the Western powers that India and Pakistan enter meaningful bilateral negotiations. Fourth, they elicited from Mr. Advani, the Home Minister , the certification that they indeed represented '60 per cent of the *jehad*' as it got said in the newspapers; one could no longer pretend that insurgency in Kashmir was the handiwork of "foreigners." On the other hand, however, it was also clear that they could not guarantee a real ceasefire without cooperation from other groups, and the Vajpayee government's ineptitude was demonstrated yet again in that one was at a loss to understand what modalities of the ceasefire the government had worked out in the first place, before expressing its enthusiasms. It soon became clear that the BJP –led government was even less serious about the ceasefire than either the Pakistan government or the Hizbul Mujahideen or its parent organisation, the Jama'at-e-Islami; it seemed to have hoped to simply split the Hizb and/or to cajole some of its major commanders to come overground—objectives in which it signally failed.[4]

The positive development, meanwhile, is that there is now in the Valley itself a palpable weariness with the constant carnage and a great desire for peace. That is why both the Autonomy Resolution and then Hizbul Mujahideen's offer of a ceasefire were greeted with waves of popular enthusiasm, and it was in response to this popular pressure for peace that even figures like Shabir Shah and Yasin Malik, hardly cohorts of the Jamaat or the Hizb, went on record regretting the collapse of the prospects for negotiations. The long-drawn process of the elections in the United States had temporarily halted the international pressure for negotiations, but the pressure has come again, with new proposals and initiatives, as soon as the new Administration was in place there. In the country at large, it is a good sign that eminent political commentators in the liberal media have been joind by the CPI(M) and Congress on the one hand, and political figures such as I.K. Gujral and V.P. Singh on the other, to impress upon the government that interlocution with Pakistan is unavoidable and that a most flexible framework for negotiations is required. So, where do we go from here?

I believe that the most important settlement in Kashmir has to be an internal one, among the Kashmiris themselves, in which the Governments of India and Pakistan can play a pivotal role and the international community can help but which will emerge out of a comprehensive and civilized dialogue among all the Kashmiris, of all regions and religious beliefs, on both sides of the Loc. But no secular, progressive, democratic and just solutions are possible without first putting in place elaborate and careful mechanisms for reconciliation. There has been altogether too much violence and cruelty, too many have suffered at the hands of the militants and the security forces alike, for it all to go away with the magic wand of a legal and territorial settlements. The dead cannot return to life but the truth about the manner of their death needs to be recorded, the guilty named and punished, and recompense offered to the survivors. The Valley will never be at peace with its own conscience, nor the great civility of Kashmiriyat be restored to it, until the pundits can be brought back to live there with their properties, liberties and security restored to them, and the violence against them accounted for. Sikhs have suffered, migrant workers have suffered, women of all communities dishonoured, and the iron has gone much too deep in the soul. We will need, I believe, something resembling the South African Commission for Truth and Reconciliation to heal the wounds. The alternative is permanence of hatred and cruelty, bifurcations, trifurcations, deeper and deeper fissures, and a real settlement infinitely postponed. Initially, such a process can be proposed and set into motion within the Indian side of the Loc but if we are able to show our own good faith in this re-building of our part of Kashmir then those on the other side can hopefully be persuaded to join in, and eventually the Pakistani State shall have to tell the truth of its own misdeeds as we require the Indian State to do so. I don't believe any initiative of that kind can come from governments; they are themselves much too immersed in acts of cruelty. The initiative shall have to come from within civil society, and if such an initiative can in fact be fruitfully pursued that will not only help the process of reconciliation in Kashmir but will also strengthen civil society in the rest of India as well, against arbitrary power of the State.

Second, we shall have to democratize the process of negotiations that are intended to yield us a just and democratic legal and territorial settlement, and to look at a whole range of possible ways of doing things. We can certainly look at the settlement in Northern Ireland for some lessons, as is often said. But there is also a wide variety of experiences in Asia and Africa at which too we may look for fresh thinking. I have already referred to the innovative way the South Africans attempted to deal with the crimes of the Apartheid era, and their work was made all the more possible because someone of Bishop Tutu's moral grandeur was there to lead the process. Elsewhere, and at the extreme end, we have the Ethiopian Constitution , the only one in the world that allows the right to secede; that's how Eritiran independence was guaranteed . And there are other quite creative instances, such as the devolution plans getting discussed in Sri Lanka, not to speak of the earlier projects of autonomy and special status for J&K within the Indian Union, which have tried to give legal and constitutional shape to the right of self-determination of regional entities within a larger union, whether federal or confederal. Even more novel forms and procedures can be devised for the special case of Kashmir which is itself divided between two nation-states and which is, on both sides of the divide, far from being homogeneous; Baltistan and the rest of what Pakistan calls 'Northern territories ' as different from the so-called 'Azad Kashmir ' proper, as Ladakh might be from the Valley. The main guiding-point here should be that we try to develop flexible ideas of sovereignty for special cases, and that we try to reconcile the need to preserve and even recreate larger unities with intricate systems of devolution of power to regions, sub-regions and localities within the larger unit.

Comprehensive peace in Kashmir can be sought along two quite different axes. In one conceptual framework , the ceasefire line itself becomes the international border with minor adjustments. India works for great autonomy for the State within the Union and for regions within the State, while Pakistan remains free to do what it sees fit with 'Azad Kashmir' and the 'Northern territories'. That is a much more limited and conventional option, and I am not sure if that is either just or workable. The dream of sharing a common social and cultural life across the LoC — in other words, some kind of re-unification—is actually very much part of the desire and hope which fuels the slogan of *'azaadi'*. Nor am I sure that it is wise to restrict the settlement of the Kashmir problem to J&K alone, without taking into account the need to include in the final settlement the Pakistani side of Kashmir as well. The Indian Government has never shown its hand on this issue. Is it willing to settle for the Loc as the final international boundary, with minor adjustments, as it informally indicates when it is trying to present its conciliatory face? Or, does it lay territorial claim to the Pakistani side of historic Kashmir as well, intending to 'liberate' it, as even BJP ministers say frequently enough? The question is in any case always posed as that of a part of Indian territorial claims of the nation-state but not the aspirations of the common Kashmiris who want to live without war and with some live relation to the whole of the historic land of Kashmir.

It is to address this more subtle aspiration that we may think of an alternate conceptual framework that would be based on a number of rather different presuppositions. First, that the Kashmir problem exists on both sides of the Loc. Second, that while the word *'azaadi'* may not actually mean full sovereignty but maximum autonomy as well as freedom from various kinds of oppressions and injustices, a key component of the Kashmiri aspiration for freedom is also some kind of unification, some common life for members of various religious groups for autonomy in their own locales; in other words, a non-denominational set of local self-governments. Finally, this alternative conception would go far beyond settling the territorial dispute between the two nation-states of India and Pakistan, and would address the issue of the shared responsibility on part of the two countries to compensate all the populations on the two sides of the Loc for the havoc this dispute has caused in their lives. That would mean a comprehensive programme for economic development, for the construction of requisite political structures, for repairing the social fractures, for rehabilitation of populations that have been evicted from their ancestral homes and properties, and compensation for families that have suffered at the hands of either the militants or the respective government forces—and all this as a joint responsibility of the two governments.

The final status of the Loc should be subject to discussion between the two governments surely but a topic of discussion above all among groups and political entities of the Kashmiris themselves. The Loc may be accepted formally as an international boundary but as an extremely soft border, together with some degree of de-militarization. Alternately, there can be various formulae for joint sovereignty, or various kinds of transitions from one kind of status to another. All that can be put up for discussion but the process through which such decisions are made is of prime importance. In this, we may learn from a remarkable experience of democratic negotiations in Somalia recently, where a large conference based upon the widest possible representation of local and regional interest groups remained in session for virtually a whole year, in order to hammer out a modicum of a system of governance in that country so ravaged by armies and warlords.

There are, in short, many possible solutions, some of which can already be glimpsed, at least partially; others that can only emerge out of widest possible democratic dialogue. For that, building a durable peace between India and Pakistan is the primary condition, because it is simply axiomatic that unless the two countries make peace with each other, quite aside from the issue of Kashmir, there will be no peace and reconciliation within Kashmir.

It is the guns—all the guns—that have to fall silent, so that the people may speak, freely at last.

References

1. The simple word 'Kashmir' is used throughout this essay to designate the whole of that historic region. Other terms—e.g. Jammu, Ladakh, Azad Kashmir, Northern Territories, the Valley, etc, are used for more specific units within that historic entity.
2. See my two articles on nuclearization in *Frontline*, June 5 and June 19, 1998.

3. See my "The Many Roads to Kargil" and "Mediation by Any Other Name," in *Frontline*, July 16, 1999 and July 30, 1999 respectively, for detailed commentary on the politics of the Lahore Resolution, as well as the Kargil War and its consequence.
4. See my "Kashmir Conundrum: India, Pakistan, the United States" and the "Question of Autonomy" in *Frontline*, August 4, 2000, for a lengthier treatment of the politics of the Autonomy Resolution; and "Ceasefire as Smokescreen," in *Frontline*, September 29, 2000 for more detailed commentary on the making and unmaking of the ceasefire.

Fourteen

Agenda for Peace

Kshitij Prabha

The Pak-based militant outfit, Hizbul Mujahideen (HM) declared ceasefire on July 24, 2000 for unconditional talks with the Government of India. Abdul Majid Dar, the Chief of HM in Kashmir Valley took the initiative for the talks, which was reluctantly approved by their counterpart in Pakistan under compulsions. The Government of India promptly responded to the initiative for dialogue with the militants. This definitely beamed positive rays of hope amidst dismay and despondency in Jammu and Kashmir (J & K). However, the hope of millions of Kashmiris suffering from the spectre of Pak-sponsored terrorism in this region was soon belied as HM under pressure from Pakistan ended the ceasefire on August 8, 2000.

The question arises what do we expect from the unpredictable sudden changes in the political weather of this region? How do we chalk out a plan for dialogue with militants in the given conditions? The intention of the Government of India is apparently to bring peace in the Valley. But the point of concern is how to go about it, especially when Salauddin insists on tripartite talks (India, Pakistan and Kashmir), whereas the Government of India has agreed for a direct dialogue with the militants? Where are we heading and how does this position take us towards peace in the Valley?

There are two ways to analyse this situation. First, was the ceasefire declared by HM a genuine urge for peace? And second, why the ceasefire ended without any discussion on issues at stake in Kashmir? Both these questions are interconnected. If there was a genuine urge for peace, the HM should have definitely taken some time to discuss current crisis and bargained with the Government of India. The manner in which the ceasefire was declared and scrapped indicates the psychology behind the game. There was no genuine urge for peace. The ceasefire was more a response to pro-active counter-terror tactics adopted by the Government of India, which has severely affected the militant outfits operating in the Valley and the US pressure on Pakistan to open a channel for discussion with India to untie the knots of Kashmir. The genuine urge for peace was one of the factors not 'the factor' for ceasefire. It is obvious that Islamabad influenced the HM for ceasefire on certain terms and conditions, i.e. tripartite political dialogue. Could it be described as the urge for peace or a game of power politics? Undoubtedly the entire exercise was a by product of the US pressure on Pakistan. And as expected, nothing came out of it. Had the ceasefire been declared for a genuine urge for peace in the Valley some long-term plan for cessation of conflict would have been worked out. Apparently, the desire for peace was missing from the agenda, the outcome of which was the end of ceasefire on August 8, 2000.

Unconditional Conditions

It is relevant to mention that the HM doesn't represent the Kashmir populace. This group is based in Pakistan and was initially created with the help of the US against the Soviets in Afghanistan during the late 1970s. Its active involvement in the Kashmir Valley began after the withdrawal of Soviet troops from Afghanistan in 1989. Until then it had very little interest in the political affairs of Kashmir. During the early phase it had more members from Afghanistan and Pakistan because they were fighting against the Soviets in Afghanistan. Later their priority shifted from Afghanistan to Kashmir. Since its future plan of action targeted the Valley, a Kashmiri-dominated mercenary force was officially created in 1990, i.e. soon after withdrawal of Soviet troops from Afghanistan. They inducted more and more members from the Pak-occupied Kashmir (PoK). Thus, it largely consists of Kashmiris from PoK and Pakistani nationals rather than the Kashmiris from the Valley. The real representative of the Kashmiri populace is the JKLF and they are not part of the ceasefire declared by HM. The HM is a religion-based mercenary force, which is more a part of Pan Islamic fundamentalism rather than global terrorism. The two phenomena are interlinked but not one and the same. The problem in Kashmir is not that of religious fanaticism but that of state-sponsored cross-border terrorism. Pakistan exploits the co-religious status of Kashmiris. The militant groups too find a sanctuary while fighting against the Indian forces. But this is not the bottom line in Kashmir. Religion is not the 'the issue' in the Valley. It is the political power and right of governance that matters in Kashmir. The HM is likely to negotiate in the interest of Pakistan not only because it is Pak-based but also because it has emerged as an organization that provides vocation for unemployed youth population in this region. How can one think of a permanent solution to the problem of Kashmir without active involvement of the local Kashmiris represented by the JKLF, the one and the only militant group, which is against merger of Kashmir with Pakistan? The JKLF shares a common platform with the All Party Hurriyat Conference (APHC), which expressed agreement with the ceasefire declared by the HM. However, it is not clear where the Hurriyat stands in the entire game plan, except that they were to negotiate with the Government of India on behalf of the HM. What are the stakes of JKLF within the Hurriyat? The APHC as we know is a common forum of seven local political parties, e.g. Ittehad-ul-Muslimeen, Jammu and Kashmir Liberation Front (JKLF), People's Conference, People's League, Awami Action Committee, Jamat-e-Islami and Muslim Conference. Besides there are number of aspiring militants belonging to different groups who have joined the political cadre to achieve their political goal. What the equation of the APHC is with the HM also needs to be thoroughly examined. The APHC is on the record of condemning the Government of India on all occasions including on the invasion of Pakistan in Kargil. But it failed to do so against Pakistan, which not merely rejected Nehru's plebiscite proposal in 1948, but is also responsible for creating the utmost hostile and violent atmosphere in the Valley that has caused immense pain and suffering to the people of Kashmir. This obviously is an example of a prejudiced approach. It would be difficult to negotiate with political leaders having this mindset.

There is a need for the APHC to work as representative of the Kashmiri people rather than that of the Government of Pakistan. Unless Kashmiri leaders maintain neutrality towards both India and Pakistan, any peace proposal would rest in limbo. All these issues are vital to peace in J&K.

The declaration of ceasefire was a positive beginning. It could have led towards a new chapter. However, since the negotiation could not take off with the Pak-based HM there is no harm in pursuing the discussion with Abdul Majid Dar, the Chief of Valley-based HM. The government needs to pursue him, Yasin Malik of JKLF and Mirwaiz, Omar Farooq for political dialogue. It needs to be clearly understood that most of the militant outfits operating in Kashmir are floated by Pakistan. Therefore, their target would be to negotiate in favour of Pakistan. They are not concerned with peace unless it accommodates Pakistan in the process. It is high time that the people of Kashmir understand that Pakistan does not want peace in the Valley and that they are not supporting them to ascertain their right of self-determination or Kashmiriyat. The day the Government of India convinces the people of Kashmir of this reality and makes a genuine gesture, that would be a real breakthrough towards a peaceful settlement of the Kashmir dispute. Until that is achieved no exercise would bear any fruit.

Permanent peace in the Kashmir Valley is possible only when there is a thorough understanding of the problem of terrorism and ideas for its eradication are implemented promptly with the utmost honesty. Haphazard execution of policy would not work in the present situation. It needs a well-concerted effort to deliberate issues with the militants. Unconditional talks are good to begin with. But once the dialogue starts certain conditions have to be attached along with their demands. The government cannot cross the boundary of the Constitution. The dialogue needs to start within the broad (not narrow framework) of the Indian Constitution, which is the most flexible constitution in the world. The talk cannot take place in the air. There has to be a certain basis for the discussion, which would follow sorting out issues involved in terrorism one by one. That would be the hour of trial for Indian skill in the art and craft of negotiation.

The issues involved in terrorism could be analysed only if there is a proper understanding of the word 'terrorism'. A dialogue for reconciliation without insight into the problem holds no relevance. Since the problem lies within the Indian subcontinent, an Indian perspective would be more effective to deal with the situation rather than imbibing novel ideas from the West. Therefore, a Vedantic understanding of terrorism and its ramifications is suggested here.

The Vedantic Understanding and Ramifications

According to the Vedanta the meaning of a word is threefold—Vachyartha, Lachyartha and Vyangyartha. Vachyartha refers to the direct meaning conveyed by the word. Lachyartha is implied meaning, i.e. meaning conveyed through its implications and Vyangyartha refers to suggested meaning, i.e. the meaning derived from its association.

Terrorism too could be understood from these three perspectives. The Vachyartha meaning of terrorism is related to the human psychology. It signifies the mental state where a person lives under the spell of fear of violence. The Lachyartha meaning of terrorism could be described in the light of its implications on politics. The political perspective on terrorism is derived from the Lachyartha meaning of the word. The understanding of terrorism as limited or proxy war by the nation-state is the logical conclusion of Vyangyartha or suggested meaning of a word.

Therefore, an eradication of terrorism, either through dialogue with the adversaries or otherwise, is possible only if the government examines and rectifies all the three issues involved in terrorism. For undermining the Vachyartha meaning of terrorism, the Government of India needs to remove the fear psychosis that prevails upon in Kashmir. The ceasefire declared by the HM is an ideal situation to achieve this goal. Second, a sequel to terrorism in accordance with the Lachyartha meaning, is that the government needs to inspire militants to join the political process on certain terms and conditions. Autonomy, devolution or delegation of power under Centre-state relationship, whatever terminology might be used, can be negotiated across the table. There is no harm in transferring more power to states. After all India has never been a Unitary state. It has been a federation of states. The only problem is that it should not be granted to just one state, but to all the states. Let Jammu and Kashmir be the beacon light of neo-federalism in India. Finally, the ramifications for the Vyangyartha meaning of terrorism could be realized through proactive counter-terrorism measures at home and active diplomacy at international fora.

All these measures need to be implemented simultaneously in coordination with different states and non-state agencies working towards peace in Kashmir. The HM has declared and withdrew ceasefire. Now is the time for all these agencies to translate the situation into a peaceful solution to the Kashmir imbroglio and put an end to the misery of the masses in the Valley. This is possible only if all the militant groups give up violence, which is the first condition for dialogue. The very fact that HM declared ceasefire for three months ought to be considered a positive signal from the militants. Even if it comes under the domestic and international compulsions of the Pakistan government, New Delhi must cash in on the opportunity and gear its machinery to bring peace in this region. Notwithstanding the fact that a lot depends on the response India gets from Islamabad on different issues likely to be discussed with the militants across the table. The current situation demands a peace process to begin. Different solutions could be explored in due course of time after a thorough examination of their demands and its overall implications on the national and regional security environment in the Indian subcontinent. Let us adopt a give and take formula to negotiate and keep them engaged in constructive talks with some genuine successes in different phases.

Proposed Agenda

The problem of terrorism could be solved in phases. No government can change the situation with an immediate effect. The problem is deeply rooted in the socio-economic and political conditions, which needs time at least five to ten years after successful implementation of the action plans.

- In the first phase government needs to control transnational terrorism by adopting an efficient counter-terror squad to fight the hard core terrorists coming from across the border. An effective intelligence network could be useful in achieving this goal.

- Implement plans to eliminate socio-economic problems in Kashmir, which is the cause of terrorism.
- Negotiate with the Kashmiri militant groups active in the Valley with the only condition, i.e. to restore peace in Kashmir. This is an important issue, because different militant groups have different agenda. Some want to accede to Pakistan, while some believe in *Azadi*. Make them sit across the table to negotiate issues for proper understanding on the Kashmir problem. We are all aware that the bone of contention is political power, which could be negotiated in different ways. In a democratic set-up there is always scope for sharing power.
- Government needs to encourage 'genuine' NGOs for direct interaction with common people. The downtrodden and the orphans ought to be protected from the roving eyes of ISI agents planted all over the state.
- Though TADA has been scrapped, important provisions of this act need to stay or bring a substitute for TADA. Modify some clauses as vetoed by the NHRC and reintroduce POT Bill for consideration or make IPC more rigorous. The existing law is not sufficient to deal with sensitive issues like terrorism.
- The Narcotic Drugs and Psychotropic Substances (NDPS) Act should continue as it has shown positive results in curbing narcotic drug trafficking, which is the main source for funding terrorism in India.
- Law enforcement agencies need cleansing operation. Corrupt officials should receive rigorous punishment. Anti-corruption cell consisting of the 'honest' officers and staff should be also posted at the borders in Jammu and Kashmir.
- The para-military forces like CRPF and BSF are not competent and honest enough to deal with cross-border terrorism. These forces need cleansing and revamping operations. The level of corruption is very high in these organizations and there is a general tendency among para-military forces to pass the buck to the army. It is high time the Government of India works towards sophistication of

para-military forces and strengthen local police in commando operation to combat cross-border terrorism. In so far as the BSF is concerned, it seriously needs an anti-corruption drive within the organization. It is an important para-military force, which needs to be more efficient and equipped to manage the borders. Corruption is the main problem with this organization and some serious measures need to be adopted to 'de-corrupt' it.

- There should be no discrimination on the basis of religion or race while dealing with drug traffickers in Jammu and Kashmir. People strongly feel that the law enforcement agencies discriminate between the Hindus and the Muslims while dealing with drug traffickers and criminals. It is relevant to mention that 80 per cent drug traffickers in Jammu and Kashmir are Hindus.
- Externally India does not have too many options except to influence the international community against terrorism as a global problem, and thereby call for global ramification at the multilateral diplomacy.
- Pressure on Pakistan against sponsoring terrorism in India and stronger ties with the US and China to balance their influence on Pakistan.
- India should initiate dialogue for compulsory extradition among the UN members for exchange of criminals.
- Finally, a nationwide anti-corruption movement is a must to root out all the evils in the present socio-economic, political and administrative system generally in India and particularly in Kashmir. All the institutions need overhauling which is possible only if we have dedicated, committed and clean governance both at the Centre and the State.

Fifteen

Kashmir—Is Peace Possible?

Asghar Ali Engineer

The Prime Minister's offer of ceasefire on the eve of Ramadan was, undoubtedly, a sound move and needed to be reciprocated. However, it was not to be. It thoroughly exposed the Kashmiri militants on one hand, and the Pakistani rulers, on the other. The militants, with the full backing of Pakistani rulers, want to make peace in Kashmir conditional. If India accepts those conditions—that Kashmir is a disputed territory and that India will agree to talk to the people of Kashmir on one hand, and to Pakistan, on the other—right at the outset, what will be India's *locus standi* then? Peace should be top priority in Kashmir today. Everything else can be settled during negotiations. And only if negotiation fails due to the unreasonable attitude of either party, should fighting can be resumed.

The holy month of Ramadan is the month of engrossing oneself in prayers and fasting. It is known as *sharullah,* i.e. the month of Allah, a month which should be devoted to all causes dear to Allah, and dearest to Allah is *salam*—peace. Some militants argued that even the Prophet fought the battle of Badr during the month of Ramadan, so what is wrong in fighting during this month? The Prophet fought a short battle to avert danger to the existence of Muslims in Madina and this battle was inevitable. It is not that he was fighting for years and that he did not cease to fight even after offer of peace by the other side. The very parallel cited is wrong. And in Kashmir the violence has degenerated into mere killing to terrorize needlessly.

Every time there is a move for peace, terror killing starts. This time too innocent Sikh drivers were pulled out of their vehicles and shot. Does it deserve to be called *Jihad*? Certainly not. I would also like to point out here that extremist violence in Kashmir cannot qualify for *Jihad*. Firstly, the Qur'an does not use the term *Jihad* for war or violence or killing, for that matter. For that other word *qital* has been used or its derivatives. *Jihad* in the Qur'an means utmost efforts to promote justice, goodness, benevolence and controlling base desires. However, what we witness in Kashmir is a mockery of *Jihad*. There it has degenerated into wanton and selfish killing. As far as *Jihad* is concerned one makes strenuous efforts not to harm anyone unnecessarily. There are several instances during the Prophet's time when Muslims did not kill their enemy when they felt it would amount to killing the enemy for selfish reasons.

Apart from the fact whether it is *Jihad* or not what is important is to note that violence will not solve the Kashmir question. What has happened is enough of violence. Ultimately it is a political solution, which will bring about the final resolution of the Kashmir problem. In an age of democracy and human rights, violence has a very limited role. If it was resorted to draw world attention to the problem it has served its purpose. The Kashmiri people have made enough sacrifice of their lives. More than 50 to 60 thousand people have already been killed in this senseless violence. How many more will have to lose their lives? And with all this can Kashmir achieve its freedom through violence? Then losing all these lives could have been worth it. Ultimately, it will have to be resolved through negotiations. Then why not negotiations now to save many more innocent lives?

The people of Kashmir are also tired of this violence. They desire peace intensely. Any survey in the Valley will establish this. But due to terror they cannot speak out freely. If the extremists are fighting—as they claim—for freedom of the people of Kashmir, why this terror? Even the newspapers from the Kashmir Valley cannot publish what they want. If they do, their editors are abducted and killed or their papers are not allowed to be sold in the market. They are ostensibly fighting for freedom and making people unfree. With this culture of violence and extremism what will be the quality of freedom in Kashmir if it is subsequently won? Violence brutalizes the human conscience. Those countries in Asia and Africa who won their freedom through violence—for example Algeria—have a legacy of violence and brutal killings. The people of Algeria never enjoyed real freedom. They have witnessed a highly authoritarian rule right from the beginning. There are many more such examples.

India won its freedom through an involvement of the masses and through democratic means and it developed a culture of democracy and this political democracy has survived in India despite many hurdles. The people of Kashmir had an excellent opportunity in 1990 to fight for their demands democratically as there was a mass uprising there against injustices perpetrated against them for all these years by the Central Government. But they lost that excellent opportunity by taking up guns. They thought, 'we will take up guns and *azadi* (freedom) will be now and here'. It was, to say the least, a gross miscalculation. Freedom for them is as far away as it was in 1990 when they took guns though more than 50,000 lives have been lost and so many women have been compelled to lose their chastity and are living a life of mental torture.

It is in view of all this that Prime Minister Vajpayee's offer of Ramadan peace should have been accepted to build peace in the Valley. The four former-Prime Ministers Sarvashri V. P. Singh, Deve Gowda, I. K. Gujral and Chandra Shekhar had also welcomed the Ramadan offer of ceasefire. When the offer was made even the Hizbul Mujahideen Chief Syed Salahuddin went into a huddle with his top commanders to consider its consequences. Some Hizbul sources said—though off the record—that a majority of those at the strategy meeting viewed the offer as exactly what they had wanted to get the negotiation process started and that Hizbul should respond positively. But the fear was that if any such public statement was issued it might split.

It was also reported that the Valley-based commander, Abdul Majid Dar, was pressing Salahuddin to take a stand, but the latter had been saying that the Indian Government should take the lead and hold out something more than a 'tame surrender'. If the latest offer had come with a package that could meet some of the Pak-based Hizbul leadership's concerns, the group could have welcomed it.

But if the package was announced, then what is there for India to negotiate? The most important thing is ceasefire and this opportunity should have been seized by the militants to build peace and also negotiate for a durable solution. The offer by Vajpayee won him support from other world leaders as well, and the militants would also have gained prestige, had they accepted the offer. It was an opportunity lost. Nevertheless India should not in any case withdraw the offer which is unlikely, at least until the end of the holy month of fasting. Not only that India, should seriously consider extending the ceasefire. It will earn even greater prestige internationally.

Indian military and para-military forces have been alleged to have indulged in excesses and killed innocent people and raped women in several instances. If the Government of India puts a stop to these gross violations of human rights of the people of Kashmir, it will earn further support not only internationally but also from the people of Kashmir themselves. The people of Kashmir, by now, know fully well that the militants cannot be their saviours, as now they are fighting for their own survival rather than for the freedom of the people of Kashmir. If there is any honourable solution within the framework of the Indian Union they will welcome it. But the very first condition for this is to stop excesses at the hands of the military and para-military forces. Today, the people of the Valley are deeply alienated from the Government of India. It is for anyone to verify. It is not a secret.

The offer for ceasefire is a necessary but not a sufficient condition for restoring permanent peace in Kashmir. For a sufficient condition the Government of India will have to reflect deeply on its policies in Kashmir, not only in respect of the behaviour of the armed forces but also in respect of a political solution. By now it should be at least clear that there is a great deal of dissatisfaction with the status quo. For a permanent solution the status quo in Kashmir must change. Whether it is complete autonomy as was demanded by the Kashmir Assembly and going back to the pre-1953 position is a matter for detailed negotiation. But the Central Government cannot insist that a permanent solution can be found without seriously rethinking the present policy framework.

The people of Kashmir have suffered intensely in the last one decade. The price has been too heavy for them, and they cannot be expected after such sacrifices to accept too little. As Mr. Vajpayee has displayed statesmanship by offering unilateral cease-fire, he should show further magnanimity by offering a package to the people of Kashmir which will be in keeping with the honour and dignity of the people of Kashmir. It will go a long way to reduce the feeling of alienation from the Central Government, if not eliminate it altogether.

Of course, it is easier said than done. Mr. Vajpayee's own party, the BJP, may not go all the way with him. Dissidence is already surfacing in the RSS. Many hard-core elements in the RSS are not happy with the Vajpayee Government on several issues, including the appeal to Muslims to support the BJP. On top of it if he crosses the Laxman Rekha on the Kashmir question there may be a virtual revolt. In fact, it is such dilemmas which continue the conflict in the Valley. It is so difficult to overcome them. The militants also face similar dilemmas. They would split if they accept solutions less than what they have been fighting for all these years. But both sides will have to take risks. No one ever achieves what one fights for. Our social stability is built on a complex set of compromises. The world would have been full of conflicts and bloodshed without these compromises. South Asia today runs the risk of becoming a nuclear flash point, if a bold compromise is not made from both sides in the interests of peace.

Sixteen

Kashmir Autonomy: National Conference Perspective

G.M. Wani

The regime of autonomy for Jammu and Kashmir has been looked with suspicion right from the day the State acceded to India. The sovereignty of the Indian State and autonomy in Kashmir were viewed as polar opposities. Article 370 was a codification of the unique socio-cultural identity of the Kashmiri people, the Valley's very special geography and economy, six centuries long resistance to incorporation under alien domination, weak integration into the colonial structure and the struggle for a special political identity in spite of accession to India.

Kashmir cannot be held hostage to continued India-Pakistan belligerence. Greater autonomy for Kashmir must be seen as part of the large desirable process of federalization and decentralization sweeping the world. In this study an attempt has been made to look at the Question of Autonomy from the National Conference (ruling party in J&K) Perspective.

Changing Concept of Sovereignty and Autonomy

The notion of state sovereignty led to the development of certain significant concepts. For example, the principle of "sovereign equality" of all states, the exclusiveness of state power over all persons and all activities in the territory; the right to use force, the absence of an obligation to submit disputes to third party adjudication, etc. Similarly, at the beginning of the 20th century an autonomous entity was one solely based on its own laws and with all the material and functional attributes of statehood. In the light of the preceding analysis of sovereignty—autonomy and sovereignty have very little in common, if anything at all. However, as is shown below, certain theorists and modern developments lend support to the view that the distance between the two nations has been considerably reduced.

First, the rise of democracy and federalism has brought a loosening of the nation of sovereignty in particular when determining who is sovereign within the state. The complex federal structure of USA made it difficult to designate a sole repository of sovereignty which led to the idea of dual sovereignty of the union and the component states. Secondly, some earlier scholars were of the opinion that sovereignty is indivisible. Sovereignty has in fact been divided into a number of historical and modern instances. Condominia, in which two or more states jointly exercise sovereignty over a territory represent one group of such cases. Finally, the theory of pluralistic sovereignty developed by Laski; in his opinion, the individual belongs to various associations.

New International System

The demise of the idea that the State has true, comprehensive and exclusive sovereignty is warranted by developments of the new international system. First, today's financial markets are globally interconnected by modern communication systems. People, ideas and criminals move across the borders in great numbers, while pollution and ballistic missiles reduce the relevance of those borders. The permeability of borders necessarily reduces the effectiveness and relevance of territorial sovereignty, while free trade agreements and common markets work to render ideas of a state's self-contained economic system obsolete. Second, the traditional implication of sovereignty, the prohibition against intervening in matters within the domestic jurisdiction of another state has also been questioned in recent times. The development of a right of self-determination, of international protection of human rights and of humanitarian law has challenged the core of State sovereignty, namely the exclusive right of the State to govern its citizens according to its own discretion. Third, the ethnic revival in the contemporary world presents yet another severe challenge to the old notion of sovereignty. To quote S. P. Huntington, "in the new world, local politics is politics of ethnicity, global politics is politics of civilization." That several thousand people or ethnic communities exist in the world, but the planet is too small to provide each of them full sovereignty over a piece of land, a compromise must be found to satisfy, at least partially the aspirations of these various groups. In the light of the above analysis, the concepts of sovereignty and autonomy could be used in a flexible manner. It is suggested that in a case of diffusion of power, the Central government and the regional or autonomous authorities could each be the lawful bearer of a share of sovereignty without necessarily leading to the disappearance or dismemberment of a state. Similarly, autonomy can be an arrangement aimed at granting to a group that differs from the majority of the population in the state, but that constitutes the majority in a specific region, a means by which it can express its distinct identity.[1]

Autonomy: An Instrument for Conflict Resolution

Autonomy is a means of distribution of power in order to preserve the unity of a state while respecting the diversity of its population. With the rise in ethnic consciousness, there is growing interest in the subject of autonomy in many parts of the world. Around the globe—from Sri Lanka to Northern Iraq, Chechnya to Bosnia, minority groups are asserting their distinctive ethnic, religious or national identity and demanding greater control over the expression of their identity. Those states that dismiss the notion of compromise must usually reckon with prolonged and violent opposition from the dissatisfied minority. Autonomy is increasingly suggested as a method of resolving these conflicts. Some have proposed to solve the Chechnya conflict by granting autonomy as a "special administrative region" in accordance with Section 31 of the Constitution of China.[2] A similar agreement was reached between Portugal and China regarding Macao which has lately been returned to Chinese sovereignty. Autonomy has also been successful in some cases such as West Berlin before the reunification of Germany.

Autonomy for Kashmir

When states were acceding to the two dominions of India/ Pakistan in 1947, Kashmir became a victim of competing ambitions of two states. Autonomy was thought to be device to conduct Indo-Kashmir relations in a friendly manner. It was a compromise solution and did not correspond to the original wishes of any of the parties involved. Sheikh Mohammad Abdullah states, "The central leadership wanted our complete merger. But our special circumstances and the objectives of our movement could not allow it."[3] As an advocate of a distinct Kashmiri identity, Sheikh Abdullah side-tracked both the Hindu-Muslim and India/Pakistan polarization around Kashmir by asking for freedom before accession.

The State of Jammu and Kahmir acceeded to the dominion of India on October 26, 1947, when Maharaja Hari Singh signed an Instrument of Accession. By the Instrument, the Maharaja accepted three subjects as one on which the Dominion legislature makes laws for the state.[4] Again by the Instrument the Maharaja clarified, "Nothing in the Instrument shall be deemed to commit me in any way to the acceptance of any future constitution of India or to fetter my discretion to enter into arrangements with the Government of India under any such future constitution".[5] The National Conference leaders did not want to exceed the items which had been transferred to the Centre under the Instrument of Accession. Negotiations on the provisions in the proposed Constitution of India that would embody the terms of the Jammu and Kashmir State's membership of the Union began when a conference of the leaders of the National Conference and of the Central leadership was held in Delhi on March 15 and 16, 1949. The State was accorded a special status under Article 370 of Indian Constitution. On January 26, 1950, the President of India made the first Constitution (Application to Jammu and Kashmir) Order 1950 under Article 370 of the Indian Constitution. It conformed strictly to the Instrument of Accession. Leaving aside the three items reserved to the Centre, everything else would be the proper concern of whatever form of Government, the Jammu and Kashmir Constituent Assembly might decide to create. Commenting on the temporary nature of Article 370, Sheikh Mohammad Abdullah said, "In actual fact, the temporary nature of Article 370 merely arises from the fact that the power to finalize the constitutional relationship between the State and the Union has been specifically vested in the Jammu and Kashmir Constituent Assembly".[6] The Constituent Assembly of India or its successor parliament have no constitutional right to abrogate or modify Article 370. The Article 368 has a proviso which says no constitutional amendment "shall have effect in relation to the State of Jammu and Kashmir unless applied by order of President under Article 370". That requires first the concurrence of the state government and subsequent ratification by its Constituent Assembly. Thus, the State Constituent Assembly's decision was to mark a finality to the exercise of the President's power under Article 370.[7] The jurisdiction of the Union Parliament to legislate with respect to Jammu and Kashmir was then clearly defined consistently with the position that emerged as a result of having ceded the powers pursuant to the Instrument of Accession. The rest of it was left for the State to take care of its own constitution. This veto power gives the Jammu and Kashmir Constituent Assembly a very special character under the Constitution of India. That Assembly ceased to exist in 1956. All subsequent central legislation has been extended to J&K, year after year without constitutional sanction.

Autonomy and Kashmiri Identity

The main issue involved in the establishment of a regime of autonomy is the division of powers between the central authorities and the autonomous entity. The powers of autonomy are usually related to matters of culture, economics and social affairs. There are, however, different degrees of autonomy and the extent of power transferred to the autonomous authorities vary accordingly ranging from very limited to larger and up to a high concentration of major powers in the above areas.

Though there was politico-ideological affinity between the National Conference and Indian National Congress, the leadership of the former did not want an instrument of accession that would obliterate their regional cultural pride and their vision of "New Kashmir" as envisaged in the 1944 Naya Kashmir programme. Thus, they favoured accession with autonomy. They demanded special status because they were afraid that the cultural glory of Kashmir would not be secure if they did not have the full freedom for their cultural prosperity in every respect. This requirement of the only Muslim majority state in the Indian union necessitated some politico-constitutional safeguards within the Indian political system. Sheikh Mohammad Abdullah states, "Indian political system can function more effectively at a regional and trans-regional level of federal units than at All India level under a unitary form of government. The actual function of an All India Centre should be weaving them into a single whole nation. The Centre should know its weaving nationalist task and should not force its values and ideas on local cultures in such a way they they feel threatened and insecure."[8]

Recognizing a Kashmiri identity and providing it vitality is a historical necessity. The broad section of Kashmiri masses have made the quantum jump by crossing over the threshold of ethnic consciousness to national consciousness. The most basic urge sustaining all movements including the present Azadi movement is freedom from subjugation. To a large extent, the entire development and definition of a Kashmiri identity has been a response to the threat of socio-political assimilation posed by an unbroken succession of imperial rulers from Mughal Emperor Akbar in 1586. The popular urge all through these years has been for self-determination. Sheikh Mohammad Abdullah states in his autobiography, "Kashmiris are heir to a peculiar individuality due to their culture and language. The learned translator of *Rajtarangni,* Stein and the great Indian historian, Tara Chand have stated it to the extent that Kashmir has never been part of the subcontinent in the geographical, cultural or historical sense".[9] A Kashmiri identity is the product of territorial homogeneity, the folk cultural specificites, the common heritage of Kashmiri civilization and its linguistic identity, uniformity of artistic, literary and aesthetic tradition and similarity in ethical-psychological make up (as well as in dress, food, habits, etc.) based on climatic, geographical conditions and socio-cultural mores evolved over the centuries. It is this identity, and the quest for its survival and growth which gave rise to subsequent demands for special status within the Indian Constitutional framework. Article 370 of the Indian

Constitution consistent with the National Conference stand throughout in respect of the right of the J&K state to frame its own constitution envisaged a Constituent Assembly. Sheikh Mohammad Abdullah saw the Constituent Assembly as a continuation of J&K freedom struggle. Kashmir had its own history of freedom movement and the New Kashmir Programme had in 1944 envisaged a National Assembly for the State of J&K. A suitable Constitution would ensure that the temporary special status indicated in Article 370 of the Constitution would in fact be permanent and would not preclude the possibility of one day full independence".[10] Sheikh Abdullah envisaged state/union relationship as "one of partners in common endeavour for the advancement of the people" and regarded "safeguarding of autonomy to the fullest extent" and suitable "constitutional arrangement with the union" as two cornerstones between partners"[11] It was against this background that the Delhi Agreement was signed.

How autonomy helped to rebuild New Kashmir during 1947-53, is a pertinent point to answer those who view it as a tool of exploitation.[12] The government because of internal autonomy registered great success. However, as already mentioned, erosion of autonomy remained a virtual state policy supported by almost all political parties.

Autonomy Eroded

The Indian state, from the very beginning denied the validity of India's multinational character and the need for a genuine federal structure. It is in this denial that national chauvinism can be located. Instead of educating the people about the need for a special constitutional position for J&K, the Indian leaders through their action created suspicion in the minds of Kashmiri leaders. Placing Article 370 before the Constituent Assembly, Gopalswamy Ayyanger had expressed the hope on behalf of "everybody here that in due course, even J&K will become ripe for some sort of integration that has taken place in case of other states."[13] Even Jawaharlal Nehru believed that there is nothing final about the Delhi Agreement. Communal elements did not approve of the Delhi Agreement. Some newspapers commented that, "instead of

Kashmir acceding to India, in fact India acceded to Kashmir".[14] In the Jammu region of the State, Praja Parishad demanded that either the Constitution of India be applied to J&K in its entirety or Jammu be detached from Kashmir and merged with the Indian Union. The Praja Parishad demanded homogeneity of the political process of Jammu and Kashmir with the rest of India. Strangely enough, the support to Praja Parishad came from Jayaprakash Narayan and Acharya Kripalani. Sheikh Abdullah believed "Nehru and Maulana Azad were interested in the preposition but did not agree with the strategy".[15]

It was in this atmosphere of political hostility towards autonomous Kashmir that erosion of the special constitutional position started. In the eagerness to create an image of cementing closer relations what followed 1952 is a series of constitutional application orders numbering as listed by State Autonomy Report (prepared by the National Conference) 42 till now which were not conceived at any point of time either in 1950 or in 1952.[16] The extent and nature of autonomy which has been left with the State as of now can be seen from the following table.[17]

I.	*Total No. of Articles*	*No. of Articles*	*Balance*
	395	260	135
II.	*Total No. of Entries in the Union List*	*Entries Applied*	*Balance*
	97	94	3
III.	*Total No. of Entries in the Concurrent List*	*Entries Applied*	*Balance*
	47	26	21

The State Autonomy Report further states that the state of J&K far from enjoying special status, was put in a status inferior to the other states.[18]

Fallout of Erosion

The process of erosion of special constitutional position hit at the most sensitive point of the Kashmiri psyche as it threatened the autonomy and identity of Kashmir for the protection of which the Kashmiris had laboured hard. "Moreover, it even made the issue of accession controversial by projecting the degree of centralization of power as a measure of patriotism."[19] Sheikh Abdullah now came to the conclusion that there was no middle course between full integration and full autonomy (which was his euphemism for independence) and as the majority of Kashmiris would not accept the first alternative, there was no choice but to accept the second. He publicly resurrected the idea of full independence, as one possible option, among several for the future of Jammu and Kashmir. The mounting discontent in the Valley against the measures and moves of constitutional integration of the State with the Centre, had one main outlet—separation. Rise of separatist sentiments in the Valley might have been one of the temptations for Pakistan to send armed infiltrators into the State in August 1965. Re-establishment of trust as expected from the Accord of 1975 could not work plunging the State into a worse turmoil in 1989. The trouble in Kashmir cannot be dismissed as ISI inspired or a proxy war by Pakistan. Pakistan only exploited a situation created by successive Indian Governments in Kashmir. No less a person than George Fernandes who was Minister Incharge Kashmir Affairs in the Janata Dal Government in 1990 said:

> "I do not believe any foreign hand created the Kashmir problem. The problem was created by us. Others decided to take advantage of it".[20]

Even Dr. Farooq Abdullah said in 1994, "It is India that is responsible for what has happened in Kashmir."[21] The former Chief Minister Mir Qasim observed: "If I dump petrol in my house and my opponent set a match to it, it is largely my fault. Wherever the entire people rise up in one voice you cannot suppress it by force."[22] The reference is towards the manner that the constitutional relationship between the Centre and state was conducted. Today we find the State has lost all resemblance to autonomy. Its erosion is the primary cause for Kashmir discontent in the eyes of the National Conference. The restoration of autonomy is thought to be a viable instrumentality for bringing peace in the State. This received both political as well as intellectual support from in and outside the State.

Political Support

Mr. Narasimha Rao, the then Prime Minister of India announced in 1995 that the Union Government would be prepared to consider autonomy "short of independence" for Jammu and

Kashmir.[23] Welcoming this on behalf of Jammu and Kashmir, the National Conference leader, Dr. Farooq Abdullah asked the Union Government to issue an order under Article 370 to restore the State's autonomy in terms of the Delhi Agreement of 1952. When this could not materialize, the National Conference boycotted the Parliamentary election of 1996. Mr. Deve Gowda as Prime Minister offered Jammu and Kashmir "maximum autonomy" which persuaded Dr. Abdullah and his party the National Conference to participate in the Assembly Elections. The party fought these elections on the autonomy plank and was returned with a massive majority. After assuming office as Chief Minister, Dr. Farooq with the approval of the cabinet constituted a committee to examine and recommend measures for the restoration of autonomy. This was exactly in accordance with the mandate given to him by the people of the State as also the assurances held out by the Union Government.

Intellectual Support

The Autonomy project has also received sufficient intellectual support. Bhikhu Parekh observes that the solution to the problem lies in the recognition by the Indian Government of Kashmir's different history, needs and circumstances and grant of differential status to the people of Jammu and Kashmir.[24] Bhabani Sen Gupta and Prem Shankar Jha assert that if New Delhi sincerely wishes to break the deadlock in Kashmir, it has no other alternative except to accept and implement what is being termed as an "Autonomy Plus", "Independence Minus" formula or to grant autonomy to the State to the point where it is almost indistinguishable from independence.[25] Praful Bidwai also pleads for "Special Autonomy" for the people of Jammu and Kashmir State.

An Autonomy project for the State can be justified on grounds of:

First, any attempt at Indo/Pak reconciliation is like wanting to treat two patients whose only disease is allergy to each other, opined G. Parthasarthy. Obviously the primary cause of hostility between the two countries is psychosomatic. India's bottom line that Kashmir is an integral part of India. Pakistan's non-negotiable position has been that according to the terms of the partition of

India, Kashmir, a Muslim majority state belongs to Pakistan. Kashmir cannot be held as hostage to the continued India/Pakistan hostility. Greater autonomy can be tested as a conflict-resolution instrumentality.

Secondly, there is an additional reason for restoring autonomy to Kashmir as the other pillar on which Kashmir's linkage with India rested, secularism is under cloud. Kashmiri leaders did not choose Pakistan despite religious affinity but opted for India on grounds of secularism. Sheikh Abdullah recognized the link between Kashmir's accession to Indian secularism. In his address to the Jammu and Kashmir Constituent Assembly in 1951, he argued:

> "Certain tendencies have been asserting themselves in India which may in the future convert it into a religious state wherein the interests of Muslims will be jeopardized. The continued accession of Kashmir to India, should however, help in defeating the tendency. From my experience of the last four years, it is my considered judgement that the presence of Kashmir in the Union of India has been the major factor in stabilizing relations between the Hindus and Muslims of India".[26]

Having seen the link, Abdullah later dithered. Should Hindu nationalists triumph in the struggle for power in Delhi, he asked, would Kashmir be secure in India. The Jana Sangh President, S. P. Mukerjee launched the Kashmir agitation in 1953, for the abrogation of Article 370. The BJP which is the political successor of the same forces for the second time since independence, marched upon Srinagar during its Ekta Yatra. At a time when Autonomy reports were presented in the state legislature, the Home Ministry under the BJP Government took serious note of it. Hence the need is for stabilizing autonomy to respect the sentiments of Kashmiris.

Third, Autonomy Project should also be looked at from the perspective of contemporary world trends. Decentralization is one of the two worldwide trends (globalization is the other). It is no coincidence that democracy and decentralization have gathered momentum together in the last decade. Both aim at empowering citizens. In Latin America the dictatorship of the 1980s have given way to democracy and new rulers believe decentralization is intrinsic to democracy. According to Freedom House, 95 per cent of democracies now hold elections for sub-national governments at the state or local levels. Dissatisfaction with big governments has spread in high-income countries too. They increasingly view decentralization as a logical extension of empowering citizens (as exemplified by new Scottish and Welsh legislatures in Britain). In India, liberalization has empowered the states to compete with one another in economiç and social policy and constitutional amendments to facilitate Panchayat Raj have created no less then three million elected leaders in local bodies, a world record.

Hence, to National Conference the most dramatic opening in Kashmir is presented by the crisis over Article 370. The best way to resolve this is to implement the article by returning to the pre-1953 situation and convening a Constituent Assembly in Kashmir to decide which central legislation should be extended to the State. This should be accompanied by a package of economic and social measures of extraordinary generosity and by an open, clean, transparent, honest and human approach to Kashmiri concerns.

References

1. Ruth Lapidoth, Autonomy: Flexible Solutions to Ethnic Conflicts w. US Institute of Peace, 1997, p. 33.
2. *Ibid.*
3. Sheikh Mohammad Abdullah, *Flames of the Chinar*, (A bridged translated from the Urdu by Khushwant Singh), Penguin, 1993, p. 113.
4. The three subjets were Defence, Communication and Foreign Affairs.
5. Clause 7 of Instrument of Accession.
6. See Report of the State Autonomy Committee, Jammu, April 1999, p. 113.
7. *Ibid.*, p. 30.
8. Cited in Prakash Chandra, "National Question in Kashmir" *Social Scientist*, June 1985, p. 49.
9. Sheikh Mohammad Abdullah, *Aatish-e-Chinar* (Autobiography), Ali Mohd. And Sons, Srinagar, 1984, pp. 247-49
10. Alastair Lamb, Kashmir: A Disputed Legacy 1846-1947 (Roxford Books, 1991), p. 193.
11. Report of the State Autonomy Committee, Jammu, April 1999, p. 41.

12. The successes of the Government during the period were:
    (a) Hereditary rule was abolished and replaced by a Constitutional head of the state.
    (b) Jagir lands confiscated without compensation. The land was distributed among tillers.
    (c) The government set up a planning system modelled on the Soviet five year plans.
13. Speech on October 6, 1949, *Constituent Assembly Debates.*
14. *Sheikh Abdullah*, n. 9, p. 118.
15. *Ibid.*, p. 118.
16. *State Autonomy Report*, p. 73.
17. *Ibid.*, pp. 75-76.
18. Reference is towards Punjab where Parliament had to amend the Constitution four times by the 59th, 67th, 68th Amendments to extend President's rule imposed in Punjab on May 11, 1987. For the state of J&K, the same result was accomplished by executive orders undr Article 370. Another case is that of the way Article 249 was extended to the State.
19. Balraj Puri, *Kashmir Towards Insurgency*, Orient Longman, 1993, p. 29.
20. George Fernandes, "India's Policies in Kashmir: An Assessment and Discourse" in Raju, G.C. Thomas, *Perspective on Kashmir: The Roots of Conflict in South Asia*, Boulder, Oxford, 1992, pp. 77-78.
21. *India Today*, 1994, p. 44.
22. Syed Mir Qasim, *My Life and Times*, Allied, pp. 302-3.
23. *Report of the State Autonomy Committee*, p. 4.
24. *The Times of India*, New Delhi, March 3, 1994.
25. *The Hindustan Times*, New Delhi, February 2, 1993.
26. Quoted byAshutosh Varshney, Kashmiriat: A Paradox of Nationalism, *The Illustrated Weekly of India*, August 31, 1991.

INDEX

D

E

Q

R